The Fiction
of Enlightenment

The Fiction
of Enlightenment

Women of Reason
in the French Eighteenth Century

Heidi Bostic

Newark: University of Delaware Press

Associated University Presses
2010 Eastpark Boulevard
Cranbury, NJ 08512

The paper used in this publication meets the requirements of the American National Standard for Permanence of Paper for Printed Library Materials Z39.48–1984.

Library of Congress Cataloging-in-Publication Data

Bostic, Heidi.
    The fiction of enlightenment : women of reason in the French eighteenth century / Heidi Bostic.
        p. cm.
    Includes bibliographical references and index.
    ISBN 978-0-87413-074-4 (alk. paper)
    1. French fiction—Women authors—History and criticism. 2. French fiction—18th century —History and criticism. 3. Reason in literature. 4. Women and literature—France—History—18th century. 5. Women—France—Intellectual life—18th century. 6. Enlightenment—France. 7. Graffigny, Mme de (Françoise d'Issembourg d'Happoncourt), 1695–1758—Criticism and interpretation. 8. Riccoboni, Marie Jeanne de Heurles Laboras de Mézières, 1713–1792—Criticism and interpretation. 9. Charrière, Isabelle de, 1740–1805—Criticism and interpretation. I. Title.
PQ648.B665 2010
843'5099287—dc22
                                    2009020791

In loving memory of my mother
Bonnie J. Bostic
(1944–2000)
for her steadfast encouragement,
her laughter and her light

Contents

Acknowledgments

My research on women and Enlightenment began to take shape at Purdue University under the guidance of Thomas F. Broden, Paul Benhamou, William L. McBride, Tracy Denean Sharpley-Whiting, and Whitney Walton. I gratefully acknowledge their pertinent questions and steady helpfulness. Thomas F. Broden proved to be an especially generous reader and a stalwart supporter.

Early versions of parts of this book found receptive audiences at annual meetings of the American Society for Eighteenth-Century Studies. Colleagues in ASECS, especially the Women's Caucus, have been particularly supportive, as have members of Women in French. I am also thankful for conversations generated at the conferences "Françoise de Graffigny: Nouvelles approches" at Oxford (2002) and "Belle de Zuylen / Isabelle de Charrière: Education & création" at Utrecht (2005). Dix-huitiémistes as a group have demonstrated exceptional kindness and generosity, embodying the best spirit of the Republic of Letters. Thanks in particular to English Showalter, Suzan van Dijk, Nadine Bérenguier, Julie Hayes, Lesley Walker, Alison Conway, and Sharon Nell, who generously supported this project through recommendations, invitations, and advice. Thanks also to Jonathan Mallinson, Downing Thomas, Reed Benhamou, Perry Gethner, and Aurora Wolfgang for conversation as well as answers to queries.

Parts of this manuscript, several years in the making, were composed in Paris and in Talca, Chile, as well as in Indiana, Minnesota, North Dakota, Michigan, Arizona, and Nebraska. I thank friends and acquaintances in all of those places for providing hospitable surroundings. Thanks to the residents of Windsor Place for helping to create an atmosphere conducive to thought. I gratefully acknowledge my teachers at the École des Hautes Études en Sciences Sociales, including Roger Chartier, Jacques Fontanille, and Luce Irigaray. I thank the students and colleagues who sustained me at Purdue University, Minnesota State University-Moorhead, Concordia College, Universidad de Talca, and Michigan Technological University. I also thank colleagues—especially Jeanne Schuler and Susan Calef—and audience members at Creighton University for their generosity and queries during my sabbatical visit there in 2007.

Without the help of librarians this project could not have been completed. I owe gratitude to librarians and other staff members at the Bibliothèque Nationale de France, the Bibliothèque historique de la ville de Paris, the Bibliothèque Marguerite Durand, the Library of Congress, the Criss Library at the University of Nebraska-Omaha, and the Beinecke Library at Yale University. I also gratefully acknowledge the assistance of librarians at the Van Pelt and Opie Libraries at Michigan Tech, including David Bezotte, *bibliothécaire extraordinaire;* Bill Sved; and the untiring Interlibrary Loan specialists Cathy Greer and Stephanie Reed.

I am grateful for a Theodore E. D. Braun Research Travel Award in 2007 from the American Society for Eighteenth-Century Studies, which supported a research trip to Paris. I am likewise thankful for a Fulbright Scholar Award in 2004 that afforded renewal and fresh perspectives.

I have had the good fortune to receive various forms of support from Michigan Tech: a sabbatical leave in 2007, Faculty Scholarship Grants from the Office of the Vice President for Research, and financial and moral support from the Department of Humanities, thanks to the good graces of its former Chair, Robert R. Johnson. Thank you to members of the Department of Humanities Gender Writing Group: Victoria Bergvall, Diane Shoos, and Patricia Sotirin, whose interest and critiques improved this project in many ways. Thanks also to the graduate students who amiably agreed to sound the depths of many of these issues with me: Kristin Arola, Katrina "Neely" Farren, Erik Hayenga, K. Alex Ilyasova, Kathryn Nelson, Karen Springsteen, and Debra Williamson.

Brief sections of this study were previously published in *Belle van Zuylen / Isabelle de Charrière: Education & creation,* ed. Suzan van Dijk et al. (Amsterdam: Rodopi, 2005); *Dalhousie French Studies; SVEC;* and *Women in French.* I am grateful to the publishers for permission to make use of this material here.

I thank Diane Gruber and Ramsey Eric Ramsey for the sustenance of *souper* and conversation over many years. Thanks also to Mark, Kristin, Zach, and Leo for their friendship; they make of hospitality an art.

Most of all, I thank Stephen Pluháček, who has taught me the possibilities of sharing as well as the impossibility of acknowledgment.

A Note on Translation and Orthography

Unless otherwise indicated, all translations from the French are my own. Orthography has been modernized throughout.

Abbreviations

CG	*Correspondance de Mme de Graffigny*
Correspondence	*There Are No Letters Like Yours: The Correspondence of Isabelle de Charrière and Constant d'Hermenches*
GP	Graffigny Papers
HC	*Histoire du marquis de Cressy*
Letters	*Letters of Mistress Henley Published by Her Friend*
MR	*Lettres de Mylord Rivers*
OC	*Oeuvres complètes d'Isabelle de Charrière*
RBSE	La Réunion du bon sens et de l'esprit
SVEC	*Studies on Voltaire and the Eighteenth Century*

The Fiction
of Enlightenment

Introduction

THIS BOOK ARGUES THAT WOMEN WRITERS OF THE FRENCH EIGHTEENTH century claimed reason and contributed to Enlightenment. It focuses on works of imaginative literature by three authors spanning the period from mid-century to post-Revolution: Françoise de Graffigny, Marie Jeanne Riccoboni, and Isabelle de Charrière. These authors refuted the ancient tradition of disparaging women's reason, a topic that sparked lively public discussion during the eighteenth century.

Approaching these issues and these authors means asking anew the question, What is Enlightenment? This project suggests why reason is worth recovering and why these women's ideas remain pertinent today. It presents the fiction of Enlightenment as a double provocation. First, what passes under the name of Enlightenment in much current critical discourse is a fiction, or a caricatured construct. Second, works of fiction can illuminate the historical and philosophical phenomenon called Enlightenment.

WOMEN IN AND OUT OF THE PICTURE

Intellectual women of the French eighteenth century continue to be excluded from Enlightenment. Their works are too often trivialized or treated as mere embellishment when they are not simply ignored. Three examples can serve as illustration. First is the anthology *Être dix-huitiémiste* [Being an eighteenth-century scholar], which contains autobiographical works offering glimpses of the lives of researchers prone to self-effacement behind their subject matter. The book implies, through omission, that there are no eighteenth-century women worthy of study. It also inaccurately depicts research on the eighteenth century as

1. Cover of *Être dix-huitiémiste*, portrait (1760) by Thomas Frey of an unknown man

an endeavor exclusive to men. The editor's introduction describes prominent critics and teachers using terms like *maître* (literally, "master") and *patriarche*. One scholar, Jean Ehrard, describes the French state, which is funding his retirement, as a *bonne fille*, that is, a "good girl" or "good daughter." Another scholar, Robert Darnton, when asked by an interviewer about the absence of women in his work, points in self-defense to his analysis of the novel *Thérèse philosophe* (1748, attributed to Boyer d'Argens), a frankly pornographic work featuring the sexual initiation of a young girl, which Darnton describes as a "manifesto for women's liberation."[1] The tenor of this collection is mirrored in its visual aspects: each selection is accompanied by a photograph of the scholar, creating a striking all-male gallery. The book's cover, a 1760 portrait by Thomas Frey of an unknown man, accurately reflects its exclusive focus on men. *Être dix-huitiémiste* is a monument to Enlightenment-as-usual.[2]

Other book covers in French eighteenth-century studies do, by contrast, attest to the existence of women. One example is *Romans libertins du XVIIIe siècle* (1993), which appeared in the popular "Bouquins" series at the Robert Laffont publishing house.[3] This book's cover features a detail from François Boucher's painting *A Woman Fastening Her Garter, with Her Maid* (1742). While the painting in its entirety includes a scene of a whole room, with the maid looking on as the woman dresses, the book cover crops the painting and dismembers the woman, featuring only her leg along with a cat and a fire. Nancy K. Miller links the book's cover image to the gender politics of libertine literature, including Denis Diderot's *Les Bijoux indiscrets [The Indiscreet Jewels]*, in which women are shown to speak through their genitals, or *bijoux*. Miller analyzes, among other aspects, the suggestive presence of the cat between the woman's legs.[4]

And yet, one could argue, surely the publisher was justified in selecting a rather licentious cover image for a collection of libertine works. But what about the cover of another book in the same series, an anthology of novels by women writers? This one is quite unbelievable. Entitled *Romans de femmes du XVIIIe siècle* (1996), the anthology includes works by Graffigny, Riccoboni, and Charrière, that is, the most prominent women writers of the French Enlightenment. For this book cover, the publisher selected Antoine Watteau's painting *La toilette intime* (circa 1716–

21), again calling to mind Diderot's suggestion that women speak through their jewels, that a woman is reducible not just to her body but more specifically to her genitals. If the nude woman in the image is meant to depict the woman writer, then the kneeling servant woman holding a washbasin and sponge, gazing affectionately at her mistress's exposed *bijoux,* is the metaphorical reader. Such a depiction obfuscates the real, active, intellectual exchange that took place between women writers and their readers (some of whom were authors themselves).[5]

Given the cover design's implicit diminishment of women writers, it is little surprise to find dismissive comments in the book's preface. There, Raymond Trousson asserts that "many of these novels have more or less obvious autobiographical origins"; that the authors mainly wrote about women protagonists because of "an incapacity to represent a truly different character." In sum, Trousson argues that these women authors "say what they lived and felt."[6]

This evidence points to a real problem. Women's works are consigned to the margins of Enlightenment. Today we remain in thrall to some of the same negative characterizations faced by women during the eighteenth century: that they were intellectually inferior to men, that their texts were mere transcriptions of their own lives, that their work did not really matter. The time has come to address the gender anxieties leading to women's exclusion from understandings of eighteenth-century thought, to redress this blind spot in the Enlightenment intellectual heritage, and to rediscover women of reason and their contributions.

BRINGING WOMEN INTO FOCUS

Over the past two decades, interest in early modern women writers has increased dramatically. Literary scholars, many working from a feminist perspective, have recovered the lost voices of eighteenth-century women authors, offering new editions and critical insights. Parallel to these developments, recent historiography has called attention to people and practices too long neglected by standard historical accounts. Phenomenologists have focused on narrative identity and on humans as historical beings, other philosophers have performed archaeologies of the self, and theorists from across the critical spectrum have investigated how discourse shapes the human world. All of these lines of inquiry have enriched the study of women's lives and works.

But too much recent scholarship on eighteenth-century women characterizes them as little more than muse, helpmeet, or hostess supporting men's undertaking of the serious work of Enlightenment. For all of this critical work's innovativeness, reason is still most often left to the men. According to the traditional account, the Enlightenment is a man-made affair. Women facilitated salon conversations and wielded what influence they had with the powerful men to whom they had access through bloodlines or love affairs. Additional effort is needed to unsettle this account. At the same time, reason and Enlightenment values have come under attack for their purported universalizing and totalizing ambitions. Such attacks oversimplify Enlightenment and flatten the complex texture of reason.

What happens when we apply some pressure to this account? What shifts in perspective and new insights emerge when we place women at the center of the exchange of ideas, rather than at the periphery? Reason is worth recovering because it is a fundamental aspect of Enlightenment, of Western thought, and of our understanding of what it means to be human. If women are to take their rightful place in the Western intellectual heritage, we need to read and understand them within this context. We will then be in a position to ask: How would our understanding of the French Enlightenment change if women's intellectual contributions were taken seriously?

After a long oblivion, Graffigny, Riccoboni, and Charrière have become part of an emerging new canon of eighteenth-century French literature alongside the men—such as Montesquieu, Voltaire, Diderot, and Rousseau—who have dominated reading lists and public perception. What unites these authors goes beyond their identity as women and their concerns reflecting that standpoint. Their works feature a thematic focus on reason and Enlightenment, which has remained hidden in plain view. They expressed their views on reason and gender in creative works that provide a counterweight to sweeping dismissals of Enlightenment. These women deserve to be recognized as Enlightenment thinkers. In fact, by exposing and critiquing gender bias, they often embraced the egalitarian ethos of Enlightenment more fully than their male contemporaries.

ANOTHER LOOK AT ENLIGHTENMENT

Three core themes—gender, philosophy, and Enlightenment—are linked through reason, the keystone of this book's analysis. Much critical work today invokes "reason" as an aside, bending it to the will of the author and the whim of the argument, but rarely addressing it directly or even acknowledging that it is a multilayered, context-specific idea. While we can say that reason was and is a cardinal virtue of Enlightenment, it is difficult to define just what this means. Both "reason" and "Enlightenment" have several distinct significations, which are explored in chapter 1. Rather than endeavoring to catalogue every possible meaning of the term "reason," this study focuses instead on reason's social function. Reason, freedom, and Enlightenment work in concert: Enlightenment entails the free use of reason. Where eighteenth-century women were concerned, "reason" often functioned as a code word, a mechanism for curtailing their freedom and excluding them from Enlightenment.

The overarching questions that frame this analysis include: What is the role of gender in the construction of knowledge, in the interpretation of this construction, and in the recognition of knowledge? How have women authors responded to the charge that women lack reason? What is the contribution of women to the debates on gender and reason? These queries in turn reveal that the question "What is Enlightenment?" could more helpfully be phrased "What counts as Enlightenment?" As explained in chapter 1, the latter questions entail both historical and contemporary dimensions. This study seeks to place the works of Graffigny, Riccoboni, and Charrière in history without abandoning them there. That is, it endeavors to reclaim something in their works that will remain meaningful for readers now and in the future. Certainly it is vital to investigate the reception of these women among their contemporaries, to discover whether they gained acceptance for their perceived adherence or nonadherence to Enlightenment ideals. But it is likewise informative to ask about the possible relevance of their ideas today. Do we, twenty-first-century readers, recognize and accept their Enlightenment? Is it possible that we have inherited more than we usually acknowledge?

As noted above, "the Enlightenment" is traditionally understood as an affair among men. Critics call it the source of masculinist universal claims and presuppositions. The argument quickly becomes circular: men are the Enlightenment thinkers and "Enlightenment" is defined as what men have written and said. So this book deals in part with the erasure of women from French Enlightenment thought. Were we to reject that tradition altogether, we would even more effectively exclude women from Enlightenment. But there is an alternative. If Enlightenment may be understood as a conversation, as both Lawrence Klein and Dorinda Outram have suggested, it is worthwhile to recognize women's role in this conversation.[7] Perhaps "the" Enlightenment is much more complex than has often been assumed. Perhaps we can simultaneously claim a place for women in Enlightenment, maintain a critical perspective, and expand our very definition of Enlightenment.

A Word on Method: Experience and Relation

Richard Rorty writes that humanistic intellectuals "read books in order to enlarge their sense of what is possible and important." They are, he continues, "trying to expand their own moral imaginations."[8] A similar spirit animates the readings of eighteenth-century works in the chapters that follow. These readings likewise owe something to Paul Ricoeur, who writes of "the intersection of the world of the text and that of the listener or reader." Ricoeur notes that "every work . . . adds something to the world which was not there previously," that every work of fiction "projects . . . ways of inhabiting the world that lie waiting to be taken up by reading."[9] Like eighteenth-century women, we live in a world partly constructed by discourse, including literary texts. These texts suggest new possibilities for ways of being in the world.

Informed by a range of critical approaches, this project's methodology acknowledges the role of texts in constructing reality as well as the links between authors' works and their lives. Thus it charts a course between two extremes: strict discursive construction, or the idea that reality is entirely reducible to texts, and autobiographical reduction, or the idea that women's texts simply and straightforwardly mirror their own lives.

A crucial yet relatively neglected part of the ongoing effort to recover eighteenth-century women's contributions is the development of appropriate methodologies: new ways of reading and new paradigms of understanding. The analysis in the chapters that follow is guided by two methodological through-lines: experience and relation. More precisely, these through-lines mark the interface between the rational and the experiential, and between the rational and the relational.

In the modern era, and certainly during the eighteenth century, epistemological questions became linked to empiricism. That is, knowledge claims came to be confirmed or refuted through tests of validation that ultimately refer back to experience. At the same time, experience has long been a central facet of feminist methodology. Notwithstanding the suspicion sometimes expressed toward appeals to experience (by historian Joan W. Scott, for example), such appeals need not be considered foundational. Nor should they be taken up in a way either simplistic or absolute.[10] That, in fact, is the shortcoming of a reading like Trousson's in the preface to *Romans de femmes*, which turns the discussion of an author's experiences—whether real or supposed—into a reductive understanding of her works.

Other thinkers have reclaimed appeals to experience—such as literary scholar Paula Moya, in a direct challenge to Scott.[11] These nuanced appeals show that experiences are always shared, always about relation, always subject to interpretation, and always open to revision. The phrase "the authority of experience" appears in a classic essay of feminist literary criticism by Elaine Showalter, in an article on feminist standpoint theory by Dorothy Smith, and in the title of a book on eighteenth-century French sensationalism by John C. O'Neal.[12] Recourse to the authority of experience links Enlightenment thought with feminist thought, both then and now. Women's experiences provide a wellspring of evidence to question the status quo and to generate alternative accounts. The commonalities among women's experiences have also provided a way to talk about women as a group,

without making purchases upon any idea of essential woman-
hood. To be very clear: women's texts may be linked to their experiences without being reduced to them. It is the texts' relation
to events in the world—whether the texts reflect that world, seek
to change it, or both—that grants them their power.

Relation, like experience, is a multifaceted dimension of this
project's methodology. It is in part because women have been read
too much in relation to men that their contributions on women
and reason have been overlooked. For example, the *Cartésiennes*,
or avowed followers of Descartes, have garnered some attention,
and Émilie Du Châtelet, a noted scientist, was long known as
Voltaire's love interest rather than on the merits of her achievements. In other words, these women's relation to an intellectual
man is often the focus of any notice paid to them. This asymme-
try is not unrelated to a problem with Nancy K. Miller's methodology of "reading in pairs," or reading a woman's text paired with
a man's.[13] Doing so has often meant allowing the man to set the
terms of the discussion. It has meant positioning the woman in
the dyad as reactive rather than creative. Women did offer responses, and did sometimes subvert what was taken as given.
But to limit the analysis to responses and subversions is still to
relegate women to a secondary role. Pairing a woman's text with
a man's text can serve the function of legitimation, but it can
likewise result in limitation.

At the same time, careful readings of eighteenth-century wom-
en's texts with an eye to relation can yield crucial insights.
Women lived and wrote in an environment of mixed-gender sociability. Their works often examine relations between the sexes.
And we can understand their unique contributions through con-
textualization with respect to other thinkers. This is why, instead of "reading in pairs," this study advocates "reading in context." These writers understood that getting along in both public
and private spheres required interaction across the lines of gender. Their Enlightenment stakes a claim for a new kind of equitable relationality, including relations between women and men.

Emphasizing experience and relation in an analysis centered
on reason may seem paradoxical, in two respects. First, reason
and experience have, in recent critical discourse, been defined as
oppositional. Feminist standpoint theory, for instance, makes
claims on the basis of experience that it understands as under-

mining what it calls Enlightenment reason. Drawing upon the rich intellectual heritage of the eighteenth century, this project suggests that such oppositions do not withstand scrutiny. Second, reason has often been considered a universal value that has little or nothing to do with relations to others or to the world. However, the meaning and possession of reason in the eighteenth century, as argued in chapter 1, was determined in part through interaction. And while men were able to prove their reason among other men, for women the proving ground was in large part controlled by the other gender. The case of eighteenth-century women provides a strong argument for taking a broader perspective, one in which reason, experience, and relation intersect.

CRITICAL HORIZONS AND CURRENT CONVERSATIONS

Three trends within current critical discourse have helped to shape this project. First, literary scholars have moved beyond initial rediscovery of Graffigny, Riccoboni, and Charrière. It is time to bring more of their texts into the critical conversation and to read them in new ways. Second, the question "What is Enlightenment?" remains open, lively, and relevant. Yet discussions of this question continue to overlook women's role in Enlightenment. Third, interest in the issue of women and reason, especially on the part of feminist theorists, continues unabated, but exploration of this interest tends to spin along a familiar track, all sides neglecting the historical role of women in these debates. All three of these perspectives stand to be significantly enriched by interacting with the others.

This project brings together insights from scholarly communities—notably literary critics and feminist philosophers—that tend not to communicate with one another. It takes up where two other books, adept explorations of men's historical prejudice against women's reason, leave off: Genevieve Lloyd's *The Man of Reason* and Geneviève Fraisse's *Reason's Muse*.[14] A number of studies have taken a one-on-one comparative approach between male-authored and female-authored texts, in the lineage of Miller's "reading in pairs." By contrast, that approach is expressly avoided here because, particularly where reason is concerned, it risks a reductive reading of women in terms of men. Indeed, one of the major biases against which this study struggles is the persistent tendency to read women's works as if all of their ideas came from their own lives or from works by men.

Critical studies to date have not treated Graffigny, Riccoboni, and Charrière together. And yet they form a coherent group, as women writers reclaiming reason during the period (in the words of historian Jeffrey Ravel) when Enlightenment ideas "went mainstream."[15] Analyses tend to focus on these women's novels, particularly the few that are the most widely known. There are no extant studies focusing on reason and Enlightenment. Erica Harth's well-researched *Cartesian Women* deals with women and reason in seventeenth-century France. It centers on the self-described *Cartésiennes,* discussing their social roles and intellectual work as overt engagements with the work of Descartes. The authors examined here, by contrast, were not professed disciples of any particular philosopher or philosophical system. Mary Trouille's excellent *Sexual Education in the Enlightenment* likewise focuses on the responses of women (none of them the focal authors of this study) to the work of a canonical philosopher, in this case Jean-Jacques Rousseau.[16] This study draws upon insights from all of these works, while offering something distinctive: a contextual analysis of three women's contributions to theorizing reason and Enlightenment, with implications for a better understanding not only of the eighteenth century but also of current controversies and concerns. Feminism originated as an Enlightenment project, and it is possible to demonstrate that Enlightenment continues to offer resources to feminism. These ideas will be explored in each of the following chapters.

A LOOK AHEAD

Chapter 1 provides an overview of eighteenth-century views on women, ranging from physiology to education. It offers signposts toward a more complex definition of the key terms "reason" and "Enlightenment." It further situates this study within contemporary debates and discusses the conditions under which eighteenth-century women wrote. Each of the three subsequent chapters focuses on one author, and particularly on those texts that best illustrate the author's unique contribution to the question of women's reason. The discussion in each case develops around a central motif that helps to elucidate this contribution. Chapter 2, on Graffigny, centers on the motif of the mask and the related themes of masquerade and gender performance. Chapter 3, on Riccoboni, draws upon the motif of the cup and the theme of reason as remedy. Chapter 4, devoted to Charrière, uses the motif of the book to introduce a broad understanding of literacy and Enlightenment. Finally, the conclusion returns to the explicit links between these women's works and current debates in feminist theory. There, it is argued that Graffigny, Riccoboni, and Charrière deserve a place in the wider history of ideas, that they contribute to debates on women's reason, and that they should rightfully be known not only as women of reason but as Enlightenment thinkers.

1
Women, Enlightenment,
and the Salic Law
of Reason

IMAGINE YOURSELF IN A WELL-APPOINTED LIBRARY READING ROOM. A volume of Denis Diderot and Jean Le Rond d'Alembert's *Encyclopédie, ou dictionnaire raisonné des arts, des sciences et des métiers* (1751–80) lies on a table before you. It is a book of impressive weight and dimension: in-folio, bound in brown leather, with gilt lettering on the spine and marbled endpapers. The luxuriousness of its binding befits the work's considerable status as the best-known monument to Enlightenment thought. You open the book to the frontispiece, an allegorical depiction of all of the domains of knowledge represented by human figures. The accompanying *explication* reads:

> "Sous un Temple d'Architecture Ionique, Sanctuaire de la Vérité, on voit la Vérité enveloppée d'un voile, et rayonnante d'une lumière qui écarte les nuages et les disperse. A droite de la Vérité, la Raison et la Philosophie s'occupent l'une à lever, l'autre à arracher le voile de la Vérité"

> [Beneath a Temple of Ionic Architecture, Sanctuary of Truth, we see Truth wrapped in a veil, radiating a light that parts the clouds and disperses them. To the right of Truth, Reason and Philosophy are occupied, the one in lifting the veil from Truth, the other in pulling it away].

2. *Encyclopédie* frontispiece, Benoît-Louis Prévost (1772) after Charles-Nicholas Cochin *fils*. Courtesy of Special Collections Library, Michigan State University

At the top of the image, Imagination appears on the left, approaching Truth with a garland and crown; Memory is located to the right of Reason. Thus the allegory highlights the trinity of faculties—imagination, reason, and memory—presented in the *Encyclopédie's Système figuré des connaissances humaines,* a sort of genealogical tree of knowledge, and in the attendant *Explication détaillée du système des connaissances humaines.* Also like the *Système,* the frontispiece depicts the various arts and sciences that spring from these three faculties. Beneath Memory, there is History. Beneath Imagination, the literary genres and fine arts. And beneath Reason, who wears a crown, Philosophy has pride of place. One feature of this frontispiece merits particular attention: all of the allegorical figures—including Reason—are female. If one were to assess the *Encyclopédie's* views on women based solely upon this allegory, one might conclude that it pays homage to some kind of gynocentric paradise, an intellectual realm where women reign supreme.

The frontispiece image, drawn by Charles-Nicholas Cochin *fils* and exhibited at the Louvre in the Salon of 1765, was engraved by Benoît-Louis Prévost in 1772. The first volume of the *Encyclopédie* had been published over twenty years earlier. The frontispiece was sent along belatedly to subscribers, who could have it bound in their existing copy. In using female bodies to depict abstract concepts, Cochin followed an ancient practice that continues to this day. Explanations for the practice in the context of ancien régime France range from the feminine gender of the nouns represented (such as *philosophie* and *raison)* to the fact that using a woman in the land of Salic law—where no woman could inherit the throne—meant that the figure would never be confused with a real-life ruler.[1] The frontispiece is subtly encoded feminine in another way, too: the backdrop features columns and capitals in Ionic style, long viewed as striving to imitate the female body.[2] Only at the bottom of the image do we see male figures: they represent actual human beings engaged in sciences and crafts, identifiable through the implements they hold.

Visual elements are a significant part of the *Encyclopédie.* There are eleven volumes of plates to accompany seventeen volumes of text. If the humble glassmaker or shipbuilder could be elevated by having his craft featured in the same work that plumbed the depths of metaphysics, why not also elevate women, who are featured allegorically as representing the supreme spheres of knowledge (Reason, Philosophy, and so forth)? But in fact, the frontispiece highlights an ironic disjuncture: reason appears as a woman, but only in allegory. When it is a question of real women, the Salic law of reason prevails. That is, although the abstract idea of *raison* is depicted in female form, women themselves were believed incapable of the highest forms of *raison*.[3] The message to women? Leave the philosophizing to men. We will use your bodies as models for our concepts, but your minds have nothing to do with reason.

So, is reason a woman? Londa Schiebinger writes that the *Encyclopédie* frontispiece depicts "feminine hegemony in science," featuring "a feminine Truth and Reason [that] reign over the sciences." She identifies this frontispiece as part of a tradition in which "science was a woman."[4] But a female allegorical figure representing a field of study does not mean that the field itself favored that gender. The case of *la raison* makes this point clearly enough. More recently and aptly, art historian Mary Sheriff has described the *Encyclopédie* frontispiece as an appropriation of femininity.[5] In other words, it encapsulates a much larger problem: the idea that women are mere embellishment to the serious work of Enlightenment.

The depiction of Reason as allegorically female in the frontispiece stands in stark contrast to the perceived opposition between reason and actual women, made clear in the *Encyclopédie*'s articles such as "Femme" and "Raisonnable," the latter of which I return to below. Desmahis writes in the article "Femme": "les deux sexes ont des avantages *presque* égaux. La nature a mis d'un côté la force et la majesté, le courage et la *raison;* de l'autre, les grâces et la beauté, la finesse et le *sentiment*" [The two sexes have *almost* equal advantages. To one, nature gave strength and majesty, courage and *reason;* to the other, graces and beauty, delicacy and *sentiment*]. Note the rhetorical construction of the second sentence: emphasis falls in each clause on the final term, *sentiment* and *raison*. This definition reflects the emerging eighteenth-century notion of complementarity between the sexes.[6] In it, women and reason are opposed. This view was particularly ironic in an age that declared allegiance to universal equality.

Eighteenth-Century Views
on Women and Reason

Women's reason was the subject of intense public debate in eighteenth-century France. Thinkers across diverse fields repeatedly proclaimed that the light of reason became distorted when it passed through the lens of femininity. Just as Salic law had, since the reign of Clovis in the sixth century, decreed that no female royal could inherit the French crown, French society denied that women were inheritors of reason on an equal basis with men. The eighteenth century defined "woman" and "reason" reciprocally and inversely. These attitudes have roots extending far into history. Eighteenth-century misogynists were never terribly original; in fact, they did not need to be. They mainly restated and reinforced ideas inherited from the tradition. And these ideas held powerful sway over women's lives. Women's inferior *raison* was perceived to be tightly linked to their *raison d'être*, permeating most every domain of life: physiology, education, marriage and law, morality, and access to public discourse.

Female Physiology: No Home for Reason

The association of men with the mind and of women with the body ran deep in French eighteenth-century thought. Women's status in society was profoundly influenced by interpretations of female physiology. Eighteenth-century anatomists reinforced ideals of feminine beauty and of women's proper role as reproducer rather than thinker. Drawings of female skeletons, skewed by ideology, gave visual "proof" in what were actually political debates. In 1759, the first known drawing of a specifically female skeleton inaccurately depicted the female skull as smaller in proportion to the body than the male skull. Although a more accurate skeleton drawing appeared in 1796, the public preferred the older version.[7]

In marked contrast to seventeenth-century Cartesianism and its tenet that, as Poullain de la Barre and other adherents famously stated, "the mind has no sex," eighteenth-century thinkers sought to demonstrate sex differences in the mind and to prove the ineluctable inferiority of women's reason. In his widely read *Système physique et moral de la femme* (1775), Pierre Rous-

sel asserts that a woman's sex is not limited to a single organ,
but rather extends to all parts of her body, over which it plays a
directing function. Women's fundamental physical *mollesse* [soft-
ness], he explains, is the cause of their great *sensibilité* [sensibil-
ity].[8] Supposed physical signs, including women's reputedly fragile bones, the abundance of nerve fibers, the dimensions of the
pelvis, and the small size of their brain, were thought to reveal
women's greater sensitivity and destination for motherhood. According to Roussel, women are "plus capable de sentir que de
créer" [more capable of feeling than of creating].[9]

Discussions of female physiology often bypassed the brain
completely, and focused on what was considered a woman's most
essential organ: the uterus. In his essay "Sur les femmes," Diderot writes: "La femme porte au-dedans d'elle-même un organe
susceptible de spasmes terribles, disposant d'elle et suscitant
dans son imagination des fantômes de toute espèce" [Woman
carries within herself an organ susceptible to terrible spasms,
controlling her and exciting in her imagination all sorts of phan-
toms].[10] And in his *Éléments de physiologie,* Diderot asserts star-
tlingly that the uterus "donne des lois, se mutine, entre en
fureur, resserre et étrangle les autres parties [du corps] tout
ainsi que le ferait un animal en colère" [dictates laws, mutinies,
becomes enraged, [and] squeezes and strangles the other parts
[of the body] as would an angry animal].[11]

Such pronouncements paved the way to declarations that
women were incapable of sound thinking, that the female body
was no home for reason. By virtue of being instantiated in this
particular (female) body, reason was stunted and simply could
not function properly. Physical attributes were linked with political rights in the popular imagination. Beginning in the 1750s,
men's seemingly superior body was cited with increasing frequency as a justification for men's social and political privileges.[12] The Salic law of reason held sway not only in physiological matters but in social matters as well, predominant among
which was women's education.

Women's Education: Nurture Meets "Nature"

The inadequate education available to eighteenth-century
women was a common theme in the writings of progressive

thinkers, who pointed out how the poor educational system per-
petuated conservative views in circular fashion. That is, the limited curriculum and circumscribed opportunities were justified
through appeals to women's "nature," which had itself been constructed through the lack of access to satisfactory education.
During the seventeenth century, the Counter-Reformation,
Jansenism, the development of new institutions of sociability, and
the growth in rates of education had all contributed to a greater
role for women in intellectual life.[13] The mid-century saw an up-
surge of interest in intellectual pursuits among women of the
upper classes, sometimes called *précieuses*. Their salons fostered
a flowering of intellectual brilliance. With the eventual decline of
humanism, however, learnedness in women was no longer admired, but became an object of scorn.[14] Women who distinguished
themselves intellectually—such as the *Cartésiennes*—risked
being branded *femmes savantes,* a stereotype immortalized in
Molière's 1672 play by that title. Anne-Thérèse de Lambert la-
mented in 1727 that women were supposed to hide their knowledge in accordance with the *bienséances*, or norms of propriety.
She asked: "Les femmes ne peuvent-elles pas dire aux hommes:
Quel droit avez-vous de nous défendre l'étude des sciences et des
beaux-arts?" [Can women not say to men: What right do you have
to prevent us from studying the sciences and fine arts?].[15] Similar remonstrances appear regularly in the writings of Graffigny,
Riccoboni, and Charrière.

Debates raged about the proper setting for girls' education—at
home or in convents. In the eighteenth century, there were probably no fewer than seventeen convent schools for girls in Paris,
one of the most famous being the abbey of Port-Royal. The curriculum included reading, writing, arithmetic, music, some geog-
raphy and history, and, above all, religious instruction.[16] The
basic mission was not to shape girls' intellectual development,
but to strengthen their moral sense and ability to teach their future children to be good members of society. Critics ridiculed convent schools on the grounds that the pupils learned nothing about
being good wives and mothers, given that the nuns who taught
them were neither. Graffigny (in her novel) and Riccoboni (in her
correspondence and in other works) joined other women in disparaging convent education, of which they both had personal experience, for its lack of intellectual rigor. In fact, most women

who managed to gain an education above the mediocre did so through independent study or a sympathetic father's intervention.

Jean-Jacques Rousseau, the eighteenth century's most famous—or infamous, depending on the perspective—pedagogue, asked, in a spectacular show of bad faith: "Et depuis quand sont-ce les hommes qui se mêlent de l'éducation des filles? Qui est-ce qui empêche les mères de les élever comme il leur plaît?" [What have men to do with the education of girls? What is there to hinder their mothers educating them as they please?].[17] At the same time, he asserted: "L'art de penser n'est pas étranger aux femmes, mais elles ne doivent faire qu'effleurer les sciences de raisonnement" [The art of thinking is not foreign to women, but they should only skim the surface of the sciences of reasoning].[18] The philosopher and mathematician marquis de Condorcet was alone among the *philosophes* in advocating something like equal rights for women, including equal access to education. He argued that "if all the barriers to women's education were lifted, their intellectual being would be exactly the same as that of man."[19] Janet Whatley speculates that it may have been his brilliant wife, Sophie de Grouchy de Condorcet, who inspired his progressive ideas.[20]

Marriage and Legal Discourse

Throughout the early modern period in France, women's identities were subsumed under those of men, in accordance with the doctrine of coverture. This doctrine was another variation on the worldview that gave rise to Salic law. Legally and economically, a woman was the responsibility of her father or husband. It is hardly surprising, then, that marriage was considered the pivotal moment in a woman's life. In the eighteenth century, women who died still unmarried constituted less than ten percent of the population.[21] The overriding concern of conduct manuals on proper behavior for girls was, in the words of Vivien Jones, how they "might create themselves as objects of male desire, but in terms which will contain that desire within the publicly sanctioned form of marriage."[22] In one sense, then, marriage was intended to control women's sexuality in the service of morality.

French laws reflected the importance of marriage for women, as well as the serious consequences that this institution entailed. Upon marrying, a woman "ceased to be an individual" and, in the eyes of the law, became "a virtual slave, whose person and assets were given over to the absolute control of another party." Eighteenth-century women had very limited or no legal ability "to litigate, to bear witness in court, to have guardianship of minors, to have [their] signature considered legally binding and valid, to witness a will, [or] to make a will."[23] Like the overt discourse on women's reason, the legal system functioned as a curb on women's freedom.

The mid-eighteenth century saw intense debates concerning the nature of marriage and the possibility of divorce. Two factors spurred the growing public discussion of divorce (which would only be legalized following the Revolution, in September 1792): first, treatises arguing that marriage was a contract, rather than a sacrament, encouraged the development of a new, secular ideal of the "modern marriage"; second, the common perception that "women were having their own way and making their own law" continued to grow despite ever-increasing legal restrictions on women.[24] The first of these factors indicates a general shift toward secularization, while the second reflects a suspicion of women's power.

Marriage contracts were widely used, especially among the bourgeoisie and the nobility, to spell out the couple's financial arrangements. Although the husband generally had control over the wife's goods, she might regain that control if granted a legal separation.[25] Hence the vested interest of men in preventing separations. These were of two types: a *séparation de corps* and a *séparation des biens*, neither easily obtained. A *séparation de corps* was possible if a woman "could prove that she was the victim of life-endangering abuse," while a *séparation des biens* required evidence that the "husband had willfully dissipated her fortune."[26] As Julie Hardwick explains, petitions for separation brought forth by wives "had to show clear proof of extreme wrongdoing by the husband." Things were easier for husbands, who could simply abandon their wives or have them committed to convents.[27] The latter scenario—imprisonment for life—was a possible consequence of a wife's infidelity (while a husband's infidelity was not even considered sufficient cause for a legal separation). All three of this study's focal authors were married, though none enjoyed a happy spousal relationship. Graffigny and Riccoboni both separated from their dissolute husbands; Charrière married late and lived out her adulthood in the company of a spouse who, while not abusive, lacked the intellectual spark to match her own.

Women's Reason and Morality

In the French eighteenth century, women's supposed lesser aptitude for reason was accompanied by a purported greater aptitude for morality. In *The Moral Sex,* Lieselotte Steinbrügge argues that eighteenth-century French women were understood as the upholders of morality, destined to obey social norms and to cultivate this obedience in their children.[28] Adherence to morality was to be judged by others, leading to a veritable obsession over women's reputation. Rousseau observed that "[i]l n'importe donc pas seulement que la femme soit fidèle, mais qu'elle soit jugée telle par son mari, par ses proches, par tout le monde" [it is not enough that a wife should be faithful; her husband, along with his friends and neighbors, must believe in her fidelity]. Thus, he continues, "leur honneur n'est pas seulement dans leur conduite, mais dans leur réputation, et il n'est pas possible que celle qui *consent à* passer pour infâme puisse jamais être honnête" [a woman's honor does not depend on her conduct alone, but on her reputation, and no woman who *permits herself* to be considered vile is really virtuous].[29]

As soon as women ventured outside the bounds of acceptable femininity—by becoming published authors, for instance—they were viewed as a threat to the moral order.[30] I will return in more detail below to the attacks against women authors. Women were thus consigned to the moral extremes: as guardians or destroyers of morality. The eighteenth-century ideals of virtue and modesty (*pudeur*)—subcategories of this wider concept of "the moral sex"—are closely linked to this book's core concerns: reason and women's writing. Placing women upon a moral pedestal, from which it was so easy to fall, was another mechanism for exerting control and limiting women's freedom.

Eighteenth-century women's reason was not systematically cultivated through education. It was not generally honored through status, position, or award. In fact, women's reason, constituted as an object of public discourse, was routinely diminished or denied. "Reason" in these contexts functioned as a code word. That is, denials of women's intellectual capacity and assertions about women's inferior reason had less to do with intellect or reason per se, and more to do with setting limits on women's freedom.

"Reasonable" Women

In eighteenth-century France, "woman" was labeled as "irrational" and intellectual "reason" as "unwomanly." But it is crucial to recognize that women of the era were also faced with something beyond the idea that their reason was inferior to men's. That is, *raison* was taken to mean something quite different for women and for men. Reason owed its substance to social convention, to the opinion of others. This was especially true for women, as I've suggested through the concepts of morality and reputation. Reason is not something that an individual woman could simply confer upon herself. Women, like men, had to bring their case before the tribunal of public opinion: reason had to be proved in public. But the public was gender biased. And women's virtue hinged on confinement to the private sphere.[31]

Consider the *Encyclopédie* article entitled "Raisonnable." It states, simply enough, that "[u]n homme raisonnable" is one "dont la conduite est conforme à la raison" [a "reasonable man" is one "whose behavior is in conformity with reason"]. The entry continues: "Ce mot a une acception un peu détournée, lorsqu'il est appliqué à la femme; une femme *raisonnable* est celle qui ne se laisse point emporter à l'esprit régnant de la galanterie" [This word's meaning deviates slightly when it is applied to woman; a *reasonable* woman is one who does not let herself get carried away by the reigning spirit of gallantry].[32] This article, largely if not utterly ignored by scholars today, is one of a precious few instances where the canonical eighteenth-century distinction between "reasonable" men versus "reasonable" women is so plainly articulated. According to the article, the *homme raisonnable* is intellectual and rational, while the *femme raisonnable* is obedient and moral. The definition of *raisonnable* is said to "deviate" when applied to women. For a woman, being *raisonnable* means behaving herself, not allowing herself to be seduced. This idea neatly reflects the eighteenth-century obsession with women's reputation and their role as upholders of morality. Eighteenth-century women were considered less rational but constrained to be more "reasonable" than men.

For a woman, what we could call the reason of convention trumped all else. Men's reason could be highly unconventional, challenging the most sacrosanct values of the society, from Church to State to hierarchy in other forms. Indeed, this critical task has been understood as reason's principal function from Descartes until the present day. But women's reason had to be channeled and controlled. And of course, those traditional social values so strenuously attacked by the *philosophes* did not include the sexism that saturated social institutions, leading to these sex-specific definitions of reason.

Here we come up against a tension at the heart of mainstream Enlightenment thought, a tension that illuminates the present study's focus on the social function of reason. Seemingly universal proclamations—of liberty, equality, and "brotherhood"—notwithstanding, the ideals of Enlightenment were not really considered to be shared by all. And so, on the one hand, there is the question of how the eighteenth century understood "reason." On the other hand, there is the question of who was considered to possess the faculty of reason, to what degree, and for what purpose.

The chapters that follow will highlight the fundamental refusal of this study's focal authors to accept a limited definition of women's reason. Their female protagonists ask questions such as "What should I do to be reasonable?" (Graffigny), make statements like "I am a woman, obliged by my status to be reasonable" (Riccoboni), and criticize "those who claim to be reasonable" (Charrière). All three authors prove to be women of reason.

By virtue of their claims to reason, Graffigny, Riccoboni, and Charrière participated in a long but often overlooked women's literary tradition that may be traced back to the beginnings of the *querelle des femmes*. In Christine de Pizan's early-fifteenth-century *Book of the City of Ladies,* the protagonist, Christine, falls into a deep melancholy upon reading a book of misogynous attacks. Three allegorical ladies appear—Reason, Rectitude, and Justice—and guide her to construct a city, a refuge for unjustly slandered women of virtue. Lady Reason explains to Christine: "I can assure you that these attacks on all women . . . have never originated in me, Reason, and that all who subscribe to them have failed totally and will continue to fail."[33] According to historian Joan Kelly, Christine de Pizan's opposition to the idea of women's inferiority "rest[s] upon a refutation of male authority as expressed in what was accepted as knowledge, or learning." As Kelly explains, her texts show that "[u]niversal as it might seem, the disparagement of women was not validated by her own and other women's experience."[34] Christine de Pizan's fight against misogyny in the name of reason, bolstered by appeals to experience, prefigured the battles that Graffigny, Riccoboni, and Charrière continued to wage more than three hundred years later.

Although these works attest to a certain continuity across time, they also call upon us to study reason within a particular context, both historical and ideological. To a significant degree, reason is less usefully understood as a transhistorical constant than as a regulative ideal that functioned to certain ends. Such close attention to reason in the eighteenth century will, in turn, reopen the crucial question of Enlightenment.

Seventeenth-Century Rationalism versus Eighteenth-Century Reason

Whether championed or disparaged, "reason" is often invoked yet seldom defined. But what does "reason" mean? Here we may usefully appeal to what philosophers David Hall and Roger Ames call a "cluster concept," or a concept that is not susceptible to definition in an absolute sense, outside of a given context.[35] Instead, as Hall and Ames suggest, we should seek to elucidate the term's functioning within a determined historical, cultural, and ideological space. This method will help us better understand just what was at stake in denials of women's reason, and just what eighteenth-century women were claiming when they claimed reason. A first step is to distinguish, in broad terms, seventeenth-century rationalism from eighteenth-century reason.

Seventeenth-century rationalists worked to construct philosophical systems through deduction. For them, the function of reason was to reduce what is complex to simple elements, an analytic method based upon the work of Descartes. Up through the seventeenth century, reason was understood not only as a quality of the mind but also as a principle reflected in the cosmic order; for Enlightenment thinkers, on the other hand, reason is a fundamentally human faculty, the capacity for analysis and discernment, for criticism and invention. In his classic study of the "crisis of consciousness" at the turn of the eighteenth century, Paul Hazard notes that the seventeenth century loved hierarchy, discipline, order, and authority, while the eighteenth century loathed automatic loyalty to such constraints.[36]

The latter idea is most famously and succinctly expressed by Immanuel Kant in his 1784 essay "An Answer to the Question: 'What is Enlightenment?,'" where he defines *Aufklärung* as "man's emergence from his self-incurred immaturity" and issues the challenge *Sapere aude,* or "Dare to know."[37] In that essay, Kant uses the German verb *räsonieren,* which means "reasoning for reason's sake," to characterize philosophical thinking. In his own essay entitled "What is Enlightenment?," to which I return below, Michel Foucault expressly takes up and discusses this use of *räsonieren.* This idea will also figure in chapters 2 and 4, on the work of Graffigny and Charrière.

Despite his call to "have courage to use [one's] *own* understanding," Kant held that some traditional limits were not to be breached. Thus, in "What is Enlightenment?," Kant also observes that "by far the largest part of mankind (including the entire fair sex) . . . consider[s] the step forward to maturity not only as difficult but also as highly dangerous."[38] This observation is disingenuous, though, given that Kant was aware of at least some women's intellectual pursuits, as revealed in his infamous attack on learned women: "A woman who has a head full of Greek, like Mme Dacier, or carries on fundamental controversies about mechanics, like the Marquise Du Châtelet, might as well even have a beard, for perhaps that would express more obviously the mien of profundity for which she strives."[39] Note that both examples are French women. For Kant, as in the minds of most *philosophes,* the only authentic *raison* is the bearded variety.

Eighteenth-century thinkers purported to use reason to overcome unreflective allegiance to any authority—though, of course,

they were largely oblivious to various kinds of traditional prejudice, including sexism. The *Encyclopédie* article "Raison" asserts:
"dans toutes les choses dont nous avons une idée nette et dis-
tincte, la *raison* est le vrai juge compétant" [in all things about
which we have a clear and distinct idea, *reason* is the true
judge].[40] The Cartesian tradition certainly persisted in the eighteenth century—hence the reference here to "clear and distinct
ideas"—but with important nuances. In his article on "Reason"
in *The Cambridge History of Eighteenth-Century Philosophy,* Michel Malherbe reminds us that pure rationalism was not a central feature of eighteenth-century thought. Malherbe adds that
eighteenth-century thinkers were interested in establishing the
scope of reason and testing its limits.[41] Calling the eighteenth
century the "Age of Reason" is inaccurate, because mainstream
Enlightenment thinkers "did not grant reason the ability to
achieve knowledge on its own, independently of the senses."[42] Enlightenment philosophers reconciled reason with sense experience. Inspired by the British philosophers John Locke and David
Hume as well as their compatriot Étienne Bonnot de Condillac,
most French thinkers of the Enlightenment adopted some sort of
empiricism, that is, the stance that our knowledge originates in
sense impressions and experiences. D'Alembert's *Discours préliminaire* to the *Encyclopédie* provides an overview of the eighteenth-century synthesis between rationalism and empiricism.
D'Alembert divides all knowledge [*connaissances*] into two types:
direct [*directes*] and reflexive [*réfléchies*], of which the former results from the senses.[43]

    In line with the materialist anthropology of the day, the *phi-
losophes* embraced sensibility and the passions. Their ideas harmonize with the theories of moral sentiments developed by thinkers such as Hume and Adam Smith. As Janet Todd explains in
her authoritative study *Sensibility: An Introduction,* the eighteenth century understood the term *sentiment* primarily in moral
terms: "A sentiment . . . is a moral reflection, a rational opinion
usually about the rights and wrongs of human conduct."[44] Claude-
Adrien Helvétius affirms that reason is not altogether foreign to
sensibility and the passions when he writes in *De l'Esprit* [*Essays
on the Mind*] that the passions are "le germe productif de l'esprit"
[the productive germ of the mind] and "la source de nos lumières"
[the source of our enlightenment].[45] Likewise, Diderot remarks in

his *Pensées philosophiques* that "[i]l n'y a que les passions, et les grandes passions, qui puissent élever l'âme aux grandes choses" [only passions, great passions, can elevate the soul to great things].[46] It is true that, echoing a long philosophical tradition harking back to Plato's tripartite division of the soul into the rational, the spirited, and the appetitive (in Book 4 of the *Republic*), the *philosophes* generally believed that reason should govern the other aspects. But they certainly did not view reason and the passions, or reason and sentiment, as unrelated, incompatible, or strictly opposed.

At the same time, it is important to recall the double standard of *sensibilité*. Although to a lesser degree than their British counterparts, French thinkers supposed that women had greater *sensibilité* than men.[47] In men, *sensibilité* was viewed as a natural complement to reason. In women, it was viewed as a hindrance to reason. When male writers placed value on *sentiment*, they were called empiricists and sensationalists. When women writers did the same, they were called emotional and said to be dominated by their feelings. This eighteenth-century truism lives on in much scholarship about Graffigny, Riccoboni, and Charrière. That is, despite ample evidence to the contrary, scholars often assert or imply that these women were solely interested in sentiment rather than reason.

Eighteenth-century reason was significantly broader in scope than its seventeenth-century rationalist cousin. Nevertheless, the standard eighteenth-century understanding of reason was not broad enough to include women. That is, canonical eighteenth-century thinkers viewed reason, at least in its most developed forms, as a capacity for creation and an instrument of analysis exclusive to men.

No writer of the age made this point more forcefully than Rousseau, who argues that because speculative studies are beyond women's reach, practical endeavors should be their focus.[48] Rousseau describes women as intellectually passive: "la femme observe, et l'homme raisonne" [woman observes, man reasons].[49] For French Enlightenment thinkers, as for Kant, the call to reason was fundamentally a call to think for oneself, independently of arbitrary authorities. But according to Rousseau, only men may use reason in this way: "[l]'homme . . . peut braver le jugement public" [men are free to defy public opinion], but women must constantly ask themselves what other people think.[50]

At this juncture, it seems fitting to ask: Which is more amenable to women's interests, seventeenth-century rationalism or eighteenth-century reason? Descartes, along with Cartesians like Poullain de la Barre and the women who described themselves as *Cartésiennes,* drew upon the idea that body and mind are separable to argue that women's reason can equal men's, despite women's supposed inferior physiology. And canonical eighteenth-century thinkers were certainly less open to women's concerns than these Cartesians.

And yet, neither the ways in which eighteenth-century reason was applied nor its evident omissions should lead us to disregard its potential. Eighteenth-century reason may be understood in two different, compatible ways: as critical and as constructive (Hazard speaks of "demolition" and "reconstruction").[51] Thinkers of the age critiqued prejudice and the power of traditional institutions. They believed that reason could lead to better human lives and a more enlightened society. Eighteenth-century reason was resolutely anti-authoritarian. It was considered a force for transforming the world. And so, in comparison with seventeenth-century rationalism, eighteenth-century reason may in principle be considered better able to promote women's interests. Counter to a feminist tenet drawn from the Cartesian mind/body distinction, Graffigny, Riccoboni, and Charrière did not hold that the solution to sexism is getting rid of sex. Reason as the eighteenth century understood it is not universal and closed, but contingent, open, and dynamic. Historicizing our discussion of reason will open up new understandings of Enlightenment.

WHAT IS ENLIGHTENMENT?

Only when we approach eighteenth-century reason within the wider scope of Enlightenment do we appreciate the full force of the attitudes, definitions, and questions discussed above. And so it is necessary to return to Kant's question: What is Enlightenment? The term can refer to a historical period as well as to a philosophical approach; the discussion that follows will engage both of these senses. Even that basic distinction—among oth-

ers—often gets lost. Current critical discourse on Enlightenment is marked by two main tendencies whose adherents may be
labeled caricaturists and apologists.

The Caricaturist Tendency

Today, across the humanities, the dominant mode of critical engagement with Enlightenment is caricature. As political scientist James Schmidt observes, only its detractors think that Enlightenment is one unified body of ideas.[52] Caricaturists often
attribute to Enlightenment the idea that reason is the sole route
to knowledge, or that reason is strictly opposed to passion or sentiment. To construct such claims is to battle a straw person,
given, as I have suggested above, that Enlightenment thinkers
espoused empiricism and embraced the passions. Most often,
caricaturists avoid dealing with particular Enlightenment
thinkers or texts. Their accounts often seem to lump together
thinkers from Descartes to Kant and every man in between.
And they routinely omit the eighteenth-century French *philosophes* entirely. Through the brief discussion that follows, I hope to
urge greater care in defining Enlightenment.

The most famous Enlightenment caricaturists are Frankfurt
School philosophers Theodor Adorno and Max Horkheimer who,
in their 1947 book *Dialectic of Enlightenment,* describe the
greatest horrors of the twentieth century as the logical outcome
of Enlightenment reason. Such an attribution, however, mistak-
enly reduces the whole of Enlightenment thought to "mere utili-
tarian means-end reasoning,"[53] or, in other words, instrumental
reason. Another group of caricaturists is comprised of postmodernists who call Enlightenment a universalizing monolith.[54]
This stance is particularly ironic, because in making the accusation, critics actually impose a narrow, universal definition on a
much more complex set of historical and intellectual phenomena.
As Daniel Gordon remarks, the notion that there is a single van-
tage point offering objective, unified knowledge "is precisely
what the *philosophes* denied." He adds that postmodern critics
tend "to identify Enlightenment thinkers with the very rationalism that they tried to avoid."[55] Furthermore, as Dena Goodman
explains, difference and diversity may be called core Enlightenment values.[56] In her book *Reading the French Enlightenment:*

System and Subversion, Julie Hayes shows that "systematizing and classifying reason could become hegemonic and coercive only to the extent to which significant strains within it are forgotten and repressed."[57] That is, those who dismiss Enlightenment reason on the grounds that it was strictly instrumental and monolithic invoke only a diminished, caricatured definition of it.

Some feminists explicitly label Enlightenment as women's enemy. Philosopher Susan Hekman, at the conclusion of an otherwise thoughtful article on feminist standpoint theory, states confidently that "the Enlightenment certainties have been exploded," but it is not clear what those "certainties" might be.[58] In her book *Gender and Knowledge,* Hekman defends postmodern feminism against eighteenth-century epistemology, which she describes inaccurately as advocating the belief that "there is only one way in which knowledge can be constituted."[59] Postmodern theorist Jane Flax denies the liberatory potential of Enlightenment while admitting to dealing with a "cluster of beliefs [she] clump[s] too simply under the rubric of the 'Enlightenment.'"[60] Arguably, for defenders of Enlightenment, it is less a matter of discounting points raised by postmodernists—for example, that we should resist any theory that attempts to impose a monolithic viewpoint—and more a matter of showing that Enlightenment thinkers do not stand in opposition to those points.

All of these caricatures invoke, in one way or another, what has been called "the crisis of reason."[61] Traditional philosophical methods that make purchases on the ideal of objectivity have been critiqued for positing as given an isolated, autonomous knower, on the grounds that they ignore the body as well as a range of identity categories that inevitably influence knowledge. For instance, Diana Meyers summarizes the feminist critique of models of the self ascribed to the Enlightenment. These models, she writes, rely upon a "decontextualized individualism," treating the self as "a free and rational chooser and actor—an autonomous agent."[62] In no way do I mean to discount such critiques, or to suggest that Enlightenment is immune to criticism. Rather, I am calling for a nuanced definition of reason and of Enlightenment, perhaps most especially in the context of critique. For example, as I have suggested, it is a mistake to equate Cartesian rationalism—the real target of the critiques of reason summarized above—with Enlightenment. When "Enlightenment

thought" is presented in these stark terms, the contributions of
eighteenth-century women are by definition ignored. Valuable
resources are missed, including resources that could help to re-
define Enlightenment and serve feminist thinking today. A central dilemma, as I discuss in greater detail below, is that caricaturists discount Enlightenment without having entertained the
idea that any women were part of it.

The Apologist Tendency

On the other side are the apologists, who argue for the complexity and ongoing relevance of the cluster of phenomena known as
Enlightenment. James Schmidt cogently describes some of the
confusion spread by invocations of "Enlightenment" in current
discussions about civil society, and asks whether "Enlightenment" has been stretched to the point of losing its meaning.
Schmidt nevertheless emerges as a champion of Enlightenment
(specifically, Kantian) justice, and remarks that the kind of "critical examination" he undertakes of the various claims made in
the name of Enlightenment "might well be characterized as the
Enlightenment project."[63]

Perhaps the most famous Enlightenment apologist is philosopher Jürgen Habermas. Like Horkheimer and Adorno, he is associated with the Frankfurt School, though of a more recent
generation. His *Structural Transformation of the Public Sphere,*
since its initial publication in German in 1969 and especially
following its English translation in 1989, has changed the ways
in which scholars think about the early modern flourishing of
public discourse and the institutions (places such as cafés and
publications such as newspapers) that fostered this discourse.
Building upon this research, Habermas's subsequent theory of
communicative reason attributes liberating potential to the Enlightenment ideal of interaction among rational participants in
the public sphere.

There is much in the work of both Schmidt and Habermas—
as well as other Enlightenment apologists—with which I am
deeply sympathetic. But at the same time, there are shortcom-
ings in these approaches. Schmidt focuses on male thinkers of
the German Enlightenment, providing a strictly androcentric
view of the era. Habermas's description of the bourgeois public

sphere and his theory of communicative reason likewise center exclusively on men and their achievements. In a careful analysis of Habermas's communicative reason, Marie Fleming shows that the theory does not provide room for a critical examination of reason itself; thus it "fail[s] to engage feminist critiques."[64] While both Schmidt and Habermas investigate what reason and the Enlightenment can offer current social theory, they remain within a traditional and limited understanding of Enlightenment as a male-only intellectual movement. Like the caricaturists, the apologists ignore the contributions of women to Enlightenment, contributions that would enrich and complicate the ways in which Enlightenment is understood.

Pro-Enlightenment Feminists

[handwritten: idea that feminism is possible because of Enlightenment]

Although Enlightenment has been subject to feminist critique, there are also feminists who take a positive view of Enlightenment, including some theorists who are in dialogue with Habermas. For example, Seyla Benhabib undertakes "[a] post-Enlightenment defense of universalism," drawing upon the thought of Habermas while working "to 'engender' the subject of moral reasoning."[65] Pauline Johnson argues that the feminist repudiation of Enlightenment rests upon a fundamental misunderstanding of the meaning of Enlightenment. Echoing the passage from Schmidt quoted above, she shows that feminist critique of some eighteenth-century ideas and of gender prejudice more generally is, in fact, "another vital episode in the unfolding of the Enlightenment project itself."[66] Taking a historical perspective, Anne Mellor states the matter plainly: "Modern feminist theory originated in the philosophies of the Enlightenment."[67]

Like other Enlightenment apologists, these feminist theorists reject the caricaturists' monolithic view of Enlightenment. Of course, they aim to include women among those who stand to benefit from Enlightenment as a liberatory ideal. But at the same time, they accept a traditional view of the collection of works thought to constitute Enlightenment. For them, it was the men of the eighteenth century who formulated Enlightenment ideas, and who still have something to say to us today. I do not mean to reject these feminists' recuperation of Enlightenment. Rather, I propose that their theories would be enriched by drawing upon a wider corpus of eighteenth-century texts. In so doing, they could also present a theoretical position that would speak more directly to feminist concerns today. Chapters 2, 3, and 4 all engage this issue, which again comes to the fore in the conclusion.

Scholarship on Eighteenth-Century Women

Thus far I have suggested that the question of eighteenth-century women as Enlightenment thinkers is overlooked by Enlightenment caricaturists and apologists alike. What about in the burgeoning scholarship on eighteenth-century women? Over the past twenty years, scholars have increasingly studied the lives of these women from historical, legal, political, literary, and social perspectives. Scholars of France have focused particular attention on the role of women during the Revolutionary period, analyzing, for instance, the symbolic function of attacks on Marie Antoinette.[68] In her groundbreaking work on eighteenth-century salon hostesses, or *salonnières*, historian Dena Goodman has drawn new attention to the role of these women in French intellectual life. And yet Goodman tends to describe them as enforcers of rules; as selfless, attentive, and silent. She argues that the *salonnières* "provided the *ground* for the philosophes' *serious* work."[69] Rather than being creative individuals in their own right, the *salonnières* appear on this account to serve a secondary, supporting role so that men could carry out the real work of Enlightenment. This may well be an accurate picture of the *salonnières;* I leave that determination to others.[70] But it does not significantly alter the traditional view of eighteenth-century women. It certainly calls upon us to look elsewhere for the original, intellectual contributions of women to Enlightenment.

Hence the present study's focus on what eighteenth-century women wrote. Indeed, the work of these writers has become increasingly visible in recent years, with new editions of texts and critical studies appearing at an ever-quickening pace. Witness the growing interest in writers like Anne-Thérèse de Lambert, Émilie Du Châtelet, and Stéphanie de Genlis.[71] And, of course, the work of literary authors, including Graffigny, Riccoboni, and Charrière, is gaining new attention, as I will discuss below and in subsequent chapters. But I want to emphasize a surprising fact: all too often—and despite some exceptions—scholars who study eighteenth-century literary women fail to claim for them the status of Enlightenment thinker.

Neither Lambert, nor Du Châtelet, nor Genlis—nor, for that matter, Graffigny, Riccoboni, or Charrière—is a household name. So far, at least, they have not broken into the orbit of those considered to be "real" Enlightenment thinkers. As I noted above, even apologists for the Enlightenment routinely leave women out of the picture. One may imagine that historians of the Enlightenment would do better. But in fact, even historical accounts, including recent debates about "conservative" (or mainstream) versus "radical" Enlightenment, largely ignore women's contributions.[72]

Curiously, in overviews of Enlightenment by historians (those sympathetic to women) as well as in overviews of feminism by feminist theorists (those attuned to history), often just one token woman is included: Mary Wollstonecraft. Her *Vindication of the Rights of Woman* (1792) is a profoundly admirable book, in both content and form. It draws upon ideals of reason, education, and citizenship in order to argue for a more equitable world for women. In it, Wollstonecraft boldly refutes the misogynous screed of Rousseau's *Émile,* often point by point. My critique has nothing to do with the quality of Wollstonecraft's thought. Rather, I object that all too often, Wollstonecraft is made to stand in for the whole of eighteenth-century feminist thought, a move we could call the "Wollstonecraft synecdoche." Among the overviews by historians, a key example is Dorinda Outram's *The Enlightenment,* excellent in many respects. But its chapter on "Enlightenment Thinking about Gender," aside from a brief mention of Du Châtelet and a short discussion of the *salonnières*, is exclusively devoted to Wollstonecraft.[73] Similarly, Wollstonecraft is the only eighteenth-century woman quoted in Anne Mellor's entry on "Feminist Theory" in the *Encyclopedia of the Enlightenment* edited by Alan Kors (there is also one sentence about Olympe de Gouges). Among the overviews by feminist theorists, a good example is Claire Colebrook's book *Gender,* in which "Enlightenment feminism" and "Wollstonecraft" are used interchangeably.[74] And this conflation leads Colebrook to assert that eighteenth-century women's thought evinces no sex/gender distinction, a claim that this book's discussions of Graffigny, Riccoboni, and Charrière will repeatedly call into question.[75]

The time has come to expand the scope of knowledge about women's thought in the eighteenth century and about their contributions to Enlightenment. The Wollstonecraft synecdoche not only elides differences among eighteenth-century women intellectuals, but it risks falling into the logic of the exception that proves the rule: there was one woman intellectual in the eighteenth century, thus women of the era were not intellectuals. The story of the Enlightenment extends beyond men, and the story of eighteenth-century feminism extends beyond Wollstonecraft.

Beyond the Wollstonecraft Synecdoche: Women, Enlightenment, and New Frameworks

And so, reading various accounts of Enlightenment, we are left to wonder: Where are the women? Common assumptions about Enlightenment—whether from caricaturists, apologists, or others—effectively erase key aspects of the past as well as the ongoing project of Enlightenment. There is a danger in failing to inquire where our definition of Enlightenment comes from and which voices it excludes. As we explore the different meanings of the term, it is helpful to ask: Whose interests does it serve to remember the historical Enlightenment, or to define the philosophical Enlightenment, in this way? We are called upon to follow Enlightenment thinkers themselves in adopting a strategy that is both critical and constructive.

Perhaps there is no convincing the most entrenched caricaturists that the Enlightenment is redeemable. But for those open to a new approach, I submit that there is a problem with simply rejecting Enlightenment. Women have been excluded from the basic interpretive schemas through which Enlightenment is understood. As feminist critics have often observed, simply adding women's voices without transforming those interpretive schemas (the "add women and stir" approach) does not suffice. A broadened definition of Enlightenment, one that truly includes women's voices, may avoid the pitfalls described by the caricaturists. Modifying a phrase from David Halperin, I suggest that it is premature to join the chorus "Forget Enlightenment" before adequately remembering it.[76] I urge that we not simply give Enlightenment over to those who hold it in such low regard.

And so I propose to take another look at the French eighteenth century, at "the" Enlightenment, from a fresh angle, bringing into the picture perspectives that are usually overlooked. A range of critics have excluded women such as Graffigny, Riccoboni, and Charrière from Enlightenment thought, while caricaturists have called into question why anyone would wish to be included under the label. I take issue with both points of view in an effort to expand our understanding of Enlightenment.

What Is Enlightenment? A Threefold Definition

In his essay "What is Enlightenment?," Foucault defines Enlightenment as an *ethos*, "the permanent reactivation of an attitude," a "critical interrogation on the present and on ourselves."[77] Julie Hayes writes that Foucault's project "speaks urgently . . . of the need for rereadings and reevaluations of Enlightenment texts."[78] With these ideas in mind, I invite the reader to consider Enlightenment in three senses. First is a historical redefining and broadening of Enlightenment to include women's intellectual contributions. Second is a sense of Enlightenment as the continual reactivation of a critical attitude, hence a mode of thinking that exceeds the bounds of one historical period. Third is a blend of the first two: considering how a new historical understanding of Enlightenment may inform and shape our current critical reactivations. The Enlightenment I discuss is rooted in eighteenth-century France, but it extends beyond a single century or national context. The interpretive approach here focuses on eighteenth-century texts, but it also suggests a fluidity between past, present, and future. It recognizes that the study of the past is, in part, a creation of the present as well as a projection of possible futures. It conceives of Enlightenment as a project both unfinished and ongoing.

WOMEN WRITERS AND THE
PUBLIC SPHERE OF DISCOURSE

This study draws upon an appreciation of the context within which eighteenth-century women wrote, the accusations made against them, and the value of turning to their literary works. As has by

now been well documented, eighteenth-century women authors
faced serious challenges, both material and symbolic. These
challenges spanned the domains of life discussed above: an inadequate educational system, legal and financial barriers, and
moral proscriptions against women's participation in public life.
Overall, a prohibition reigned against women's ambition. Joan
DeJean explains the vilification of women writers, particularly
novelists, on the grounds that it was believed their texts could
lead to "social unrest and societal . . . transformation."[79] Novels
were also considered especially dangerous for female readers, as
Rousseau warned ominously in the preface to *Julie:* "Jamais fille
chaste n'a lu de romans" [No chaste girl has ever read a novel].[80]
Writing by women was well tolerated only in circumscribed contexts, such as letter writing.

Lambert's "Réflexions nouvelles sur les femmes" begins: "Il a
paru, depuis quelque temps, des romans faits par des dames,
dont les ouvrages sont aussi aimables qu'elles" [There have appeared recently some novels written by ladies, whose works are
as likable as they are]. However, Lambert notes: "Quelques personnes, au lieu d'en examiner les grâces, ont cherché à y jeter du
ridicule" [Some people, instead of examining the graces of these
works, have sought to heap ridicule upon them].[81] Some thirty
years later, Rousseau would register his scorn for the woman
who, neglecting her motherly duties, may be found "écrivant des
vers sur sa toilette, entourée de brochures de toutes les sortes et
de petits billets peints de toutes les couleurs" [writing verses at
her toilet table surrounded with pamphlets of every kind and
with notes on tinted paper].[82] In 1777, Restif de la Bretonne published *Les Gynographes*, a mockery of women writers that urged
them to return to their proper place in the home in the service of
reforming moral values. Elsewhere, Restif argued that because
women writers "s'exposent" [expose themselves] publicly, they
are like actresses or prostitutes—that is, immoral.[83] The vehe-
mence with which women writers were attacked suggests the
threat that these women posed to the values of the status quo.

To be fair, we must acknowledge that not all men simply rejected women's right to take up the pen. In his six-volume work
Le Tableau de Paris (1781–88), Louis-Sébastien Mercier included
an article on "Femmes auteurs," defending women authors
against their male detractors. Although his defense now seems

condescending (he asks "pourquoi serait-il défendu à l'esprit de passer par une belle bouche?" [why should intellect be prevented from passing through a beautiful mouth?]),[84] Mercier criticizes men who invoke female modesty to forbid women from writing. Women's works, he observes, are judged severely: "Dès que les femmes publient leurs ouvrages, elles ont d'abord contre elles la plus grande partie de leur sexe, et bientôt presque tous les hommes" [As soon as women publish their works, they have most of the members of their own sex against them, and soon almost all men].[85] Mercier's essay ends, however, on an equivocal note. He suggests that the ideas and feelings that reside in women's soul "se développent peut-être avec plus de franchise dans leurs écrits que dans leurs regards et dans leurs paroles" [are perhaps developed more honestly in their writings than in their looks and words].[86] Here, he alludes to the idea of feminine dissimulation, which is another crucial aspect of the question of women's reason.

Women authors were denounced not only as a threat to morality but also as fakes. Women—including Graffigny, Riccoboni, and Charrière—were often accused of passing off men's works as their own. At best, they were considered closet autobiographers or imitators of men. Even today, much critical literature about these three authors belies a fixation on the question: From what man did this woman get her ideas? The belief persists that these women lacked the intellectual acuity—the kind of reason—that would enable them to create original works.

Women, Coquetry, and Faking Reason

Above, I invoked Kant's use and Foucault's discussion of the verb *räsonieren*, "to reason for reason's sake." Here, it will be instructive to link that discussion to Restif de la Bretonne's *Les Parisiennes* (1787), in which the author offers a pitiable parade of wifely types to avoid. The chapter entitled "L'épouse dominatrice et la raisonneuse" [The Dominating Wife and the *Raisonneuse*] features an *épouse raisonneuse* named Valentine-De-Voulut (her last name is a form of the verb *vouloir*, "to want") whose fault is her penchant for playing devil's advocate. Of this reasoning wife, Restif writes: "Si l'on proposait une partie, même la plus agréable à Valentine, elle raisonnait à perte-de-vue, pour prouver qu'il valait mieux faire autre chose" [If one proposed an activity, even one very agreeable to Valentine, she reasoned as far as the eye could see, in order to prove that it was better to do something else].[87] We are told that she had perfected "cet insupportable talent de raisonner" [this insufferable talent for reasoning] among her brothers, and that she had thus become "savante au-delà de ce qu'une Femme doit l'être" [more learned than a woman should be]. That is, she had become a *femme savante*. Valentine uses her reason to question a wife's duty to be faithful, then turns to proving the opposite idea, but not before scandalizing her interlocutors, who conclude "qu'elle avait . . . point ou très peu de principes de morale" [that she had no, or very few, moral principles].[88] In short, it is unseemly and immoral when a woman reasons for reason's sake. This judgment rests in part upon the stereotype that women are inconstant, an idea addressed again in chapter 2.

As I have explained, this study's focus is the social functioning of reason, particularly in terms of the cultural work accomplished by women who claimed reason, but also in terms of men's denials of women's reason. Sometimes this denial was carried out by attacking women through association with derogatory concepts. Chief among these was coquetry. The *Encyclopédie* defines coquetry as "le défaut le plus méprisable qu'on puisse reprocher à une femme" [the most despicable flaw of which a woman may be accused]. It is "un tissu de faussetés" [a fabric of falsehoods] born of a woman's "dessein de paraître aimable à plusieurs hommes" [intention to seem agreeable to several men].[89] Quite unlike *raison, coquetterie* is virtually never invoked in a positive sense. The notable exception to this rule is Rousseau. In fact, there are two competing views of the *coquette* in *Émile*. On the negative side, following tradition, Rousseau attacks the kind of coquetry that he says "produit tous les travers des femmes et fait les plus extravagantes petites maîtresses" [produces every kind of misconduct, a coquetry which turns out girls who are the most ridiculous little madams].[90] Rousseau observes: "Le même tour d'esprit qui fait exceller une femme du monde dans l'art de tenir maison, fait exceller une coquette dans l'art d'amuser plusieurs soupirants" [The same turn of mind which makes a woman of the world such an excellent hostess, enables a *coquette* to excel in the art of amusing a number of suitors].[91] He means that women are experts at deception, the corrupt foundation of coquetry. On the positive side, a woman's desire to please her husband should make her a secret coquette. Rousseau writes about Sophie: "Il n'y a pas une jeune personne qui paraisse mise avec moins de recherche et dont l'ajustement soit plus recherché. . . . Sa parure est très modeste en apparence, très coquette en effet" [No girl seems more simply dressed, but no one could take more pains over her toilet. . . . Her dress is very modest in appearance and very coquettish in reality].[92] It is allowable for Sophie to "employer la coquetterie aux intérêts de la vertu" [employ coquetry on behalf of virtue].[93] In any case, Rousseau writes: "La femme est coquette par état" [Woman is a coquette by profession].[94] So there is a bad kind of coquetry (immoral, overt, and on display) and a good kind (honest, covert, and enticing). Which points to a fundamental irony: coquetry is disparaged because it grows from dissimulation, yet Rousseau's "good" coquetry is precisely the type that hides itself. Openly displaying one's coquettish talents is what leads to moral corruption. And why would a woman act like a coquette? Wollstonecraft suggests that coquetry "is not natural; but arises . . . from a love of power."[95] Perhaps this insight can help us to understand why women of reason were susceptible to being attacked as coquettes: their claims to reason were viewed as plays for power.

Here I will hazard a rather provocative idea: not every coquette is a woman of reason, but every woman who reasons acts like a coquette. Coquetry, like reason, was defined in terms of women's relation to men. Like coquetry, the dictates of reason may lead to a frequent shifting of perspective that generates more doubt than certainty. The coquette fakes her beauty and fakes an interest in a man. And what about reason? Can it, too, be faked?

Corrine Harol has elucidated what she calls the "epistemological crisis" centered on proving the virginity and virtue of the protagonist in English writer Samuel Richardson's enormously popular novel *Pamela* (1740). Harol's analysis shows that there is an epistemological distinction to be made between *factual* questions (science—determining virginity) and *ethical* questions (morality—determining virtue). In the realm of reason, this distinction corresponds to the difference between physiological

issues—women's cranial capacity, for example—and social issues—women's education, for instance. Harol suggests that both
virginity and virtue can be faked. Extrapolating a bit, we may
ask: Can reason be faked? In Pamela's case, faking it means
conforming, or at least seeming to conform, to male norms. But
the female protagonists populating the chapters that follow dif-
fer from Pamela. They are less intent on trying to "fake it"—
that is, passing for what men want them to be (virtuous,
virginal)—than on something more interesting and potentially
more liberating: proving what they actually possess and making
their own claim to reason. In fact, as we will see, calling women
of reason coquettes is an attempt to deny the power and reality
of their reason.

The *Encyclopédie* article "Philosophe" begins by warning
readers against fake philosophers: "Il n'y a rien qui coûte moins
à acquérir aujourd'hui que le nom de *philosophe;* une vie obscure
et retirée, quelques dehors de sagesse, avec un peu de lecture,
suffisent pour attirer ce nom à des personnes qui s'en honorent
sans le mériter" [Today, nothing is more easily acquired that the
name of *philosophe;* an obscure, solitary life, the appearance of
wisdom, along with a little reading, suffice to confer this name
on people who honor themselves with it without deserving it].[96]
Graffigny, Riccoboni, and Charrière all created fictional examples of silly, solitary, misguided men who fancy themselves philosophers. It is within this larger discourse on determining philosophical authenticity that we can understand the repeated
insistence that women are not philosophers.

Critical commentary on Graffigny, Riccoboni, and Charrière
often entails the rather incongruous assertion that "she was not
a *philosophe.*" The evidence offered sometimes incorporates the
author's own remarks to this effect (which, of course, may be explained in terms of social pressure toward modesty) and most
always includes the fact that she "did not create a system."[97] And
yet, many prominent male *philosophes*—Voltaire and Diderot,
for example—likewise created no philosophical system. The *En-
cyclopédistes* famously declared themselves allergic to *l'esprit des
systèmes,* even while embracing *l'esprit systématique.* That com-
mentators even feel compelled to invoke the question of philosophy tells us something important about these women. The denial
of their status as philosophers goes hand in glove with the re-

fusal of their significance as writers or as thinkers. Moreover, as gender outsiders, these women cannot always be allied comfortably with dominant eighteenth-century trends.

ENLIGHTENMENT AND LITERATURE

That finding brings us to the question: Why turn to literary texts? In Gravelot and Cochin's *Iconologie par figures* (1791), Truth is paired with Fable, which is described as "an ingenious fiction that conceals a useful lesson."[98] In his *Essai sur l'origine des connaissances humaines* (1746), Condillac likewise describes the embellishment of truth. His description, in fact, calls the coquette to mind. He writes: "L'imagination est à la vérité ce qu'est la parure à une belle personne; elle doit lui prêter tous ses secours pour le faire paraître avec les avantages dont elle est susceptible" [Imagination is to truth what *parure* is to a beautiful woman. It should lend every aid to set her off to best advantage].[99] Both of these observations (Condillac's gender stereotype aside) suggest that creative works—fables fueled by imagination—can reveal truth. Likewise, in the *Encyclopédie* frontispiece, Reason and Imagination work together, showing that "truth [is] enhanced, rather than tainted, by artful embellishment."[100] All of these examples suggest that stories and other artistic creations can serve enlightened ends.

The French Enlightenment was a fundamentally literary phenomenon. Works of imaginative literature were understood not as mere diversion, but as a means for reflection, self-knowledge, and analysis. Authors sought to respect the twin Horatian dictates to please and instruct the reader. And the borders between currently well-defined genres were much more fluid in the eighteenth century. Georges May writes, for instance: "That the *Encyclopédie* was in the mind of its creators a work of literature is obvious." As evidence, May cites the title page's reference to "une société de gens de lettres" and Voltaire's *Encyclopédie* entry on "gens de lettres." This was, in the words of May, a group united by "the ability to write, and to write well."[101] Lionel Gossman concurs, noting that the French Enlightenment was basically "a literary movement aimed at the conversion of readers."[102] And, at least among those who focus on France, literary critics—for example, Julie Hayes and Daniel Brewer—seem more willing than scholars in other fields to embrace and promote a relatively broad sense of Enlightenment.[103]

As historian Daniel Gordon explains in the introduction to his edited volume *Postmodernism and the Enlightenment*, it has become fashionable among historians to study the textual Enlightenment solely through pamphlets and other ephemera from the Revolutionary period. Scholars, he explains, have lost sight of the rich insights about Enlightenment to be gained through the careful study of more extended works, including literary texts. Although Gordon mentions only "the writings of the major *philosophes*,"[104] the following chapters will suggest that works by women authors also contribute fundamentally to a more nuanced understanding of Enlightenment.

Interestingly, at the same time, some philosophers have recently turned to literature, both to gain moral insights and to elaborate a notion of "narrative identity," or an understanding of self through the stories that we tell and that others tell about us. Paul Ricoeur is probably the best-known representative of this literary turn; others include Seyla Benhabib, Alasdair McIntyre, Martha Nussbaum, and Charles Taylor.[105] Now, I do not claim that philosophers are always good readers of literature.[106] Rather, I mention these examples to show that there is a growing interest in what we can learn philosophically by reading literary works.

Literary Texts, Women's Ideas:
The World-Creating Function of Literature

Thanks to the work of scholars like Joan DeJean, Katharine Jensen, and Nancy K. Miller, today we are aware of French women's crucial role in the rise of the novel. But we have not yet fully appreciated the links between women's literary production (in its many guises) and Enlightenment. Above, I discussed the attacks on eighteenth-century women literary authors. These attacks, in fact, targeted women writers in general, because the vast majority of women who wrote did so in literary form. Women were not supposed to create philosophical treatises, and so they expressed their ideas in other genres. These included letters and overtly educational works.[107] But most often, they were

works of imaginative literature. And these literary texts should
not be viewed as the poor cousins of more formal philosophical
treatises. Literature permitted women to treat the topic of reason
in rich, varied ways, emphasizing its impact on women's lives.
These authors put female characters in dramatic situations, mirroring real-life occurrences or preoccupations, placing the reader
(or spectator) imaginatively in the discourse. Their texts also
permitted women to imagine new worlds.[108]

It may seem a curious choice to analyze reason in literary
works of which several have often been called "sentimental." Critics and literary historians have long used this term to refer to
texts that depict feelings and manners and that are primarily associated with women, both as writers and as readers. Sentimental works—at least those authored by women—are often considered to have no real relevance to the world outside their pages.[109]
This bias has functioned to elide the broader relevance of issues
taken up by French women writers. The rediscovery of women's
works solely under the rubric "sentimental," like the recuperation
of *salonnières* only to emphasize their secondary status behind
men, risks cementing women more firmly in traditional subordi-
nate roles. Such categorization occludes women's contributions to
debates on reason and trivializes the breadth of women's experiences. It is not a matter of dismissing the sentimental angle, but
of reframing it.

Why are works by eighteenth-century women writers so often
dismissed as "sentimental"? I want to highlight three categories
of factors: social, generic, and hermeneutic. First, there is the social conditioning and constraint within which women were
raised. They were trained to be feminine and to think of themselves in such terms, and so it is unsurprising when their works
reflect this social conditioning. Moreover, literary sentiment
could be analyzed in terms of Joan Riviere's "womanliness as
masquerade," or an exaggeration of femininity to ward off potential retribution for intellectual achievement, an idea to which I
return in chapter 2. Second, there were generic constraints. The
genres available to women—the novel, prose narrative, prose theater, the letter—were simultaneously less prestigious and more
receptive to expressions of sentiment. Third, there is a hermeneutic factor. Readers and critics have simply tended to view
women's works through a soft-focus lens of gender bias, to read

them (irrespective of the evidence) as being more sentimental than works by men.

In his *L'idée du bonheur au XVIIIe siècle*, Robert Mauzi notes that imaginative literature "remains one of the best sources for understanding souls, by revealing to us what they dreamed about, what they would have liked to be, what bothered them among the received ideas."[110] The texts that Mauzi cites as examples were all written by men. Men's literary works are routinely assigned philosophical importance, but women's works are not. This may be in part because men's literary works are read in the light of their more formal treatises. In the absence of such treatises by women (with a very few exceptions, such as Du Châtelet's *Discours sur le bonheur*),[111] we should not neglect the philosophical contributions to be found in women's literary texts.

Focused on unearthing these contributions, the following chapters are not restricted to analyzing one particular genre. This is a unique approach, as studies of these authors nearly always focus solely on their novels. Instead, these chapters consider works across genres—novels but also stories, plays, essays, and letters—in order to suggest the breadth of each author's work and to provide an overall sense of her most crucial contribution to the question of women's reason. Just as there are several Enlightenments, there are several Graffignys, Riccobonis, and Charrières. This study focuses on a particularly rich yet neglected aspect of their work.

Today, we are in a position to widen the range of works to which we may appeal for philosophical insight. In order for women authors to take their place in Enlightenment, we need to read more of their works and try to analyze them on their own terms. These authors' contributions to the debates on gender and reason become much more evident when we look beyond their texts that attract the widest readership today. Perhaps this is not a coincidence. In *How to Suppress Women's Writing,* Joanna Russ notes that those few works by women that become widely known tend to be those that best conform to preconceived ideas about what women *should* be and what they *should* say.[112]

There is no denying that literary texts are cultural forms specific to certain social classes. Their creation necessitates literacy, time, and habits of expression, aside from the more obvious gift of talent. I do not claim that Graffigny, Riccoboni, and Charrière spoke to the lives of women of all conditions and walks of life. But for these relatively privileged women, literary forms enabled them to make philosophical contributions. At the beginning of this chapter, I invoked the lack of originality among eighteenth-century men who espoused misogyny. These women, on the other hand, needed to be highly creative and resolutely original to overcome the sediment of centuries. Giving primacy to women's texts, what (different) story emerges? Is there a distinctive kind of reason held up as the ideal in these women's works? And what do we learn from them about Enlightenment?

Unlike the docile and voiceless female figures that adorn the *Encyclopédie* frontispiece, women's texts offer us women's words and ideas, rather than their mute bodies. Writing is a means of remembering, but it is also a way of knowing and a way of creating new knowledge. Women's texts are their continuing testimony to us: scholars, students, and other readers. Without in any way discounting the sociohistorical context, we need not *limit* women to it, in parallel fashion to the way in which women have often been limited to the body and to autobiography—mired in immediacy, fixed (and forgotten) in history. As readers, we can have a relationship with these texts today. If we understand these women as philosophers of a sort, can't we think of their ideas as possessing value beyond the historical period of their creation? They remain compelling and their texts are still worth reading, not just because they shed light on history, but because they can inform our present understandings and future possibilities. They participate in the ongoing project of Enlightenment.

In the introduction, I invoked this project's methodology of "reading in context" as a way to move beyond "reading in pairs." The analyses in the chapters that follow will situate each text not as a direct response to one man's text, but rather in dialogue with and helping to shape the context of an entire *ethos*. As Madelyn Gutwirth observes of the eighteenth-century literary tradition, "canonic structures, despite important emendations, still basically persist." She continues: "This is why new paradigms of Enlightenment that might melt our rigid categories seem . . . so necessary."[113] In an important sense, we have yet to read eigh-

teenth-century women writers. I am issuing a call: no more Enlightenment-as-usual. Taking women's texts seriously will allow
us to reassess women's relation to reason in eighteenth-century
France as well as women's role in Enlightenment: then, now, and
in the future.

2

Reason, Gender, and Masquerade in Françoise de Graffigny's "La Réunion du bon sens et de l'esprit" and *Phaza*

IN HER PLAYS "LA RÉUNION DU BON SENS ET DE L'ESPRIT" (THE Reunion of Good Sense and Wit, before 1733) and *Phaza* (1753), Françoise de Graffigny presents tales of reason and disguise. This chapter will engage those issues in her work by drawing upon the motif of the mask and the idea of masquerade. Anne-Marie Fiquet Du Boccage, a playwright and poet, composed verses praising *Cénie,* Graffigny's successful play first staged at the Comédie Française in 1750. In the following excerpt from those verses, the character Comedy describes her own role in the play:

> Changer de masque est ma manie; / Je veux, dans ma coquette-rie, / Plaire à l'esprit, toucher le coeur, / Pleurer, rire à ma fantai-sie: / Quand j'amuse le Spectateur, / Je suis sûre d'être applaudie; / Qui le prouve mieux que *Cénie?*

> [Changing masks is my mania; / I wish, in my coquetry, / To please the mind, to touch the heart, / To cry and laugh on a whim: / When I amuse the Spectator, / I am sure to be applauded; / What proves it better than *Cénie?*][1]

Like the *Encyclopédie*'s frontispiece, in which the figure of Comedy holds a mask, these verses explicitly link comedy and masquerade. To this pairing, Du Boccage adds coquetry. The mask, like coquetry, suggests dissimulation. Indeed, all theater

3. Portrait of Graffigny from Lunéville museum, attributed to
Charles-François Chéron. Photograph Françoise Balleraud.
Courtesy of English Showalter

is dissimulation because it involves people pretending to be someone they are not, speaking words in the sincerest tones that they
do not necessarily believe to be true. The mask also suggests
something about the world beyond the playhouse. Things are not
as they appear. A mask may hide an individual quality or an entire identity. It may be playful but it can also be sinister. The
mask does not always fool others, yet it can even fool the wearer.
Social norms are a kind of mask, which can be imposed from the
outside or maintained from within. For example, eighteenth-century women from Graffigny's social milieu were expected to assume a comportment reflecting modesty and virtue. On the other
hand, women may mask their ambition if it is unpalatable for
public consumption. So the mask can be strategic. Reason, too,
may be concealed beneath a mask: of gender, of sentimentality, of
coquetry, or of comedy.

Who was Françoise de Graffigny and under what mask do we
know her? The authenticity of the beautiful portrait thought to
be of Graffigny—a pastel by Maurice Quentin de la Tour—that
graces several of the early volumes of her published *Correspondance* has been convincingly called into question by Colin Harrison.[2] Because it is such a lovely picture, readers were quick to
assume that it was an image of their favorite author. In more recent volumes of the *Correspondance,* this portrait has been replaced with another whose authenticity is more certain; it is also
less beautiful. Poignantly, this more authentic portrait was de-
stroyed by fire in 2003; what remains now are only photographic
reproductions.[3] The story of the Graffigny portraits is a reminder
that readers sometimes hastily accept a questionable representation of an author. Women of letters have often been read through
the lens of stereotypes; we would do well not to mistake a preconceived image or mask for the author herself.

Graffigny wrote a number of plays; only two, *Cénie* and *La
Fille d'Aristide* (1758), were ever publicly produced.[4] The rest
were performed, if at all, on private stages; several were never
published and some never completed. Graffigny's writing for the
theater belongs to more than one theatrical tradition. "La
Réunion" conveys the flavor of the commedia dell'arte, a type of
comedy employing a stereotyped plot, broad humor, and stock
characters. *Phaza* is a *féerie* (fairy play), characterized by the use
of supernatural elements, in a lineage of plays and fairy tales by

other women writers of the seventeenth and eighteenth centuries. In this sense it is similar to *Ziman et Zenise* (1749), one of the edifying plays Graffigny wrote on commission to be performed by children at the Royal Court of Vienna. And *Cénie,* identified by Graffigny in the published text as a *pièce nouvelle,* was indeed something new, helping to establish the emerging genre of the *comédie larmoyante,* which stressed social and emotional realism as well as characters' relationships within a social network.

Beyond the theater, it is possible to situate Graffigny within still other traditions. Her prolific output as a letter writer aligns her with the seventeenth- and eighteenth-century predilection for the epistolary form. Women such as the famed Marquise de Sévigné were thought to possess a special talent for writing letters. Graffigny's only novel, *Lettres d'une Péruvienne* (1747 or 1748), is a philosophical tale in epistolary form, employing a naive outside observer—in this case, a transplanted Peruvian princess—to expose the foibles of French society.[5] It may therefore be located in the lineage of Montesquieu's *Lettres persanes* (1721), anticipating Voltaire's *Ingénu* (1767). But the novel, like many of her other works, also participates in another tradition, spanning the whole history of the *querelle des femmes,* in which women authors renounce sexism in the name of reason. They not only reject the denials of their reason, but set out to create strong, philosophical women of reason, imagining possible futures in which such women could flourish. That tradition, too, is alive and well in the two plays that will be the focus of this chapter.

GRAFFIGNY'S MILIEU

Throughout the nineteenth century and most of the twentieth, Graffigny languished in near-oblivion. Prior to the rediscovery of her works by English Showalter beginning in the 1960s, she was remembered only as a onetime houseguest of Voltaire and Émilie Du Châtelet.[6] In fact, however, Françoise de Graffigny was the most prominent woman of letters in mid-eighteenth-century France, and perhaps in all of Europe. Born Françoise d'Issembourg d'Happoncourt to a family of the provincial *petite noblesse,* she became a resolutely independent woman. She left her native Lorraine after the dissolution of the ducal court there in 1738. Freed from an abusive marriage, she made her way to Paris alone. There, she sought and secured the financial and social means necessary to live as a single woman. The hundreds of letters she wrote to her closest friend and fellow Lorrainer François-Antoine Devaux, alias "Panpan" or "Panpichon," brim with witty observations and spicy anecdotes. In a familiar style by turns poignant, humorous, and critical, the letters chronicle the social, political, and literary life of eighteenth-century France.

Graffigny became famous following the publication of *Lettres d'une Péruvienne* and the triumph of *Cénie*. Graffigny's novel is by far and away the work for which she is best known today. It recounts the story of Zilia, an Inca princess who is kidnapped from her native Peru by Spanish invaders and then brought to France by a French sea captain. The text consists primarily of Zilia's letters to her Inca fiancé. In the end, having honed her talents as a social critic, Zilia decides to pursue a solitary life of reasoned introspection; the novel is thus the tale of her coming to reason.

Lettres d'une Péruvienne has earned critical attention principally among feminist scholars, including Janet Altman, Joan De-Jean, Julia Douthwaite, Nancy K. Miller, and Aurora Wolfgang. These scholars have enhanced our understanding of Graffigny's novel as social critique, particularly as a denouncement of sexism. Thanks in part to their work, we are now in a position to question facile interpretations according to which Graffigny's protagonist, Zilia, aligns with "female 'feeling' or *sentiment,*" in contrast to Usbek's "masculine Reason" in Montesquieu's *Lettres persanes,* of which Graffigny's novel was too long considered a pale imitation.[7] We can similarly move beyond the notion of Zilia as "victim to the lies of reason."[8] We can also see past the love-story plot. When the novel is read within the wider context of Graffigny's other works and mid-eighteenth-century French intellectual life more generally, its most crucial thematic focus proves to be not love but learning, not sentiment but reason.

It should not surprise us to discover philosophical reflections throughout the work of someone so active in the life of the mind. Graffigny read widely and acted as a literary and theater agent. She frequented the most renowned thinkers of her day. She knew Marivaux, Mirabeau, d'Alembert, Duclos, Helvétius, Diderot, Rousseau, and Voltaire, most of them regulars at her successful

Parisian salon of the 1750s. Of all the prominent *philosophes* in Graffigny's circle of acquaintances, none was more important in her life than Helvétius, nicknamed "the Genius," with whom Graffigny eventually arranged a brilliant marriage for her younger relative, Anne-Catherine de Ligniville, alias "Minette." Following a conversation with Helvétius in December 1744, Graffigny wrote to Devaux:

> Je ne sais par quel hasard je m'avisai de nommer la métaphysi-que. . . . Il parle, il ouvre son âme. Il me fait le résumé d'un livre qu'il va faire imprimer. Ah, quel livre! . . . Le grand Locke, cet homme que jusqu'ici j'ai seul admiré, sera toujours grand, mais ce sera d'avoir indiqué ce que le Génie devait dire.

> [I don't know by what chance I dared to mention metaphysics. . . . He spoke, he exposed his soul. He summarized for me a book that he is going to have printed. Ah, what a book! . . . The great Locke, that man who was the only one I admired up until now, will always be great, but it will be for having indicated what the Genius would say.][9]

The book was none other than his *De l'Esprit*, ultimately published in 1758. It articulates Helvétius's materialist philosophy, according to which all human knowledge and consciousness originate in the senses. In a subsequent letter, Graffigny describes another conversation with Helvétius:

> [J]e raisonne métaphysique tant qu'il veut, et jusqu'à perdre ha-leine. Son livre lui tourne la tête et me la tournera si cela dure, car tout ce qu'il m'en raconte m'enchante. Tu sais que c'est là ma chevallerie.

> [I reason about metaphysics as much as he likes, so much that I run out of breath. His book has his mind spinning and will do the same to mine if this lasts, for everything he tells me about it enchants me. You know that is my obsession.][10]

Graffigny was said to have described *De l'Esprit* as "les bal-ayures de [s]on appartement" [sweepings from [her] apartment]. The remark is likely apocryphal, or at any rate would have been delivered tongue in cheek, in part because Graffigny was well aware that Helvétius had developed the book's ideas prior to the heyday of her salon. But, as English Showalter speculates, if the phrase seemed worth passing along, it was because it accurately reflected the intellectual tenor of the conversations hosted by Graffigny.[11]

Beyond her admiration for the philosophers she read and frequented, what was Graffigny's view of reason? How did her decidedly independent streak shape her view of women's situation in society? What was her contribution to Enlightenment thought? "La Réunion" and *Phaza,* read with an eye to masquerade, will provide guidance in answering these questions.

"LA RÉUNION DU BON SENS ET DE L'ESPRIT": REASON AS A WOMAN

This one-act play, divided into sixteen short scenes, has remained not only unpublished but unexamined by scholars, with the exception of English Showalter's brief discussion in his 2004 biography of Graffigny. The manuscript is part of the Graffigny Papers held at the Beinecke Library. Information about the work's genesis remains sketchy. It was composed before autumn 1733, after Graffigny's *séparation de corps et de biens* from her husband in 1723 and prior to her arrival in Paris in 1739. Graffigny mentioned the play in an October 1733 letter to Devaux, now lost, which we can reconstruct based upon Devaux's response. The play apparently originated in a collaboration with Devaux. Showalter remarks that a handful of Graffigny's early works, including "La Réunion," may have been cowritten with Devaux and likely were edited according to his criticisms. Nevertheless, these works were always described in the Graffigny-Devaux correspondence "as her works alone."[12] For instance, Devaux writes of "La Réunion": "vous avez tort de désespérer du succès de votre pièce, j'en pense bien différemment; je crois qu'elle ira à merveille" [you are wrong to despair over the success of your play; I am of a quite different mind; I think that it will succeed marvelously].[13] We cannot be certain why the play was written—perhaps Graffigny imagined submitting it to the Comédie italienne for possible performance.

"La Réunion" treats a popular eighteenth-century theme: the perceived separation of good sense and wit in society. This debate exercised the minds of such luminaries as La Mettrie in his *Essais sur l'esprit et les beaux-esprits* (1740) and Helvétius in *De l'Esprit*. It frequently opened upon larger discussions about reason, sentiment, the passions, and faith. But Graffigny's play is original in bringing this theme to the stage and in using it as a springboard for treating gender issues, particularly women's reason. The play introduces this and other topics, such as the critique of French society and of women's place in it, that would reappear more than a decade later in *Lettres d'une Péruvienne*.

In the play, Jupiter has ordered Mercury and Momus to reunite Good Sense and Wit, who have been separated for some time. Mercury sets off to pursue Wit, while Momus strikes up a conversation with the allegorical figure of Reason. She is a woman; as if to underscore this point, Momus always addresses her as "Madame Reason" [*Madame la Raison*]. Reason promises to send him Good Sense, who, in fact, soon appears. Meanwhile, Momus encounters two young women, Silvia and Lucilie, who are arguing about their tastes and their suitors. Silvia, who adores literature and theater, represents wit, while Lucilie, reasonable and abrupt, embodies good sense. Their suitors, a count and a marquis, possess the same contrast of character as the young women: the dreamy Silvia is paired with the level-headed count, and the sensible Lucilie with the poetry-loving marquis. The remaining cast of characters includes a young woman, Angélique, who seeks advice about social comportment, and *le métaphysicien*, a rationalist philosopher. After Mercury reappears with Wit in tow, Reason presides over a double reunion: between the pairs of young lovers, and between the two allegorical characters Good Sense and Wit.

From one perspective, "La Réunion du bon sens et de l'esprit" is traditional. Of a genre commonly destined for the Comédie italienne, the commedia dell'arte, it presents stock characters (including Arlequin, the French equivalent of the Italian Arlecchino and the English Harlequin; Momus, god of satire; and an ingénue named Silvia); it ends with a *vaudeville,* or strophic song;[14] it is funny; and its plot turns on love. But the play is written in prose, and for that reason—in addition to its unusual thematic focus—breaks with tradition. Although verse plays were more highly regarded, such writing on the part of women was not easily tolerated; as Graffigny observed: "Les vers affichent

l'auteur, la savante; la prose ne dit que la femme du monde"
[Verse indicates an author, a *savante;* prose just suggests a
woman of the world].[15]

"La Réunion" involves masquerade on the part of gods, allegorical figures, and humans alike. Momus is disguised (though
we are not told how; we learn only that Reason is able to see
through the disguise). Good Sense, *Bon Sens,* is dressed as Arlequin and named as such in the script. Arlequin was the most
popular character of the commedia dell'arte; his traditional suit
of multicolored diamond patches mirrors the diversity of roles he
assumed. We may suppose that *Bon Sens* appears as Arlequin to
create a sense of lightheartedness and sympathy on the part of
spectators. "La Réunion" also deals with masquerade more subtly and metaphorically, by way of misunderstood attributes, false
appearances, and the role playing that constitutes gender. The
discussion that follows will focus on three episodes from the play:
first is a conversation between Momus and Reason, second is a
scene featuring the rationalist philosopher, and third is the appearance of Angélique.

Momus and Madame Reason: Four Accusations

"La Réunion" is reminiscent of what we now call readers' theater: large sections seem less like scenes to be staged than like a
philosophical dialogue. This is particularly true of the scene between Reason and Momus, the only character audacious enough
to question Reason directly, as befits the "dieu de la raillerie et
des bons mots satyriques" [god of jest and satirical witticisms].[16]
Reason remarks: "En vérité, ceci est nouveau; il n'y a que Momus
qui soit capable de demander compte de sa conduite à la Raison
elle-même" [Truly this is something new; there is none but
Momus who is capable of calling Reason herself to account for
her behavior].[17] Here, Graffigny underscores something important. The eighteenth century elevated reason as an ideal that
generated questions, but that was not itself subject to being questioned. By turning the tables on reason, Graffigny opens a space
for recognizing that reason is not a monolith, that it functions
within distinct social contexts. As Graffigny emphasizes, the definition of reason can vary according to the parties and purposes
involved.

reason questioned

The appearance of Madame Reason here recalls the conversation between the protagonist and Lady Reason in Christine de Pizan's *Book of the City of Ladies*, described in chapter 1. We have no evidence that Graffigny read Christine de Pizan or even knew of her existence; this is hardly surprising, given that it was not until the nineteenth century that French intellectuals rediscovered and embraced the literature of the Middle Ages. But there is an unmistakable, even if unintended, echo between Pizan and Graffigny, not simply in the appearance of Reason incarnate, but in the position ascribed to this overtly female character.

Momus describes four key accusations against reason. The first two are general, while the second two are specific to given social settings. The first accusation is that reason has lost the uniformity in her behavior that she had in ancient times. Second, Momus says: "vous criez contre les passions et vous vous raccommodez avec elles un moment après" [you alternately cry out against the passions and then make up with them]. Third, people turn reason to their own purposes in debates about how to raise a daughter. Some people, says Momus, invoke reason to convince mothers that keeping a daughter away from society too long, "c'est l'exposer à y faire de plus grande faute quand elle y paraîtra" [means exposing her to making even greater mistakes in the future]. Conversely, others use reason to argue that a daughter should be shielded from society until a marriage has been arranged for her, that "lui donner le goût du monde avant de lui avoir choisi un établissement, . . . c'est courir risque de n'en trouver aucun" [giving her a taste for society, . . . risks finding no marriage for her at all] (*RBSE* 3).[18] The fourth accusation is crucial and surprising. Momus reports that because there are "tant de disputes publiques et particulières où [la raison se] prêt[e] également aux deux partis" [so many public and private disputes in which reason lends herself equally to both parties], a number of "honnêtes gens . . . n[']admettent [la Raison] que *comme une coquette* dans une société pour entretenir des gens désoeuvrés" [gentlemen and -women . . . admit [reason] only *as a coquette* to entertain the idle in social gatherings] (*RBSE* 3, emphasis added). That is, people call reason a coquette because they believe she is too changeable.

In fact, a quick survey of the history of philosophy turns up invocations of reason's mercurial nature. As philosopher Pierre Bayle observes in his *Dictionnaire historique et critique* (1697), "notre raison n'est propre qu'à brouiller tout, et qu'à faire douter de tout: elle n'a pas plus tôt bâti un ouvrage, qu'elle vous montre les moyens de le ruiner" [our reason is only good for muddling everything, and for making us doubt everything: it has no sooner built something than it shows us how to ruin it]. He continues by calling reason "une véritable Pénélope, qui pendant la nuit défait la toile qu'elle avait faite le jour" [a veritable Penelope who during the night undoes the work she had done during the day].[19] Here is a link between Restif de la Bretonne's *épouse raisonneuse* (discussed in chapter 1), Bayle's Penelope, and Madame Reason according to her detractors: when reason is called inconstant, it is categorized as female.

Descartes writes in his *Meditations* that in philosophy, "chacun croyant que tout y est problématique, peu de personnes s'adonnent à la recherche de la vérité; et même beaucoup, se voulant acquérir la réputation d'esprits forts, ne s'étudient à autre chose qu'à combattre avec arrogance les vérités les plus apparentes" [since it is believed that there is no issue that cannot be defended from either side, few look for the truth, and many more prowl about for a reputation for profundity by arrogantly challenging whichever arguments are the best].[20] For these philosophers, the attempt to win a reputation for intelligence is often successful, though undeservedly so. But what happens when women similarly reason in public? I wish to emphasize Descartes's reference to "reputation." If we compare the observation by Descartes on the one side, and the sentiment recorded in Graffigny's play on the other, we notice something peculiar, though far from unpredictable. The same behavior (namely, reasoning) earns a man a reputation for profundity, but earns Madame Reason a reputation for coquetry. Graffigny's play illustrates the suspicion cast upon reasoning women.

Following the litany of accusations, Reason asks Momus, with delicious irony: "L'éloge est complète; m'est-il permis d'y répondre?" [The tribute is complete; am I permitted to respond?] Retaining her aplomb (she is Reason, after all), she remarks that the faults Momus described come not from her, but from those who invoke reason carelessly: "je ne saurais empêcher les hommes de se servir de mon nom pour autoriser leurs sottises" [I cannot prevent men from using my name to authorize their foolishness]. She explains:

> [S]i le hasard les conduit dans mon temple, je les éclaire, ma lumière leur déplaît, l'amour-propre les entraîne, ils sortent et ne reviennent plus, le même amour-propre les engage à parler de moi, et c'est alors qu'ils donnent de belle couleur à leurs faux raisonnements et qu'il en résulte toutes les fautes que vous m'attribuez.

> [If chance brings them to my temple, I illuminate them, my light displeases them, egotism carries them away; they leave and never come back. The same egotism leads them to speak of me, and it is then that they give beautiful color to their false reasoning: this is the source of all of the faults you attribute to me.] (*RBSE* 3)

Madame Reason suggests that people often do not want to listen to reason. They proclaim nonsense and call it reasoning. In sum, Reason explains that the failings of which she is accused lie not in the faculty of reason, but in the use to which reason is put. Upon hearing this explanation, Momus implores Reason: "[F]aites publier . . . que vous n'avez aucune part à toutes les sottises qu'on vous attribue" [Announce publicly . . . that you have nothing to do with all of the foolishness attributed to you] (*RBSE* 3). Graffigny's play may be understood as just such a public declaration.

The Ridiculous Metaphysician

Graffigny possessed the rare gift of not taking herself too seriously. Following a fire in her house, she found herself theorizing in a letter to Devaux about why there was so much soot: "Voilà comme les raisonneuses s'amusent à raisonner physique pendant que la maison brûle" [You see how the *raisonneuses* amuse themselves reasoning about physics while the house is burning down].[21] This self-deprecating stance makes palatable one of the most biting yet delightful aspects of Graffigny's theatrical works: the parade of ridiculous philosophers.

Showalter traces part of the inspiration for such figures to plays that Graffigny admired, including works by Molière as well as Regnard's *Démocrite* (1700) and La Drevetière's *Timon le misanthrope* (1722), both of which feature ancient Greek philosophers whose cynicism is highlighted to great comic effect.[22] After describing her own melancholy in a letter to Devaux, Graffigny remarked: "En vérité l'homme est une étrange machine. Démocrite avait raison d'en rire" [Truly man is a strange machine. Democritus was right to laugh about it].[23] In the 1730s, Graffigny drafted a never-completed play called *Héraclite, prétendu sage,* which features "a cynical pessimistic philosopher, whose gloomy attitude and austere principles make everyone around him unhappy."[24] Some elements of *Héraclite* reappeared in her last play, *La Fille d'Aristide.* In 1749, Graffigny wrote to Devaux about an idea for a Greek novel; she sought his suggestions about "a stoic philosopher, or at least a strict and austere moralist, who would be exposed as a fool."[25] She explained: "Je ne veux pas sortir de mon caractère, du sentiment, de la naïveté et de la philosophie. J'ai beau champ pour prendre à la barbe un philosophe et le mettre en danse, il en pleuvait en Grèce" [I want to respect my own character, to respect sentiment, naiveté, and philosophy. I can easily grab a philosopher by the beard and make him dance. Greece was full of them].[26] Another of Graffigny's plays, *Les Saturnales* (1752), features the philosopher Cato, whose shortfalls include pride, drunkenness, and avarice.

None of these examples is as funny as the metaphysician, or rationalist philosopher, of "La Réunion," who steals the show in scenes six and seven. He says aloud to himself that he is traveling to Reason's temple and apostrophizes: "Ô divine raison, que j'ai de grâces à vous rendre" [O divine reason, what thanks I must give you]. When Momus overhears and asks him to explain, the metaphysician sneers: "Il faut que vous ne soyez jamais sorti de la dépendance de vos sens pour me faire cette question" [You must never have escaped dependence upon your senses, if you ask me such a question]. When Momus says he still does not understand, the metaphysician retorts: "Hélas, je vous plains; vous êtes de ces êtres bornés qui n'ont jamais vu d'autre monde, que celui de l'univers" [Alas, I feel sorry for you; you are one of these stunted creatures who have never seen a world other than that of the universe]. Momus replies as if directly addressing the specta-

tor: "Voilà un plaisant raisonnement" [Now there is a funny rea-
soning] (*RBSE* 6).

In their brief remaining dialogue, Momus continues to profess
confusion. He says: "M'apprenez ce que vous êtes. . . . La sérenité
que je vois dans vos yeux contrarie quelques idées qui m'étaient
venues sur votre façon de parler" [Tell me what you are. . . . The
serenity that I see in your eyes contradicts some ideas that had
occurred to me about your way of speaking]. The metaphysician
responds with rationalist platitudes: "Avez-vous bien distingué si
ces idées sont d'une nature simple ou complexe? Êtes-vous dans
une identité assez parfaite avec vous-même pour n'y trouver
aucune contradiction?" [Have you distinguished whether these
ideas are of a simple or complex nature? Are you in a sufficiently
perfect unity with yourself in order to find no contradiction
there?]. Momus observes: "il faut que vous soyez bien obscur pour
que je ne vous comprenne pas" [you must be very obscure, if I
cannot understand you], to which the metaphysician again replies with disdain: "Vous conserveriez ce que je dis si vous aviez
accoutumé de bonne heure les fibres de votre cerveau à ne rece-
voir d'impressions que des choses purement intellectuelles" [You
would grasp what I say if you had accustomed, early on, the fibers of your brain to receive impressions only of purely intellectual things] (*RBSE* 6). The metaphysician's dogged allegiance to
rationalism makes him reject any appeal to the world outside of
his own mind.

Good Sense, masquerading as Arlequin, enters the stage in
scene seven; the metaphysician's exchange with him is even
more pointed and comical than the conversation with Momus.
Gesturing toward the metaphysician, Arlequin says to Momus:
"je gage que c'est un de ces habiles fous qui croient tout savoir
sans moi" [I bet that is one of those clever fools who think they
know everything without me]. Momus replies: "vous l'avez
deviné; j'essayais de le ramener sous vos lois quand vous êtes ar-
rivé" [you guessed it; I was trying to bring him back under your
laws when you arrived] (*RBSE* 7). When told that he is in the
presence of Good Sense, the metaphysician responds: "Vous, le
bon sens? Comment prétendez-vous le prouver? Remontons au
principe des choses" [You, good sense? How do you claim to prove
it? Let's go back to the principle of things]. Arlequin's retort
plays upon the verb (*remonter*) that the metaphysician has just

invoked: "Remonte dans ton cabinet; toi, tu m'ennuies. Va donner la torture à ton imagination, pour trouver de nouvelles obscurités à répandre sur la clarté de la nature" [Go back to your study; you annoy me. Go torture your imagination, to find new obscurities to spread over the clarity of nature]. The scene ends with the stage direction: "Il le chasse" [He chases him away] (*RBSE* 7).

Through the metaphysician, Graffigny satirizes rationalist philosophy. This episode alone provides a response to the caricaturists who collapse seventeenth-century rationalism and eighteenth-century reason. Graffigny's play defines Enlightenment reason in a way sharply distinct from Cartesian rationalism.

Angélique, or How to Be Reasonable

The ridiculous metaphysician serves as a foil to Madame Reason, a way to emphasize her admirable qualities. Within the world of the play, she is portrayed in a distinctly positive light. At the same time, according to Momus, society calls her a coquette. Which leads us to the third episode from "La Réunion," focused on the sexual double standard. In scene thirteen, the appropriately named, rather innocent Angélique arrives onstage. She explains: "je viens faire des voeux à la raison pour être éclairée . . . sur bien d[es] choses qui m'inquiètent" [I have come because I want Reason to enlighten me . . . about many things that worry me]. Angélique says that she wants Reason's help in resolving the contradictions faced by young women like her. She "voudrai[t] avoir des règles sures pour [s]a conduite [mais elle] n'en trouve nulle part" [would like to have reliable rules for [her] behavior, but [she] cannot find them anywhere] (*RBSE* 13).

While Momus described general attitudes toward reason in a vicarious mode, Angélique is clearly motivated by personal experience. In a metatheatrical moment, she expresses frustration that theatrical works criticize vices and faults but offer no "règle pour les éviter" [rule for avoiding them], while these works simultaneously present virtues so pure that spectators become discouraged by "l'impossibilité d'y atteindre" [the impossibility of attaining them]. Angélique then describes her two main problems. First, she reports that if she rejects a man's gallant advances, she will be considered a "prude." But if she welcomes them, she will be labeled—this term again—a "coquette." Second, Angélique describes a problem linked to an intellectual pursuit: reading. She dislikes novels, but their more philosophical alternative, "livres raisonnables" [reasonable books], are "interdits" [forbidden] to women: "on me dit sans cesse que si j'en lis je deviendrai savante et ridicule par conséquent" [I am told ceaselessly that if I read them I will become learned and ridiculous in consequence].[27] Finally, she poses the key question underlying not only her discourse but the play as a whole: "Que faire pour être raisonnable?" [What should one do to be reasonable?] (*RBSE* 13).

In the first situation described by Angélique, the coquette is she who evinces an interest. The coquette falls short of the *Encyclopédie*'s definition of a *femme raisonnable*—that is, she fails to resist gallantry. She thus neglects to exhibit the appropriate *pudeur,* defined by the *Encyclopédie* quite explicitly—and negatively—in terms of suppressing womanly desire. The message? Watch out, women: your desire is showing.

Angélique's description of the second problem—reading—functions as a symbol of protest against a larger network of social norms. Women's education and intellectual opportunities are thrown open to inspection. Angélique asks Madame Reason what she must do to be *raisonnable* because the answers supplied by society have not satisfied her. Thus she goes directly to the source: to Reason herself.

As suggested in chapter 1, coquetry is a phenomenon of dissimulation. Being called a coquette means being accused of masquerade. When reason is a woman, or when a woman reasons, she is presumed to be faking it, and thus she is a coquette. And so "La Réunion" illustrates the slippage from woman of reason to coquette. Although both Angélique and Madame Reason are called coquettes, only the latter responds to the charge in a systematic way. She uses her interview with Momus to explain that, in fact, she is not inconstant. Rather, the fault lies in the use and misuse of reason. Those making the accusation of coquetry against reason are living under social conditions in which good sense and wit are separated. Their judgment is skewed, they cannot think clearly, and they have banished reason from their midst.

Angélique has no such opportunity to defend herself explicitly. But then, it would seem strange and certainly out of character if the play's ingénue articulated such an apologia. I propose that we, the readers or spectators, are meant to understand what goes unstated here: that, like Madame Reason, Angélique is blameless. She describes the paradoxes and contradictions that she faces; it is our task to draw the conclusions, to recognize the no-exit situation in which she finds herself. We find her innocent and blame the circumstances.

In the end, "La Réunion du bon sens et de l'esprit" suggests that it is a reason full of good sense that will benefit human beings. Something in the world has to change in order for both Madame Reason and Angélique to be considered in the proper light. The person of good sense—for whom Momus and Arlequin are spokespeople within the play—can recognize the unfairness of Angélique's plight. And even Angélique herself is invited to turn inward, rather than outward toward society, to find solutions to her problems. Arlequin tells her: "[C]'est dans le secret du coeur que je donne mes leçons; allez, madame, suivez le penchant du vôtre; vous m'y trouverez pour diriger toutes vos actions" [It is in the secret of the heart that I give my lessons; go, Madame, follow the penchant of your own heart; you will find me there to guide all of your actions]. It is worth emphasizing that he calls her "Madame," rather than the more appropriate "Mademoiselle," as if to suggest her link to Madame Reason. Angélique exclaims: "Je sens déjà que vos lumières éclairent mon esprit; puissant dieu ne m'abandonnez pas" [I already feel that your lights are enlightening my mind; powerful god, do not abandon me] (*RBSE* 13).

Angélique and Madame Reason each contribute something distinctive to the play's message. Angélique provides a concrete example; she is a "real" person, critical of social pressures she herself has faced. Madame Reason offers an explicit, constructive response to the phenomena described by both Momus and Angélique: no reform of reason is needed, but rather a reform of reason's use. Here, it is the social function of reason regarding women that is called into question. And so these two women present both critical and constructive aspects of the debate. Their stories are a kind of "gender fable"—in other words, a tale that elucidates the operation of gender roles while calling those roles into question.[28] This aspect of gender as masquerade comes into focus even more clearly in *Phaza*.

PHAZA AND GENDER PERFORMANCE

More than a decade separates "La Réunion" from the first drafts of *Phaza*, another play by Graffigny that remains undeservedly little-known. Much had happened in Graffigny's life, including the move to Paris, the establishment of her household and a new circle of acquaintances there, and the ongoing trials of daily existence recorded in a steady output of letters to Devaux. During this period, her thought developed, as did her skill and scope as a writer. At the end of it, she would emerge a famous author, transformed from provincial obscurity to Parisian celebrity.

In "La Réunion du bon sens et de l'esprit," although women are accused of coquettishness, actually men are the ones who disguise themselves and trick others. That is, men wear the masks. The women of the play are, by and large, guileless. In *Phaza,* things are different and more complex. In what follows, I elucidate *Phaza* as a staging of gender masquerade and performance. *Phaza* yields rich insights about disguise, authenticity, and relations between the sexes; in so doing, it teaches us about women's relationship to Enlightenment.

"These Disguises and Secrets": The Genesis of Phaza

August 1747 found Graffigny enthusiastically at work on a play, originally intended for a Parisian audience, which would later become *Phaza*. A letter to Devaux suggests the uniqueness of the plot: "Je vais travailler à une petite pièce pour les Français. . . . Je veux que la Gautier y soit, habillée en homme" [I am going to work on a little play for the Comédie Française. . . . I want Mlle Gautier to perform in it, dressed as a man]. Françoise-Marie-Jeanne-Elisabeth Gautier was a famous actress whom Graffigny would later befriend. Graffigny soon discovered that Voisenon had submitted a similar play to the Comédie Française, which had rejected it.[29] Undaunted, she set to work on a revision. Actually, she was happy to abandon the original outline, which "comme il était sans féeries, et qu'alors il faut des raisons suffisantes de ces déguisements et du secret, cela devenait trop sérieux" [as it was without a fairy plot, and thus needed sufficient reasons for these disguises and secrets, was becoming too serious].[30]

Graffigny's letters track her progress on this manuscript, her setbacks and satisfactions, and her solicitation of feedback. The play, which Graffigny sometimes called "[s]a fille en garçon" [her girl dressed as a boy],[31] was unusual, and Graffigny had to stand by her own instincts rather than listen to some of the advice offered by friends. For example, the comte de Caylus, "en vrai romancier qui ne connaît pas le théâtre" [like a true novelist who does not know the theater], informed her "que ce n'était pas une pièce" [that this was not a play], that she would do better to think of writing a theatrical version of one of Mme d'Aulnoy's fairy tales. Graffigny explained: "Je pris la liberté de lui dire que mon idée était plus nouvelle que celles de Mme d'Aulnoy" [I took the liberty of telling him that my idea was newer than those of Mme d'Aulnoy].[32] She later learned that Caylus had ulterior motives: he himself had just written a comedy on a somewhat similar topic (which, as it happens, was never performed or published).[33] In mid-March 1749, elated, Graffigny announced to Devaux that the play was finally finished and that she would send it to her protector, the comte de Clermont. She wrote: "j'en ferais honneur à ma raison si je voulais" [I would honor my reason with it if I wanted to].[34]

Graffigny and the Queer Fairy

In Graffigny's *Ziman et Zenise,* another short play from the same period, the fairy Bienfaisante ("Do-Gooder") raises a prince, a princess, and a peasant boy and girl, while hiding their social status from them, following the dying wish of the prince's father. Through a series of trials, the nobles' inborn virtue distinguishes them; similar to "La Réunion," the play ends happily with a double wedding. Like *Ziman et Zenise, Phaza* is a one-act *féerie* in prose. As Charlotte Simonin remarks, during the first half of the eighteenth century, the genre enjoyed a robust popularity in venues such as the Théâtre de la Foire, the Opéra, and the Comédie italienne.[35] But *Phaza* is distinctly stranger than *Ziman et Zenise.* Graffigny sent Devaux the plot outline while the play was still a work in progress:

C'est une fée qui, indigne de l'abaissement des femmes, prétend qu'en les élevant en homme . . . les choses deviendraient égales.

Pour cet effet, elle élève une fille sous des habits d'homme, et cette petite fille se croit elle-même un garçon.

[There is a fairy who, indignant about women's subordination, claims that by raising them as men, . . . equality would be achieved. To this end, she raises a girl in men's clothing, and this little girl herself believes that she is a boy.][36]

That girl, a princess, is Phaza. (Because Phaza is male for most of the play, I will often refer to this character using masculine pronouns.) And the mastermind of this odd arrangement is the fairy Singulière. She steals female babies from their parents, conceals from them their true sex, and raises them in "solitude qui l'assure du secret" [isolation that preserves the secret].[37] According to the *Dictionnaire de L'Académie française* (1762), *singulier, -ière* means "unique, particulier, qui n'a point son semblable, rare" [unique, exceptional, which has no peer, rare] as well as "bizarre, capricieux" [bizarre, capricious]. In other words, it would be fitting to call Singulière a Queer Fairy. Her machinations prefigure twentieth-century theories of gender as masquerade (for example, in the work of Joan Riviere) and performance (for example, in the work of Judith Butler), to which I return below. Clémentine, the other fairy in *Phaza*'s four-member cast, explains that Singulière's goal is "la réforme du genre humain" [the reform of the human species] (*Phaza* 2). Singulière herself never appears in person; she has left the more benevolent Clémentine in charge during her absence. The two other characters are Zamie, Clémentine's niece, and Azor, Clémentine's son. The plot is straightforward and canonical: Phaza and Azor meet, overcome obstacles, and marry.

In framing these plays as fairy stories, Graffigny was drawing upon a rich French literary tradition in which women played a central role across the seventeenth and eighteenth centuries. I have already mentioned Marie-Catherine d'Aulnoy, whom Caylus encouraged Graffigny to take as a model. Madame Leprince de Beaumont created the famous fairy tale "La Belle et la bête," or "Beauty and the Beast." Marie-Madeleine de Lubert, a Lorrainer and friend of Graffigny, also composed popular fairy tales. Perhaps women were drawn to the form thanks to the unique possibilities it affords. Fairy-tale texts offer immediately recognizable links to real life, playing the "sociological role of a mirror" held up to society.[38] Moreover, the fairy-tale setting is ripe for testing and transgressing limits, thanks to its otherworldliness and attendant suspension of normal laws and rules. As Raymonde Robert notes, texts of the *merveilleux* genre "enable the fulfillment through fantasy of unsatisfied desires and ungratified aspirations."[39] Lewis Seifert adds that the fairy has also been viewed as a metaphor for the woman writer herself.[40]

Phaza was eventually performed in 1753, on the comte de Clermont's private stage at Berny. Such *théâtres de société* afforded authors a "freedom from decorum and the proprieties unthinkable at the Comédie Française and other establishment theaters."[41] Along with *Ziman et Zenise*, *Phaza* was later published in 1770 in a volume entitled *Oeuvres posthumes de Madame de Grafigny*. That volume contains an unsigned *Avertissement* that ends with a comment on Graffigny's style: "A la légèreté, à la délicatesse du pinceau, le lecteur sensible reconnaîtra le coeur d'une femme" [From the lightness [and] the delicacy of the brush-strokes, the sensitive reader will recognize the heart of a woman].[42] So the published text of *Phaza* was framed in terms of authenticity, and what's more, in terms of proof: this play was written by a woman. Such insistence becomes all the more interesting in light of the play's focus on disguise and masquerade.

Singulière's Educational Plan:
Phaza and the Masquerade

Clémentine, acting as narrator and interpreter, explains the logic behind Singulière's weird experiment: if girls were offered the education usually given to boys, they would no longer cultivate "la timidité, la douceur et la modestie" [timidity, gentleness, and modesty], but rather "de la valeur, de l'ambition, de l'indépendance" [valor, ambition, independence]; above all, Clémentine explains that women would become "bien inconstantes, bien perfides en amour" [very inconstant, very false in love], just like men (*Phaza* 52–53). Along with the invocation of positive qualities, what emerges here is an undercurrent of critique against the way men are educated. Men's inconstancy was a perennial theme in women's texts of the French eighteenth century. It is the decisive attribute of Zilia's fiancé in Graffigny's novel, and a theme in several works by Marie Jeanne Riccoboni. Clémentine sums up: "les choses devenant égales, la société en tirerait de grands avantages" [if things became equal in this way, society would gain great advantages] (*Phaza* 53).

In such a topsy-turvy world, women would learn the tricks of gallantry. Azor, the mouthpiece of the reader or spectator, is taken aback by Singulière's educational philosophy: "Quel travers! nous serions des barbares si les femmes pensaient comme nous" [But that's wrong! We would be barbarians if women thought like we do] (*Phaza* 53). This remark calls for at least two observations. First, Azor focuses not on women's actions, but on their thoughts. Second, the *nous,* or "we," is different in the two clauses: the second *nous* is "we men" while the first *nous* refers to the society as a whole. Thus, society would be barbaric if everyone thought like men. And Clémentine herself is not simply an impartial reporter of Singulière's schemes. She explains to Azor that he has probably already observed the ill effects of Singulière's perverse work in action, hinting that the *petits-maîtres* one encounters in society are really cross-dressed women.

The play not only joins a chorus of other voices in critiquing women's education, but, as noted above, adds a twist by critiquing men's education as well. Both aspects come to the fore in the following exchange:

> Phaza: On vous élève si mal! vous êtes d'une ignorance! le plus sot des hommes peut vous tromper, et c'est l'amour qui vous perd.
>
> Zamie: Mais où prenez-vous ce que vous dites?
>
> Phaza: Dans la bonne éducation que j'ai reçu, et tout homme d'esprit pense comme moi.
>
> [Phaza: You are so poorly brought up! You are so ignorant! The most foolish of men can trick you, and love is your downfall.
>
> Zamie: But where do you get what you are saying?
>
> Phaza: From the good education I have received, and every educated man thinks like I do.] (*Phaza* 73)

The play suggests that men's education leads to the mistreatment of women.

By his own admission, Phaza is a typical man, which is to say a misogynist. Phaza's belief in this male identity provides fodder for some rich situational irony as Phaza holds forth on the topic of women. Zamie is in love with Phaza and tells him she supposes that he loves her too. Phaza retorts: "Moi! que je vous aime! . . . Ah! Les femmes sont trop coquettes" [Me! that I love you! . . . Ah! Women are too coquettish] (*Phaza* 6). Here, *coquette* means "presumptuous," describing women who suppose that they have the same power of seduction as men. In a later scene, Phaza exclaims: "Les femmes sont si faibles!" [Women are so weak!] (*Phaza* 71). But these comments actually belie an acknowledgment of women's power and the fear it engenders.

Singulière's machinations prefigure Joan Riviere's celebrated psychoanalytic account of the phenomenon she calls "womanliness as a masquerade"—the title of an article originally published in 1929 and rediscovered by critics in the 1980s. According to Riviere's theory, a woman who aims to occupy a "masculine" position of power may take on a persona, or mask, of exaggerated femininity. This "mask of womanliness" serves to "avert anxiety and the retribution feared from men."[43] In the scene from Graffigny's play that was just mentioned, Phaza does indeed lash out at Zamie, whom he perceives to possess a kind of power (here, a confidence that he loves her). Note that Zamie defies the *Encyclopédie's* dictates about being a reasonable woman: not only does she fail to avert gallantry, but she openly professes her desire. We could read this scene as Phaza's (the man's) retribution against Zamie's (the woman's) perceived power. Of course, the irony underlying this drama intensifies thanks to our knowledge of Phaza's "real" identity as a woman, an issue to which I return below.

Love and the Question of Garçonnerie

The gender confusion—masquerade under various guises—in *Phaza* involves two amorous links: between Phaza and Zamie and between Phaza and Azor. They are of interest especially because the economy within which the play functions certainly does not seem to envision any love possibility other than a heterosexual one. In *Phaza's* second scene, Azor announces to Clémentine: "J'adore une jeune Amazone!" [I adore a young Amazon!] (*Phaza* 50). From the beginning, he has been able to perceive that Phaza is actually a woman. Clémentine and Azor conspire to reveal the truth during Singulière's absence. Any outright declaration is made impossible by the spell that Phaza is under; if she learns her true sex before turning fifteen, she will die.[44] This could be a nod to the fairy-tale tradition, in which the age fifteen is often important for girls; it may also be a covert message about chastity. In any case, the spell can only be broken if Phaza kneels in the presence of the man she loves.

While composing the play, Graffigny wrote to Devaux of the Phaza/Azor relationship that it was "furieusement difficile à traiter" [damnably difficult to treat]: "Un jeune homme et une fille en homme se font l'amour. Tu conçois combien il est difficile d'y mettre de la décence et d'éloigner l'idée de la garçonnerie, mais j'en viendrai à bout" [A young man and a girl dressed as a man are courting. You see how difficult it is to do this with decency and to banish the idea of *garçonnerie*, but I will manage it].[45] Graffigny apparently invented the word *garçonnerie*, from *garçon*, "boy."[46] The neologism refers to sexual love between men. And, outwardly, Azor's love for Phaza does look like a gay male relationship. At the same time, Zamie loves Phaza, forming, in the eyes of readers and spectators, an apparent relationship of love between women.

Consider what Graffigny wrote the first time she saw a performance by the actress Jeanne Quinault, who would later become her close friend: "Ah, mon Dieu, quelle surprise et quel enchantement! Cette fille me transporte. Si j'étais un homme j'en serais fou . . . je voudrais aller l'embrasser et lui dire qu'elle est un chef d'oeuvre de la nature" [Oh, my God, what surprise and enchantment! This girl sends me into raptures. If I were a man I would be crazy about her. . . . I would want to go and embrace her and tell her that she is a masterpiece of nature].[47] This remark could possibly be read as a queer moment, an expression of sexual desire for Mlle Quinault. In any case, it is clear evidence that Graffigny sometimes used a gender-bending motif, the idea of inhabiting the other sex, as a rhetorical strategy to make a point.

Eighteenth-Century Cross-Dressing, Onstage and Off

One form of gender transgression, cross-dressing, was more common among early modern women than we may suppose; it provided ease of movement in social space as well as greater safety than going out dressed as a woman. However, it was illegal, which Graffigny acknowledged: "Tu sais qu'il n'est pas permis de se déguiser en public" [You know that it is forbidden to disguise oneself in public].[48] In England particularly, the biblical injunction against cross-dressing (Deuteronomy 22:5) was often invoked in public debates on the topic. The most famous reputed cross-dresser of the eighteenth century was the Chevalier d'Eon, minister to Louis XV, who was rumored to be a woman passing as a man. Transvestism by both men and women was frequent at masquerade balls at court and throughout Paris.[49]

At the premiere of *Cénie,* a disruptive cabal (rumored to be Voltaire's doing) broke out when someone in the theater shouted: "Y a-t-il ici des femmes habillées en homme?" [Are there women here dressed as men]?[50] The suggestion was not so far-fetched; sometimes women cross-dressed for the chance to attend the theater from the *parterre,* the area both cheapest and closest to the stage. Graffigny was astonished to hear that her acquaintance Mme de Preysing had masked herself in this way at the Théâtre Italien.[51] The cross-dresser was discovered and escorted out. And Graffigny had other real-life encounters with women in male drag. As a joke, her protégée Minette once arrived at her house disguised as an abbé.[52]

Though proscribed in everyday life, cross-dressing was a routine occurrence on the stage: a male actor would play a female role (in Shakespearean plays, for instance) or a female a male role, sometimes called a "breeches role" (practitioners included the renowned English actress Sarah Siddons, as well as French actresses including Marie Jeanne Riccoboni). And a number of other literary works featured characters in gender masquerade. Some seventeenth-century French women writers created cross-dressed female characters as a way to pose questions about identity and social status.[53] Male-dressed women also appeared in works by eighteenth-century men. Marivaux's play *La Fausse Suivante* (1724) features a transvestite Chevalier. The picaresque heroine in Prévost's *Manon Lescaut* (1733) dresses as a man to flee the Hôpital, or detention center for women of questionable morals. On September 13, 1747, Graffigny described the play *L'École amoureuse* by Le Bret: "Ce sont trois femmes qui se travestissent en homme pour parler de l'amour plus à leur aise" [Three women dress as men in order to speak of love more freely].[54] In April 1748, she mentions the play *L'Année merveilleuse* by Abbé Gabriel-François Coyer, which she hadn't found particularly funny. Coyer's play predicts that on August 1, 1748, men will turn into women, and women into men. As a result, women will leave novel writing to men and will instead compose history and study science.[55] Such satire gives a taste of the social threat posed by women who took up intellectual activities considered to be the province of men. Below, I will return to this question more directly in the context of authorship and Graffigny's remarks on the matter. Here, I have invoked these examples of cross-dressing partly to contextualize *Phaza*'s use of the technique. But the most crucial point is the play's uniqueness, even among these examples. Phaza is disguised not only to others, but in her own eyes. The unknowingly female-to-male cross-dressed character distinguishes Graffigny's play from other works of the era.

Masquerade en Abyme

Hoping to pique Phaza's interest, Clémentine proposes inviting guests from throughout the kingdom for a masquerade ball. Phaza says that he doesn't understand why such a ball, socializing among strangers, would be enjoyable. Clémentine explains: "Sous le masque on est sincère par gaieté, et gai par enivrement. Les coeurs se développent, les secrets se révèlent" [Under the mask one is sincere through mirth and gay through intoxication. Hearts blossom, secrets are revealed] (*Phaza* 65). Sarah R. Cohen notes that eighteenth-century masquerade balls "promoted the greatest possible license in costume and performance."[56] In *Phaza,* the masquerade ball and its attendant dissimulation become the heart of the play. Although the play ends before the ball begins, that event becomes *Phaza*'s vanishing point, the moment toward which everything tends, always imagined though never seen. Of course the situational irony is that Phaza is already a masquerader, which sets up the masquerade ball as a *mise en abyme,* an embedded commentary on Phaza's identity.

Following Clémentine's persuasive description of the proposed masquerade ball, Phaza eagerly agrees to participate. It becomes evident that there is someone he would like to invite; Clémentine asks whether he is in love. Phaza rejects the suggestion, saying:

"l'amour est un vice, je l'ai en horreur. L'amitié est une vertu, je m'y livre de toute mon âme" [love is a vice, I am horrified by it. Friendship is a virtue, I give myself over to it with all my soul] (*Phaza* 66). Here, Phaza echoes what Singulière had taught him: to value friendship over love. This preference was a hallmark of the *précieuses,* echoed in many texts by seventeenth- and eighteenth-century French women writers. Phaza does admit to having a virtuous friend: "si parfait qu'il ne partagera jamais avec personne les sentiments que j'ai pour lui" [so perfect that no one else will ever merit the feelings I have for him] (*Phaza* 66). This man is none other than Azor, whom Phaza had met while hunting in the forest (in one scene, Phaza emerges onstage wielding a javelin, a none-too-subtle symbol of male identity). Phaza and Azor had pledged never to fall in love with women, so that nothing would interfere with their friendship.

Clémentine proposes a test of Azor's commitment to this pledge. Zamie will disguise herself and see whether Azor will be tempted by her charms. Phaza has an even better idea. He himself will perform the test: "C'est moi qui prenant des habits de femme, saurai bien sous ce déguisement tirer la vérité de son coeur" [It is I who, wearing women's clothing, will manage, under this disguise, to extricate the truth from his heart] (*Phaza* 67). In sum, a woman, Phaza, who believes she is a man, will masquerade as a woman. Which irresistably calls to mind Stephen Heath's gloss on Riviere: "A woman identifies as a man—takes on masculine identity—and then identifies herself after all as a woman—takes up a feminine identity."[57]

In *Lettres d'une Péruvienne,* Zilia pronounces a scathing critique of marriage: "il semble qu'en France les liens du mariage ne soient réciproques qu'au moment de la célébration, et que dans la suite les femmes seules y doivent être assujetties" [it seems that in France the bonds of marriage are reciprocal only at the moment the wedding is celebrated, and that thereafter only women must be subject to them].[58] Similarly, Phaza says to Zamie that for men, being married or unmarried is a matter of indifference. But a married woman gives up her rights and her freedom. Phaza adds: "Si je n'avais d'ailleurs une raison essentielle de ne point me marier, que m'importerait de prendre un joug qui ne serait que pour vous?" [If, moreover, I did not have an essential reason for not marrying, what would it matter to me to take on a yoke which would only apply to you]? (*Phaza* 72). This "essential reason" is his pledge of fealty to Azor. Here, the play explicitly invokes desire and faithfulness between men. *Garçonnerie*, indeed.

One scene in the play is composed entirely of a brief soliloquy by Phaza. Its theme: "que ne suis-je une femme!" [if only I were a woman!] (*Phaza* 75). The wish springs from Phaza's love for Azor. The subsequent scene is a duo between the two of them; if it is really friendship they are talking about, they do so in unabashedly sensual terms. Phaza says: "je ne saurais vivre sans vous; en garde contre les passions, l'amitié m'en tenait lieu. J'en faisais mes devoirs, mes plaisirs, mon bonheur" [I could not live without you; on guard against the passions, friendship took the place of them for me. I made of it my duties, my pleasures, my happiness] (*Phaza* 77). Sounding like a jealous lover, Phaza accuses Azor of falling for Zamie, and even threatens to marry her to prevent Azor from doing so: "demain, si je le veux, je puis être son époux" [tomorrow, if I want to, I can become her husband] (*Phaza* 78).

The distinguished subjects of the kingdom arrive; Phaza goes to greet them. Azor despairs at the thought that Phaza may want to flee. Actually, he is not thinking clearly; Phaza cannot leave due to the spell placed upon him by Singulière. To reassure Azor, Clémentine waxes philosophical:

> Ce n'est point aux circonstances que sont attachés le bonheur ou le malheur des mortels. . . . Si elles semblent bizarres, ce n'est qu'autant que les faits sont annoncés dépouillés de leurs rapports nécessaires avec leurs causes. Sont-ils arrivés, le merveilleux disparaît, ils rentrent dans la classe des événements les plus ordinaires.

> [It is not to circumstances that the happiness or unhappiness of mortals are linked. . . . If they seem bizarre, it is only insofar as occurrences are revealed stripped of their necessary relationship with causes. Once these have happened, the marvelous disappears, [and] they again come to seem like the most ordinary events.] (*Phaza* 97)

Here, Clémentine assumes a role quite similar to that of Madame Reason in "La Réunion." She remains calm and focuses on principles and ideals rather than getting lost in the apparent problems at hand. Impatient, Azor retorts sarcastically:

Oh! oui, Madame, c'est ici le moment de Philosopher, je suis fort
en état d'écouter un raisonnement bien suivi, bien conséquent.
Ah! songez plutôt aux moyens de retenir Phaza et de lui cacher
son sort qu'elle commence à soupçonner.

[Oh! Yes Madame, now is the time to Philosophize, I am in a good
state to listen to such a coherent and consequential line of reasoning. Ah! Think instead about the way to restrain Phaza and to hide
from her the fate that she is beginning to suspect.] (*Phaza* 97)

Phaza in Women's Clothing

Meanwhile, Phaza's actions seem to be leading her closer to the
truth about her identity. Phaza is offstage dressing for the ball.
Ill acquainted with the arts of womanly attire, Phaza needs a
stylist. Soon Zamie appears and asks Clémentine to send her
away, reporting that Phaza "est plus insupportable que jamais"
[is more unbearable than ever]. Phaza had asked Zamie to teach
him how to "se coiffer en femme" [style his hair like a woman]
(*Phaza* 99). Azor exclaims, his interest stirred: "Comment! il
s'habille en femme! il doit être charmant" [What! He is dressed
like a woman! He must be charming]. Zamie replies dryly: "Il
croit l'être au moins. En me disant que j'aime à plaire, que je suis
une coquette, il mettait du rouge et des mouches avec une attention la plus ridicule" [He believes he is, at least. All the while
telling me that I like to please, that I am a coquette, he was ap-
plying rouge and beauty spots with the most ridiculous care]
(*Phaza* 99). Zamie's quotation of Phaza's words provides a definition of "coquette": to like to please, and to dress oneself with care
in an exaggerated feminine style.

This explicit mention of coquetry brings us back to a kind of
masquerade that Riviere's work can illuminate. Riviere cites the
case of a professional woman whose work gave her frequent opportunities for public speaking. After each such public appearance, the woman was overcome with anxiety; her need for reas-
surance led to "flirting and coquetting" with men from the
audience. Riviere interprets this behavior as "an unconscious attempt to ward off the anxiety which would ensue on account of
the reprisals she anticipated from the father-figures after her intellectual performance." This same woman had dreams of people
donning masks in order to protect themselves from disaster. Riv-

iere concludes: "Womanliness therefore could be assumed and worn as a mask, both to hide the possession of masculinity and to avert the reprisals expected if she was found to possess it."[59] As Stephen Heath elaborates, "[i]n the masquerade the woman mimics an authentic—genuine—womanliness but then authentic womanliness is such a mimicry, is the masquerade . . . ; to be a woman is to dissimulate a fundamental masculininty, femininity is that dissimulation."[60] Now that Azor knows Phaza is dressed in feminine clothing—wearing the mask of womanliness, one might say—he can scarcely contain his enthusiasm. He tells Clémentine that he wants to run to see Phaza: "Laissez-moi jouir de sa vue. Sous l'habit de femme elle doit être mille fois plus belle" [Let me delight in looking at her. In women's clothing she must be a thousand times more beautiful] (*Phaza* 101). Surely here we may surmise that Graffigny is having fun.

We can better understand the inclusion and function of the masquerade ball if we approach *Phaza* as a "gender fable" in the sense that Judith Butler uses this term. In *Gender Trouble,* Butler "trace[s] the way in which gender fables establish and circulate the misnomer of natural facts."[61] Butler draws upon the work of Riviere and others to show that gender is a performance: "identity is performatively constituted by the very 'expressions' that are said to be its results."[62] *Phaza* suggests that gender is not an inborn, immutable fact, but rather, as Butler writes in *Bodies That Matter,* "a process of iterability, a regularized and constrained repetition of norms." Butler explains that cross-dressing is not necessarily subversive of gender norms, but that it does have the power to reveal "the 'normal' constitution of gender presentation."[63] That is, transvestism—which Phaza carries out through the machinations of Singulière and for the masquerade ball—suggests that all gender is performance.

Breaking the Spell

In the play's penultimate scene, Phaza appears transformed: he comes back onstage as she. At the sight of his beloved Phaza in womanly attire, Azor is at pains to conceal his passion. Phaza makes a proposition. He wants Azor, at any rate apparently the only other man present, to take his place in assuming the throne—that is, to pass for the king. Stunned by this generous offer, Azor balks. Phaza kneels to punctuate the request, and in so doing breaks the spell. At long last, Azor may tell Phaza the truth about her identity and profess his love. Clémentine says to Phaza: "Vous êtes libre, soyez heureuse" [You are free, be happy] (*Phaza* 105). This is the first moment in the play when Phaza is addressed using an adjective marked feminine: *heureuse*. She is called "free" because she has escaped Singulière's spell. And her dream of becoming a woman has come true. So, interestingly enough, becoming a woman equals freedom. Phaza knows the truth; Azor will become not only her husband but her king. Clémentine's previous prediction to Azor is realized: this dissimulation project "se détruira de lui-même. L'art peut dans quelques moments surmonter la nature, et jamais l'anéantir" [will fall apart on its own. Artifice can overcome nature at certain moments, but never destroy it] (*Phaza* 53). And yet, are things really so simple? Azor and Phaza act out roles and then inhabit the roles: Phaza dresses like a woman, then becomes a woman. Azor is to act like the king, and he in fact becomes the king. Social roles are assumed. One becomes an identity through performing it. Clémentine's confident prediction notwithstanding, the play shows that artifice and nature are not so easily distinguishable.

Phaza's conclusion is tempered by conservative declarations from Clémentine, who remarks that Singulière's goal "était de changer les lois de la nature, [mais] elles seront toujours les plus fortes" [was to change the laws of nature, [but] they will always be the strongest] (*Phaza* 106). Butler explains that, under conditions of compulsory heterosexuality, gender is narrowly relational: "one is one's gender to the extent that one is not the other gender, a formulation that presupposes and enforces the restriction of gender within that binary pair."[64] Phaza does not have a blurred gender identity, but rather two different and distinct identities: Phaza-as-male and Phaza-as-female. Of both *Ziman et Zenise* and *Phaza,* Showalter observes: "Both plays purvey a fundamentally conservative view of humanity and the social order. In the contest of nature and nurture, nature wins every time." Focusing on *Ziman et Zenise* but still discussing both works, Showalter adds: "It is almost as if Mme de Graffigny were interested only in the final scene, where the legitimate pretenders to the throne and to the other's heart are confirmed in their rights."[65] To evaluate this analysis, it is useful to remember two factors. First is social convention. As Grayson points out, "having braved tradition in the new and relatively experimental novelistic genre, Graffigny knew that such a course in the theatre would lead only to ridicule and failure."[66] Eighteenth-century theater was an inherently conservative form, with special pressure placed upon the rare women playwrights. Second, it is instructive to recall a remark made by Friedrich Nietzsche in an essay on history: "If the value of a drama lay solely in its conclusion, the drama itself would be merely the most wearisome and indirect way possible of reaching this goal."[67] The dénouement is not always the most interesting or most important aspect of a theatrical work. The play's conclusion must bow to convention, but the author is allowed to take a circuitous path getting there. Surely it matters not only where the players end up, but where they have traveled along the way.

Clémentine, charged merely with overseeing the place in Singulière's absence, has instead inverted this topsy-turvy world to restore the order she envisioned. In the play's final scene, she says: "charmante Phaza, il faut chercher un autre déguisement" [charming Phaza, now you must look for a different disguise] (*Phaza* 107). Given that he has become a woman, Phaza's feminine costume will not suffice for the masquerade. Artifice has ceded to reality. The performance of one's own gender is not enough—according to Clémentine—for a masquerade ball, although the play has suggested that there is nothing but masquerade in real life. But, we may ask, why would Phaza still need a disguise? Will she wear a disguise to her own wedding? What kind of costume will she choose—men's clothing, perhaps? And will Azor be the one in the dress? I mean to suggest that the play's seemingly conventional restoration of the normal order of things is actually quite ambivalent and unfinished. Although the ball will begin only after the play ends, it forms *Phaza*'s horizon, that toward which everything tends.

Graffigny Author: "I want to be a man"

The performativity highlighted in *Phaza* may be understood within the wider context of women's participation in Enlightenment. Authorship, like gender, is a performance. One becomes an author through the process of authoring. In her earliest extant letter to Devaux, Graffigny writes: "Croyez-moi, mon cher Panpan, je ne suis pas la seule femme qui pense bien. Quand vous serez répandu dans un plus grand monde, . . . vous me trouverez un peu au-dessus du commun de notre sexe, mais bien loin du galant homme qui est le but où j'aspire" [Believe me, my dear Panpan, I am not the only woman who can think. When you are out among a wider group of people, you will find me to be perhaps a little above the average of my sex, but quite far from the gallant man, the goal to which I aspire].[68] In another letter composed a decade later, Graffigny describes her desire to become an author, playfully glossing a line from Molière's *Femmes savantes* as she concludes: "Je veux enfin être homme à la barbe des gens" [I want to be a man right under people's noses (literally, under people's beard)].[69] In other words, Graffigny is describing authorship as a cross-gender masquerade.

What does it mean when Graffigny says she wants to "be a man"? Riviere writes: "Not long ago intellectual pursuits for women were associated almost exclusively with an overtly masculine type of woman, who in pronounced cases made no secret of her wish or claim to be a man."[70] In *How to Suppress Women's Writing*, Joanna Russ asks rhetorically: "What to do when a woman has written something? The first line of defense is to deny that she wrote it. Since women cannot write, someone else (a man) must have written it." Graffigny, Riccoboni, and Charrière were all subjected to this line of attack. Or, Russ continues, sometimes this stance is slightly modified: "[S]ome critics have invented a subtler version which appears to restore agency to the female author while actually insisting that some 'he' had to write it, that is: *The man inside her wrote it.*" As a corollary, for a woman author, Russ observes, "it is possible to answer *Women can't create* with *I'm not a woman.*"[71] And so there is no simple answer to the question with which this paragraph began. Graffigny does not seem to fit Riviere's category of a "masculine type" of woman. She adopted something closer to the fall-back strategy described by Russ. Yet Graffigny never claimed not to be a woman. Rather, she sought the creative license and public authority more readily available to men.

Graffigny was deeply aware of the need of the woman author to wear a mask. Admittedly, literary transvestism was commonplace in the eighteenth century. Aurora Wolfgang, in her book *Gender and Voice in the French Novel 1730–1782,* explores the literary use of a female voice by both female and male writers. But Graffigny turns this practice on its head; she is a woman author interested in passing herself off as a man. Note that her story "Nouvelle espagnole" was published anonymously in a collaborative anthology entitled *Recueil de ces messieurs,* or "Collection by These Gentlemen." Wanting to be like a man could be interpreted as shorthand for claiming the right to have a voice in setting the terms of a debate, to be an author without fear of reprisal.

Although eighteenth-century society acknowledged that some women were skilled writers (particularly of letters), becoming a public author—through publishing texts, having one's plays performed, being recognized as the author of one's works—was still deemed a man's prerogative. And so I interpret the two passages from Graffigny's letters, not to mean that Graffigny wished to be a man in every respect, but rather that she wished to assume the role of author. Her turn of phrase, *à la barbe des gens,* suggests that the public whose ridicule she fears is a public of men. As Butler writes of Riviere's schema: "One possible interpretation is that the woman in masquerade wishes for masculinity in order to engage in public discourse with men and as a man as part of a male homoerotic exchange."[72] *Garçonnerie* appears again.

A year after writing of her desire to "be a man," Graffigny confessed: "Je crains trop le nom d'auteur" [I fear the name of author].[73] She did not say that she feared *being* an author; rather, she feared being *perceived as an author.* And, indeed, she had reason to worry about her reputation. She was plagued by attacks promulgated by Émilie Du Châtelet, who suspected Graffigny of leaking details of a manuscript by Voltaire during her stay at the Châtelet estate at Cirey, and whom Graffigny called "le Monstre" [the Monster].[74] We have seen that Graffigny satirized rationalist philosophers and that she was even willing to mock herself as a *raisonneuse.* As a woman of reason, Graffigny was also mocked by others. But this was not lighthearted satire: Graffigny's detractors undertook their attacks with the venom of long-fermented misogyny. English Showalter suggests that Graffigny was the model for a character in Charles Palissot's satirical play *Les Philosophes* (1760): the silly salon hostess and *femme savante* Cydalise.[75] Palissot was once a friendly acquaintance of Graffigny's; he frequented her salon and she helped his playwriting career, though this relation was sometimes strained. In November 1750, she wrote to Devaux about Palissot: "il ne saurait penser fort, il ne peut guère raisonner" [he is incapable of sound thinking, he can scarcely reason].[76] Graffigny broke off ties a few years later.

In Palissot's play Cydalise speaks of a book she authored: "J'y traite en abrégé de l'esprit, du bon sens" [There, I treat briefly wit and good sense], that is, topics considered inappropriate for a woman author, the very ones engaged in Graffigny's play some thirty years earlier.[77] Palissot's play mocks the feminine *bel esprit,* or "fine mind," as "une maladie inconnu à vingt ans / Mais bien forte à cinquante" [an illness unknown at twenty years of age / But very strong at fifty].[78] In a similar vein, Pierre-Charles Roy published an epigram following the production of *Cénie:* "Vieille et pauvre, on n'a que l'affiche / De dévote ou de bel esprit" [As an old and poor woman, one can only show off / as being devout or a fine mind].[79] Following the failure of *La Fille d'Aristide,* Chevrier rehashed in 1762 the idea that Graffigny hadn't really composed her works, calling her a "prétendue bel esprit" [fake fine mind].[80] These comments echo Abbé Raynal's review of Graffigny's novel, where he claimed that she "s'est jetée dans le bel esprit" [threw herself into being a fine mind] with literary pretensions because she lacked the beauty that normally constitutes a woman's worth.[81]

Palissot also attacked Graffigny in his *Mémoires littéraires* (1773) and in his *Dunciade* (1771), where he wrote: "Ce fut jadis la prude Scudéri / Qui commanda cette troupe Amazone. / A cet emploi succéda Gr-f-gny" [It used to be the prude Scudéry / Who commanded this Amazon troop / Gr-f-gny was her successor].[82] It is a sign of a writer's stature to attract such enemies. And Palissot pays Graffigny an unintended compliment by placing her in the same tradition as the great seventeenth-century writer Madeleine de Scudéry. Palissot's attacks appeared in print after Graffigny's death (in 1758), to be suffered by her friends and admirers, while the author herself was spared confronting them. The viciousness of these attacks, though, reminds us of the obstacles faced by Graffigny, whose works critiqued a social system that denied women the access to education and social roles that would lead to the full flowering of their reason. It is worth invoking these attacks to better understand the stakes involved, the challenges confronting writers like Graffigny, and the courage necessary for her to write.

To contextualize Graffigny's remarks about authorship, it is useful to consider Marivaux's disparaging comments about authors in his *Spectateur français*. After claiming that "[u]n auteur est un homme . . . qui, dans son loisir, . . . réfléchi[t] à propos de rien" [an author is a man . . . who, in his leisure, . . . reflect[s] about nothing], Marivaux concludes: "Je veux être un homme et non pas un auteur" [I want to be a man and not an author].[83] Marivaux meant to break free of older traditions, staking his claim as a Modern against the Ancients. Women were even more absolutely thrown back on their own resources to create a path for themselves as authors. Graffigny had to assume an air of modesty thought to befit women. Paying homage to her novel, Louis de Boissy wrote a comedy entitled *La Péruvienne* in which a character praises Graffigny; in response, Graffigny protested to Devaux: "Mais je ne veux point être louée" [But I do not wish to be praised].[84]

In a 1749 review of Graffigny's novel, Fréron wrote of women authors:

> Avec le goût, l'imagination, et la sensibilité qu'elles ont reçus de la nature, leur sera-t-il interdit de se mettre au rang des auteurs? Avons-nous une loi salique, qui les prive des couronnes du Parnasse?

> [With the taste, the imagination, and the sensiblity that they have received from nature, why would it be forbidden [for women] to place themselves at the rank of authors? Do we have a Salic law that deprives them of the crowns of Parnassus?][85]

According to Vera Grayson, Fréron's review "suggests that women authors were well tolerated in the *ancien régime*."[86] But I urge greater circumspection: after all, if women authors were as well received as their male counterparts, there would be no need to include such an apologia in the review. Graffigny's successful play *Cénie* appeared in print in 1751. In a highly conventional dedication to the Comte de Clermont,[87] Graffigny alludes to the count's battlefield triumphs, though in a decidedly oblique manner. She notes that it certainly offends the *bienséances* for a woman to describe military campaigns; indeed, the public "pardonne difficilement aux femmes de penser et d'écrire sur des matières qui sont à leur portée" [pardons with difficulty women's thinking and writing on matters *within* their reach].[88] Indirectly, then, she asks: What lies within the appropriate field of discourse for women? And what lies beyond?

GRAFFIGNY AS PHILOSOPHER

On July 11, 1747, putting the finishing touches on her novel, Graffigny wrote: "Je me force quelquefois à me faire une volupté d'être seule. . . . Je fais abstraction de l'horreur de ma vie et je pense au plaisir d'exister. C'est le dernier effort de ma philosophie" [I make an effort sometimes to take exquisite delight in being alone. . . . I set aside the horror of my life and I think about the pleasure of existing. It is the highest effort of my philosophy].[89] Her words recall those she would ascribe to Zilia in the utopian conclusion of her novel. Celebrating the life of reasoned introspection that she will pursue, Zilia exclaims:

> Le plaisir d'être; ce plaisir oublié, ignoré même de tant d'aveugles humains; cette pensée si douce, ce bonheur si pur, *je suis, je vis, j'existe*, pourrait seul rendre heureux, si l'on s'en souvenait, si l'on en jouissait, si l'on en connaissait le prix.

> [The pleasure of being—a forgotten pleasure not even known to so many blind humans—that thought so sweet, that happiness so pure, "I am, I live, I exist," could bring happiness all by itself if one remembered it, if one enjoyed it, if one treasured it as befits its worth].[90]

Graffigny frequently invoked *raison* as a guide and philosophy as a goal. Life-weary and frustrated with various projects, she writes: "Si un effort de raison ne m'aidait à me tromper moi-même, j'en conclurais qu'il faut partir pour la montagne sans . . . soutenir une fausse espérance" [If an effort of reason did not help me fool myself, I would conclude that I should go into exile without . . . holding out a false hope].[91] A few days later, she notes: "Si je ne succombe pas à mes maux, tu pourras m'appeler une femme forte, car je tire tout de moi sans aucun secours" [If I do not succumb to my troubles, you may call me a strong woman, for I draw everything from myself without any help].[92] Following the success of the first edition of *Lettres d'une Péruvienne,* Graffigny wrote to Devaux: "Mon ambition était d'avoir du pain. J'en ai. Si je n'ai point de beurre à mettre dessus, je m'en passerai. Oh, je suis à présent bien convaincue que je suis une très véritable philosophe" [My ambition was to have bread. I have that. If I do not have any butter to put on top, I will do without. Oh, I'm quite convinced now that I am very truly a philosopher].[93]

A young German man who was a frequent visitor to Graffigny's salon wrote to a friend: "She combines with a correct, enlightened, and unforced reason (such a rare quality, especially in a lady), the integrity of the most virtuous man, the modesty of unknown merit, and the cheerfulness and liveliness of a twenty-year-old. . . . Here she is . . . the pleasure of reasonable people, who yearn for her company."[94] After Graffigny's death, Minette wrote to Devaux, urging him to come to Paris to prepare an obituary notice: "Attachez-vous surtout à faire connaître cette douce et sublime philosophie du coeur qui caractérisait ses moeurs et ses ouvrages" [Devote yourself above all to making known that sweet and sublime philosophy of the heart that characterized her behavior and her works].[95]

I offer these vignettes to suggest that, in addition to the appeals to reason and to philosophy in her literary works, Graffigny herself made such appeals a guide to living her own life. Like her literary heroines, Graffigny understood herself as a woman of reason. In addition to her plays and her novel, her private thoughts and social interactions were recognizably infused with an Enlightenment perspective.

Conclusion: Performing Gender, Reason, and Enlightenment

At the beginning of this chapter, I posed the question: Under what mask do we know Graffigny? That "La Réunion" and *Phaza* should be virtually unknown, whereas the more conservative and traditional *Cénie* was publicly performed and acclaimed, should not come as a surprise. What is easily digestible and what harmonizes fluidly with the public's tastes and attitudes is what gains adherents, then as now. Likewise, it should not be surprising that more daring ideas appear in the lesser-known theatrical works.

These two plays perform a crucial epistemological task with regard to being and knowing. They uncouple both attitude and aptitude from bodily identity, advancing a distinction between sex and gender. According to the plays, education and upbringing make people who they are. For example, Phaza's conditioned misogyny illustrates Angélique's complaints. By this logic, on a more positive note, a woman could develop her reason just as well as a man. This message is strengthened by the two plays' powerful women: Singulière and Madame Reason. Graffigny, like Christine de Pizan before her, reunites the female phenotype with the ability to reason and to speak for oneself. She explicitly aligns women with reason. The plays dramatize women's capacity for reason and their ability to turn that reason toward a project of Enlightenment that includes the emancipation of women.

In "La Réunion," Reason speaks for herself. There, reason *is* a woman, much more significantly so than in the mute depiction of female Reason in visual works like the *Encyclopédie*'s frontispiece. Angélique receives an Enlightenment apprenticeship. Amusingly, it is she—the ingénue—who speaks from experience, rather than the metaphysician. Clearly, she is a better philosopher than he. In response to Angélique's question about what women should do to be reasonable, the play calls for both internal cultivation and social transformation.

"La Réunion" endorses a reason that does not simply follow abstract, universal rules but that flexes with the social context, of which an important element is gender. *Phaza* emphasizes this point above all others. *Phaza*'s masquerade ball, along with the preparations for it, provides a context for Phaza to come to terms with his or her identity. He is unmasked. He becomes she. And then she dons the mask of femininity. Phaza finds freedom in becoming a woman. Gender is performance; the masquerade ball is society in a microcosm. Through it, Graffigny subjects gender norms to a test that reveals the masquerade. Those involved learn the "truth," only to go on masquerading.

Both "La Réunion" and *Phaza* criticize the education available to women. But *Phaza* goes even further, exposing the misogyny in education for boys. And this double critique points to a crucial parallel between Enlightenment and education. In both cases, Graffigny simultaneously claims for women the right to access what was only available to men, and critiques the version of the institution—education and Enlightenment—created by, through, and for men.

In light of the problems Angélique describes in "La Réunion," *Phaza* proposes another solution for bringing up young women. We may think of Singulière as cruel. But then again, perhaps all eighteenth-century women were in some sense raised by Singulière: a gender identity was imposed upon them. Even though the experiment is ultimately abandoned (when Phaza becomes a woman), in some sense it succeeds: Phaza successfully became a man through education. Her example implies that other women could do the same.

Singulière's bizarre masquerade was meant as a cure, but for it to succeed she has to keep Phaza hidden away from society, and that is not a solution endorsed by Graffigny. The author's admission that she wished to "become a man" (read: "author") was an acknowledgment of gender as masquerade. Women becoming men (one possible meaning of *garçonnerie)* is not the answer; as Azor exclaims, it leads to barbarism, that is, a society of between-men. Both in Graffigny's own life and in her literary works, there is never a lack of recognition that men form the base of social power; women cannot succeed without cultivating allegiances with men. In this sense, her life and her work were fundamentally relational. Graffigny was aided by Voltaire at Cirey, by the Emperor of Vienna through his commissions, and by Devaux through his advice and friendship. The rare eighteenth-century women playwrights relied upon the support of male friends to present their plays. And Graffigny not only benefited from the aid of powerful men; she herself helped some men, whether by admitting them to her salon, acting as a literary agent, or working to get their plays performed.

Reading "La Réunion" and *Phaza* together suggests a new vision of reason, gender, and Enlightenment. These gender fables, which grew out of unequal social relations, break away from strict eighteenth-century understandings of sex differences in social roles. We can read *Phaza*'s gender-bending masquerade as a corrective to the charge of "coquette," as a way to de-essentialize gender, and eventually as a way for women to claim reason.

These two plays suggest the link between performativity and women's participation in Enlightenment. As Madame Reason teaches us, cultivating a reason full of good sense will show us that gender discrimination runs counter to Enlightenment.

All literature involves some kind of masquerade, but nowhere is this fact more evident than on the stage. The next chapter turns to the work of Marie Jeanne Riccoboni, a successful actress turned writer. Among the threads that connect the two authors is Graffigny's acquaintance with the family of Riccoboni's husband. Graffigny knew his actress mother, who often went by her stage name, Flaminia, as well as his actor-director father, known as Lélio, whose *Observations sur la comédie et sur le génie de Molière* (1736) she read and appreciated in April 1748.

But more important are the intellectual links between the two writers. Both of them highlight the performance of reason. Their works show that reason may not simply be claimed for oneself; it is a matter of relation and of others' judgment. What is treated in a comic light in Graffigny's work takes on a tone more realistic and sometimes even tragic for Riccoboni. She illustrates women's experiences in the world of men and turns to reason as a remedy.

3

Reason as Remedy:
Marie Jeanne Riccoboni's *L'Abeille*,
Histoire du marquis de Cressy,
and *Lettres de Mylord Rivers*

MARIE JEANNE RICCOBONI SENT ONE OF HER EARLY WORKS (WE DO not know which) to her friend David Garrick, the famous actor-manager, in 1765. She included a letter where she wrote, in her approximate English: "There is my drug, my stuff, my foolery, what call you it?"[1] Put another way, Riccoboni understood her writings as a remedy. In narrative works crossing disparate genres, dramatic shifts in tone, and two decades of literary endeavor, Riccoboni explored gender, reason, and Enlightenment. The troubles to be remedied through these texts center on challenges women faced in a society organized to their disadvantage. The texts show that women's reason can be an effective remedy to the extent that social arrangements make it possible.

Riccoboni's essay *L'Abeille* [The bee] (1761) and her novels *Histoire du marquis de Cressy* (1758) and *Lettres de Mylord Rivers* (1776 or 1777) present ills that are physical, social, and philosophical. This chapter will elucidate the idea of remedy through the motif of the cup. This motif is sometimes quite explicit, as when one of Riccoboni's characters finds her cure in a cup of tea. At other times, the remedy is subtler, achieved through education and introspection. As a motif, the cup can signify nourishment, abundance, and the sustenance of life itself. But it can likewise suggest death. Commenting on the *Encyclopédie*'s frontispiece, Georges May notes that the allegorical figure representing Tragedy holds "a cup (presumably filled with poison?)"[2] Both the illuminating and the nullifying aspects of this motif will emerge in the analyses that follow.

Whether material or psychosocial, the remedy in these works intersects with several key ideas, including the notion of women as creators of knowledge and adherents of reason. These ideas also include the importance of relation and the tonic potential of experience. Highlighting the link between the relational and the rational, Riccoboni explores the intersection, overlap, and interference between love and reason. She offers reason as the remedy that will promote women's self-determination. While emphasizing the unequal social conditions facing the two genders, she just as crucially points to the possibility of learning something useful from the negative examples such conditions provide. In other words, from poisonous circumstances, she endeavors to extract a remedy.

Riccoboni has not been read as an author concerned with the interplay between gender, reason, and Enlightenment. In fact, Riccoboni is unique even among the focal authors of this study in being most in need of critical rehabilitation. Unlike Graffigny and Charrière, Riccoboni has not become the focus of editorial and critical efforts by an international team of scholars. A handful of her novels have been acknowledged and studied, and her other works largely ignored. Admittedly, it can be more difficult to identify the redemptive moments in her writings. This chapter is intended in part as a remedy to such critical neglect.

Riccoboni composed essays and translations as well as eight novels, most of them bestsellers. Even after she stopped writing, her popularity continued to blossom; during the ten-year period beginning in 1780, an amazing seven editions of her complete works were published. Riccoboni's early novels appeared at a crucial juncture in the history of the French novel: following the success of French translations of English novelist Samuel Richardson (beginning in 1741), and preceding the publication of Rousseau's *Julie, ou la Nouvelle Héloïse* (1761).[3] This chapter will analyze two of Riccoboni's novels, but it begins with the essay *L'Abeille*. That text introduces core themes—the denial of women's reason, women's poor education, the challenges and rewards of philosophy—following which *Histoire de Cressy* provides the tragic example (culminating in a remedy of last resort) and *Mylord Rivers* the positive example (offering a more hopeful turn to reason as remedy).

The negative current in Riccoboni's work is often overemphasized by her readers. She is frequently misunderstood as possessed of a single-minded fixation on men and their treachery in love. One simple explanation is that, among all of her works, the novels that center on this theme have garnered the widest readership. It is true that Riccoboni's texts are less utopian than Graffigny's, for example, and closer to the realism of everyday experiences. But the war between the sexes that is presumed to rage in them is not the whole story; the cup does not always contain poison. What Riccoboni critiques is not simply men, but more generally the relations between the sexes produced by unequal social conditions, and the resultant limits placed upon women's freedom. This finding animates the more complex account offered here. In her exploration of the rational and the relational, Riccoboni does not simply report experiences; she transforms them into remedies.

Reason's Milieux:
The Turn to Authorship

An actress turned author, Riccoboni succeeded in two careers, an especially remarkable achievement for a woman—the illegitimate daughter of an unloving mother—to whom life had offered few advantages. Born in 1713, Riccoboni debuted on the stage in her early twenties. Her husband was the volatile and dissolute Antoine François Riccoboni, of a famous theater family. Their marriage, though unhappy, did earn her entry into a Parisian intellectual milieu of famous writers and theater professionals, where she gained valuable experience, made contacts, and honed her literary talents. Prior to the 1750s, Riccoboni's activity as a writer was limited to coauthoring a few plays and composing some of the brief *compliments* pronounced at the Théâtre Italien at the opening and closing of each season; she herself performed these *compliments* in 1739 and 1744.[4]

Riccoboni's modestly successful career on the stage was followed by a spectacularly successful career as an author. Her experience in the theater had a notable influence on her literary writings, which tend to evince a theatrical structure, a unity of presentation, and great economy of expression. Onstage, Ricco-

boni often played the role of *seconde amoureuse* in comedies by
Marivaux. She began her career in narrative fiction in 1751 by
writing, as a sort of parlor game, a continuation to his popular
novel *La Vie de Marianne* (1731–41), which even today often appears in editions of the text. Though Riccoboni skillfully copied
Marivaux's style in her *Suite de Marianne*, the voice she gradu-
ally developed as an author is distinctive rather than imitative.
Riccoboni explained her career change from stage to writing desk
in a letter to Garrick: "Le désir de quitter la comédie, de vivre
sans assujettissement m'a conduit à écrire. . . . J'ai acquis de la
considération, c'est beaucoup. En cessant d'être jeune une femme
n'est plus rien; j'existe encore" [The desire to leave the theater, to
live without subjection, led me to write. . . . I acquired distinction; that is a lot. In ceasing to be young, a woman is nothing; I
still exist].[5]

Riccoboni was admired by some of the most prominent literary
figures of her day. Mercier said that her novels were "écrits d'un
style si pur" [written in a pure style].[6] Grimm's *Correspondance
littéraire* noted that she possessed "[l]'art de narrer avec beaucoup de concision et de rapidité, celui de semer dans son récit des
réflexions fines et justes, beaucoup de finesse et de grâce dans le
style, et un ton très distingué" [the art of narrating with great
concision and speed, that of sowing in her narration much fine-
ness and grace in the style, and a very distinguished tone].[7] But
she was also subjected by Palissot, in his *Dunciade,* to the typical accusation of not really having composed her own works. In
response, she wrote angrily: "[T]hey deny that I am the author of
my own work, they insult me, and no one says anything."[8] This
issue of reputation emerges not only in the author's life but as a
theme in her works.

Beginning in 1755, Riccoboni shared an apartment with a
close friend and fellow actress, Marie Thérèse Biancolelli. The
two women remained devoted to one another for nearly forty
years, until Riccoboni's death in 1792. Riccoboni craved seclusion
and preferred socializing with a small, intimate circle of friends,
who often gathered at the home she shared with Thérèse in Paris
on the rue Poissonnière. She referred to this group as her *société.*
When she went out, she frequented the renowned *coterie* of the
Baron d'Holbach, which met from approximately 1750 to 1780.
The regular participants numbered some fifteen individuals, in-

cluding Friedrich Melchior Grimm, Jean-François Marmontel, Abbé Raynal, André Morellet, Abbé Galiani, Helvétius, and Denis Diderot. It was there that Riccoboni first met Diderot, who admired her work and even offered comments on manuscripts of her early novels.[9] A haven in Paris for Anglophone visitors, the *coterie* also gave Riccoboni the opportunity to meet Garrick, the philosopher David Hume, and the young Scotsman and future diplomat Robert Liston. She cultivated friendships through correspondence with all three men. These rapports fed her Anglophilia, a phenomenon sweeping through France at mid-century, which led her to people many of her novels, including *Mylord Rivers,* with English characters. The *coterie* is inaccurately remembered as a male-only affair, another instance of the erasure of women from the French Enlightenment.[10]

As of this writing, the most recent biography of Riccoboni remains Emily Crosby's still aptly titled 1924 *Une romancière oubliée: Madame Riccoboni* [A forgotten woman novelist: Madame Riccoboni]. In a chapter entitled "La philosophie de Mme Riccoboni," a curious tension appears around the question of Riccoboni's philosophical status. The chapter begins by announcing that "Mme Riccoboni would have been the first to refuse the title of 'philosopher.'"[11] As I have suggested, this is a stale truism often encountered even today in scholarship on eighteenth-century women writers. Crosby acknowledges that Riccoboni frequented some of the *Encyclopédie* group, but asserts: "She could not . . . follow them in the upper regions of thought."[12] And, after noting Riccoboni's affinity with philosophers of the seventeenth and early eighteenth centuries, Crosby observes: "yet she scarcely has the right to be named among them because she never undertook the profession of philosopher."[13]

Assuming that philosophy could, indeed, be called an eighteenth-century "profession," how exactly could a woman of that era have made herself a professional philosopher? And why does Crosby even find it necessary to make such a statement? Continuing in this vein, Crosby nevertheless contradicts her own analysis as she lays out some of Riccoboni's distinctly philosophical ideas, on happiness and love, on justice in private relationships, on women's education, and on women's rights. Crosby also acknowledges Riccoboni's wish to urge others toward self-improvement: the goal should be "[f]aire le bien dans un petit cercle, tout autour de soi, voilà l'essentiel" [to do good in a small circle, near to oneself, that is the essential thing].[14] Crosby does not acknowledge the rather evident parallel here with at least one strain of Enlightenment philosophy, exemplified by the closing scene of Voltaire's *Candide* (1759) in the exhortation to cultivate one's garden. In essence, having declared that Riccoboni is no philosopher, Crosby unwittingly shows that the author is irrefutably philosophical. She even acknowledges that Riccoboni "proposes reason as a guide to conduct."[15] And yet, Crosby closes the chapter by declaring that Riccoboni suffered from a "lack of imagination" and a "natural laziness" that prevented her from developing "new systems."[16] Of course, as explained in chapter 1, the canonical *philosophes* themselves professed an allergy to systems.

It is not my aim here to argue with a work of criticism nearly one hundred years old. Rather, I invoke it in part because, unlike Crosby, more recent critics have tended to neglect entirely the philosophical themes and discussion of reason in Riccoboni's works. A few critics invoke the texts' philosophical underpinnings only to diminish them—witness Joan Hinde Stewart's brief description of Riccoboni as an example of "novelists . . . who ironize in passing about an oppressive Enlightenment 'reason' that controls female destiny."[17] A notable exception to this tendency is Olga Cragg. But Cragg addresses the issue of reason in Riccoboni from a limited perspective, to which I return below in my analysis of *Histoire du marquis de Cressy*.

One early-twentieth-century critic asserted that Riccoboni wrote only one story—her own—and another referred to Riccoboni's novels as her "memoirs."[18] This unapologetic collapse of Riccoboni's fiction into autobiography has been debunked by Aurora Wolfgang as a "myth of authenticity," but it persists in some quarters nevertheless.[19] Of course, narrowly biographical interpretations selectively emphasize certain aspects of the author's life while ignoring others. In Riccoboni's case, readers tend not only to focus on her denunciation of men but to assume that it is a catalogue of her own heartbreak. At the same time, readers neglect the more philosophical messages to be found in her writing. I will not suggest that we should disregard the author's life when analyzing her texts, but rather that we should read the life from a broader and more generous perspective. Just as the author praised the value of experience through her works, we may usefully attend to the author's own experiences. We should also remember—and this is crucial—that letters and life stories themselves are narrative creations.

L'ABEILLE: A PRIMER ON GENDER, REASON, AND ENLIGHTENMENT

Riccoboni's official retirement from the stage in 1761 coincided with the publication of *L'Abeille* in a periodical edited by Jean-François de Bastide entitled *Le Monde*. Bastide's foreword expressly situates the volume as a contribution to philosophy: "Le but qu'on se propose dans cet ouvrage est de donner l'exemple du véritable esprit philosophique" [The goal that we propose in this work is to give an example of the true philosophical spirit].[20] Riccoboni's text was republished in 1765 along with the *Suite de Marianne*, the story "Lettres de la princesse Zelmaïde," and the novella *Ernestine* in an anthology of her works entitled *Recueil de pièces détachées*.[21]

Despite *L'Abeille*'s accessible style and engaging content, it was marginalized by critics from the start. The review of the *Recueil de pièces détachées* that appeared in the *Correspondance littéraire* does not even mention *L'Abeille*.[22] To this day, the text is rarely studied. But it seems significant that *L'Abeille* was placed first in the eight-volume Volland edition (1786) of Riccoboni's collected works. The text serves as a kind of primer, introducing the most crucial topics that the author addressed.

L'Abeille in many ways echoes the tenor of Joseph Addison's and Richard Steele's *Spectator;* indeed, Riccoboni's preface (which appears in the Bastide edition but not in the *Recueil*) explicitly mentions the popular British periodical. The major difference is *L'Abeille*'s focus on women. Suzan van Dijk argues that *L'Abeille* is a piece of feminist journalism, by virtue of the attention it pays to women's situation in French society.[23]

In *L'Abeille*, the Bee serves as an Enlightenment persona explicitly adopted by the narrator, who draws our attention to experience and relation, to reason and remedy. At the same time, we know little about the narrator, who writes: "Je tais mon sexe, seulement pour laisser le plaisir de le deviner" [I remain silent about my sex, solely to grant the pleasure of guessing it].[24] A similar gender ambiguity reigns in the foreword to the original *Le Monde* edition of *L'Abeille,* which includes letters exchanged between Bastide and the anonymous Riccoboni. She hides her gender from him, although he guesses she is probably a woman, calling her a "beau masque" [beautiful mask]. But he isn't sure. He writes, amusingly: "Au reste, Madame, il est possible que vous soyez un homme" [Moreover, Madame, it is possible that you are a man].[25] Riccoboni retorts by professing to be angry and threatening that she "s'envolera" [will fly away]. In an icy tone, she writes: "renoncez, je vous prie, à votre petit projet de découverte" [kindly give up your little project of discovery].[26] In *L'Abeille,* the narrator highlights his or her explicitly ambiguous persona, and then states simply: "j'imiterai l'abeille, en travaillant comme elle" [I will imitate the bee, by working like she does] (*L'Abeille* 230).

L'Abeille includes the narrator's metatextual commentary to the effect that readers, seeing the short extent of the essay, may "former des doutes sur [s]on esprit" [form some doubts about the narrator's mind] (*L'Abeille* 226).[27] The narrator assures us that he or she has the intelligence to write more, but kept the text succinct for fear of boredom. The narrator professes to lead a simple life and to enjoy sound health. Like Riccoboni herself, the narrator has only a few good friends and believes in moderation, or control of desires, in order not to feel poor or deprived (*L'Abeille* 229). These are philosophical themes with a venerable past, stretching back at least as far as Plato's *Republic* and continuing through Aristotle, the Stoics, and the Epicureans. The narrator's other traits include modesty and a dislike of flattery.

Riccoboni's appeal to the bee as a title and a persona aligns with her love of animals and her frequent assertions of their superiority over human beings (*L'Abeille* 229). On a broader scale, her appeal also resonates with debates in early modern Europe over the cultural significance of the bee. Although the bee was traditionally a symbol of royal authority, the community of bees came to be viewed in some eighteenth-century quarters as a republican ideal, in which a leader elected by the group presided over its harmonious functioning. Some writers explicitly acknowledged the queen bee's female gender, though, as Kevin Bourque argues, in such cases the queen's work was often inscribed within the parameters of customary female roles. In any case, Riccoboni's use of the bee may be understood against this backdrop of the beehive as a symbol of republican—as opposed to monarchical—sociality.[28]

For eighteenth-century readers, the title *L'Abeille* would have invoked Bernard de Mandeville's scandalous 1723 book, *The Fable of the Bees: or, Private Vices, Publick Benefits*. But Mandeville argued that society is composed of self-interested individuals (the bees) bound together only by envy and competition, and that, paradoxically, this proliferation of vices is beneficial to society.[29] Riccoboni's bee, by contrast, proves to be a singularly virtuous and thoughtful philosopher, expressly sympathetic toward others.

A work from a century earlier offers a parallel more pertinent than Mandeville's text. The British philosopher Francis Bacon—whose work would become a crucial influence on the French *philosophes*—argued in his *Novum Organon* (1620) that advances in natural philosophy would not be made by the rationalists, those "men of dogma" whom he likened to spiders because they spin cobwebs "out of their own substance." Nor would advances come from strict empiricists, who are like ants because they simply amass a jumble of observations and experiences. Rather, those who seek knowledge should emulate bees: not only gathering pollen, but also transforming and assimilating it, making it into useful honey.[30] While it is unclear whether Riccoboni read Bacon, his work was certainly known to members of her milieu, including those she frequented at the d'Holbach *coterie*.

Like Bacon, the narrator of *L'Abeille* admires the bee because it is hardworking and useful. The bee doesn't harm others without just cause; it simply sets about its work. In *L'Abeille,* the narrator's ethos, revealed little by little as the text unfolds, revolves around Enlightenment ideals: tolerance, the betterment of society, a faith in experience, reliance on reason, and the belief that a remedy is available and achievable. That is, the bee represents Enlightenment philosophy.

L'Abeille *on Philosophy, Experience,*
and Writing as Remedy

In a letter to Bastide, Riccoboni writes that she wanted *L'Abeille* to be an "ouvrage raisonnable" [reasonable work].[31] The evidence would suggest that she succeeded. According to *L'Abeille*'s narrator, it seems that everyone is writing these days, including the Bel-esprit, who wishes to amuse, and the Philosopher, who wants to enlighten. But the public often pronounces the Bel-esprit "plat" [dull] and the Philosopher "ennuyeux" [boring]. Moreover, writes the narrator: "le monde va comme si personne ne s'était donné la peine d'écrire" [the world goes along as if no one had ever taken the trouble of writing] (*L'Abeille* 232).[32] People do not benefit from the wisdom to be found in good books because they do not read them: "Cette réflexion rend l'Abeille bien incertaine dans son vol" [This reflection makes the Bee very uncertain in her flight] (*L'Abeille* 232). What, then, is the use of writing? People act as if there is nothing to read, as if texts offer nothing to guide their thoughts or behavior. The narrator arrives at a possible explanation: "Tous les sujets sont épuisés; on nous présente depuis si longtemps les mêmes objets!" [All subjects are worn out; we have for so long been presented with the same topics!]. Readers are told constantly about their faults and the need to correct them, leading the narrator to wonder: "A quoi servent les avertissements de tant d'orgueilleux philosophes?" [What good are the warnings of so many arrogant philosophers?] (*L'Abeille* 232–33, 233).

As a remedy to the texts of these pedants, the narrator encourages readers to turn instead to the book of the world: "Jetons les yeux autour de nous; quel livre que le monde! qu'il est facile d'y lire, et combien il nous instruit si nous l'examinons!" [Let us look around; what a book the world is! It is easy to read, and it can teach us so much if we study it!] (*L'Abeille* 233). In other words, we can learn through experience. There is, however, an apparent paradox at the heart of this counsel: the author herself is offering a text that she hopes readers will heed. It is philosophical, to be sure, but it eschews the pedantic style of the texts she critiques. And reading a text can itself be an experience, particularly for those (including women) whose freedom to explore the world is restricted.

In this text, Riccoboni joins other philosophers who have urged readers to study the book of the world. But she overtly parts company with Descartes who, in his *Discourse on Method* (1637), writes that he studied "le grand livre du monde" [the great book of the world] but ultimately rejected its lessons gained "par l'exemple et par la coutume" [through example and custom], and instead made his famous inward turn, developing a rationalist epistemology in which truth may be reached through pure introspection untainted by experience.[33] The specific target for critique in *L'Abeille* is dogmatic rationalist philosophy—the kind created by system-builders. Riccoboni's strategy is also distinct from a remark that Rousseau would make in *Émile* (published a year after *L'Abeille*):

> Le monde est le livre des femmes: quand elles y lisent mal, c'est leur faute; ou quelque passion les aveugle. Cependant la véritable mère de famille, loin d'être une femme du monde, n'est guère moins recluse dans sa maison que la religieuse dans son cloître.
>
> [The world is woman's book; if she reads it ill, it is either her own fault or she is blinded by passion. Yet the genuine mother of a family is no woman of the world, she is almost as much of a recluse as a nun in her convent.][34]

As becomes clear in the second half of *L'Abeille*, Riccoboni makes no such sexist distinction. In fact, her text suggests that reading the book of the world is particularly beneficial for women. It is necessary to understand that for Riccoboni, *le monde*—"the world"—refers not to the natural environment but primarily to the social world, the world of people, as the term was usually employed in eighteenth-century French society. *L'Abeille* fittingly first appeared in a publication called *Le Monde*, which professed to observe human behavior and to analyze it philosophically.

Continuing in a Socratic style—using an implicit dialogue between teacher (the bee) and student (the reader)—the narrator asks rhetorically: "Mais quel doit être le fruit de l'étude que nous sommes maîtres d'en faire? de le haïr, de l'éviter, de le considérer avec horreur?" [But what should be the fruit of the study we are capable of making of the world? To hate it, to avoid it, to consider it with horror?]. The vivid answer follows immediately: "ce serait tirer du poison d'une plante dont on pouvait exprimer un suc salutaire" [this would mean extracting poison from a plant that can instead provide beneficial sap] (*L'Abeille* 233–34). The leitmotiv of poison appears regularly in Riccoboni's narrative works, an idea to which I return below. According to *L'Abeille*, the challenge is to find the proper remedy in the correct dosage, ingesting medicine rather than toxin: "Vivons dans ce monde, n'adoptons point ses erreurs, et gardons-nous de penser en les évitant, que nous ayons le droit de mépriser les faibles qu'elles ont séduits" [Let us live in this world, let us not adopt its errors, and let us refrain from thinking that by avoiding them, we have the right to despise the weak ones seduced by them] (*L'Abeille* 234). Here, the narrator sounds every bit the high-minded Enlightenment thinker, warning readers that "la philosophie, si noble dans ses principes, si douce dans ses maximes, si indulgente dans ses leçons, se confond insensiblement avec la triste misanthropie" [philosophy, which is so noble in its principles, so mild in its lessons, gets imperceptibly confused with sad misanthropy], then calling upon readers to cultivate a nonjudgmental and accepting ethos (*L'Abeille* 234). *L'Abeille*'s viewpoints on reason, experience, and reading the book of the world are illustrated and reinforced by the work's three embedded stories.

Three Tales of Reason, Experience, and Relation

The second half of *L'Abeille* is devoted to three stories about women's experiences and education, stories that link the rational with the relational. They are bitter tales turned into remedies through reasoned analysis. While Susan Lanser describes these stories as "private discourses" in which "authorial voice diminishes," my interpretation suggests a different conclusion: by highlighting women's experiences, *L'Abeille* legitimates their importance.[35] The stories are introduced by a revelatory preamble: "Il est surprenant de voir la plupart des hommes, surtout de ceux que la naissance ou la richesse distingue, profiter si mal des efforts que l'on fait pour les rendre sages et habiles" [It is surprising to see most men, especially those distinguished by birth or wealth, profit so little from the efforts undertaken to make them wise and capable]. Furthermore, men believe that their knowledge "les autorise à regarder leurs compagnes comme subordonnées à leur génie, condamnées à en reconnaître la supériorité" [authorizes them to regard their female companions as subordinated to their genius, condemned to recognize its superiority] (*L'Abeille* 255, 256). In fact, the three tales not only illustrate the preamble's promise, but offer women an opportunity to respond to these injustices.

Let us call the first story "The Irony of Ignorant Men." In it, the narrator overhears, at a lady's house, a group of men whose discussion of current events reveals their utter ignorance. The hostess later remarks to the narrator: "voilà pourtant les êtres . . . destinés à commander, à régir, à guider notre sexe, et à le maîtriser! on fait tout pour eux; dix ans sont employés à leur donner de l'esprit, de la raison ; . . . le monde semble créé pour eux seuls" [yet these are the beings . . . destined to command, to govern, to guide our sex, and to control it! Everything is done for them; ten years are spent to form their mind, their reason; . . . the world seems created for them alone] (*L'Abeille* 256–57). The lady contrasts this situation with the pitiful education offered to girls, left to "une vieille femme de chambre" [an old chambermaid], an "inepte gouvernante" [inept governess] who undertakes, unsuccessfully, "l'emploi difficile d'éclaircir nos premières idées" [the difficult task of illuminating [their] first ideas] (*L'Abeille* 257). Girls are then placed in convents, "où des filles, qui ne connaissent point le monde, [leur] enseignent à le haïr, [leur] répètent de le craindre, sans [les] prévenir sur ses véritables dangers" [where nuns, who do not not know the world at all, teach [them] to hate it, tell [them] repeatedly to fear it, without warning [them] about its real dangers]. In the convents, girls learn nothing except "une contenance modeste" [a modest countenance] and "quelques principes respectables, étouffés par mille préjugés" [a few respectable principles, stuffed with a thousand prejudices] (*L'Abeille* 257–58). Riccoboni wrote from experience, having herself been subjected to the drudgery of convent education, which she describes in a letter to Garrick.[36] In short, a sheltered life in the convent is the exact opposite of an outward-looking life spent learning from the book of the world.

The end of the hostess's story is a familiar one: the girl is sent back home and promptly married off. Thus, "c'est un prodige si à trente ans, une femme est parvenue . . . à penser . . . qu'elle est formée pour acquérir les connaissances" [it is a miracle if, at the age of thirty, a woman has reached . . . the conclusion . . . that she was made to acquire knowledge]. The narrator remarks: "Cette dame avait raison; communément les hommes sont élevés, et les femmes s'élèvent elles-mêmes" [That lady was right; customarily men are raised, and women raise themselves] (*L'Abeille* 258). An effort is made to develop the reason of men, but not that of women. The further tragedy is that men fail to use the reason that schools try to cultivate in them. This story conveys the gender inequalities in education and other injustices that are their result.

The second embedded story could be called "Beauty or the Brain?" In it, a male friend had reported observing a very agreeable woman who spent all of her time on her appearance; the friend wrote to this woman to encourage her to "donner un peu de temps à des soins plus sérieux" [give a little time to more serious concerns] (*L'Abeille* 259). She wrote him back; her letter, comprising about three-fourths of the story, is a veritable tour de force. Recognizably Riccobonian in style, the letter creates an embedded dialogue by including the interlocutor's words in italics. In it, the lady admits a devotion to her *toilette*. She writes: "mais que ce temps *perdu* fût mieux employé à *lire, à penser, à réfléchir, former mon caractère, cultiver mes talents, orner mon esprit, assurer mon goût;* vous me permettez, Monsieur, de n'en rien croire" [but that this *wasted* time would have been better spent *reading, thinking, reflecting, forming my character, cultivating my talents, adorning my mind;* you will permit me, Monsieur, not to believe a word of it] (*L'Abeille* 260). She explains that women would spend more energy improving their minds if men actually valued such an endeavor: women in that case, "sûres de trouver des amis, . . . dédaigner[aient] l'art d'attirer des amants" [sure of finding male friends, . . . would disdain the art of attracting lovers] (*L'Abeille* 261). This is the *précieuse* value of preference for friendship over love, previously invoked in chapter 2. And this statement clearly highlights the relational. The letter continues: "Si vous étiez sensés, les femmes seraient *raisonnables;* la façon dont elles vivent, n'est pas un défaut de leur naturel, mais la suite inévitable de votre conduite avec elles; . . . corrigez-vous!" [If you [men] had any sense, women would be *reasonable;* their way of living is not a defect of their nature, but the inevitable consequence of your conduct with them; . . . cure yourselves!] (*L'Abeille* 262, emphasis added). Men should (but apparently do not) seek a remedy to their failings; meanwhile, women can find a remedy in the education offered by this tale. The narrator explains: "Mon ami voulut répondre, [mais] il ne trouva rien à dire" [My friend tried to respond, [but] he found nothing to say] (*L'Abeille* 262). This unnamed friend stands in for the reader, who can only agree with the woman's retort. The lady's epistolary reply shows to what degree everything pivots on the relational: if men "had any sense," women would develop their reason. Women's apparent faults actually result from a social structure they did not create.

The third and final story, which we may call "Lipari's Daughters," is introduced by the narrator as follows: "Pendant que je suis sur la différence des soins que l'on croit devoir à ses enfants, suivant celle de leur sexe, je donnerai ici quelques lignes des Mémoires du comte de Lipari" [While I am on the topic of the different care believed to be owed to one's children, following their difference in sex, I will include here a few lines from the Memoirs of the Count of Lipari] (*L'Abeille* 262). Lipari is a gentleman appalled by the notion that a father would be unhappy to have a daughter. Such was his future father-in-law's reaction upon the birth of the girl who would become Lipari's wife. Lipari writes for the benefit of his own two daughters. He rejects the idea that men want only to pass along their name to a son; he writes: "mon nom mourra parmi les hommes; mais ma mémoire vivra dans vos coeurs" [my name will die among men; but my memory will live on in your hearts] (*L'Abeille* 266–67). He deemphasizes social convention while affirming relation (here, between parent and child). He also notes the large number of sons—inheritors— who prove to be worthless. Lipari intones Enlightenment values when he says: "L'inconséquence naturelle des hommes peut leur faire adopter un préjugé; mais quand il est absolument injuste, comment le temps et la réflexion ne parviennent-ils pas à le détruire?" [Men's natural thoughtlessness may make them adopt a prejudice; but when it is absolutely unjust, how do time and reflection not manage to destroy it?] (*L'Abeille* 265–66). Here, clearly, Riccoboni is turning crucial Enlightenment tenets back on the sexist men who often espouse them: among the prejudices needing to be cleared away by the light of reason is the unjust bias that favors men.

L'Abeille, a primer on Riccoboni's thought, offers a feminist critique of men's views on women, women's inadequate education, and men's wasting of their own advantages. It underlines the social function of reason. And it clearly puts forth a sex/gender distinction: men and women become who they are in large part due to social conditions. *L'Abeille* urges us to seek medicine rather than poison in society, emphasizing experience and reason as remedies for ignorance and the social ills following from it. These topics are further explored and expanded in *Histoire du marquis de Cressy* and *Lettres de Mylord Rivers,* Riccoboni's most philosophical novels.

"This Salutary Remedy": Reason and Gender in *Histoire du marquis de Cressy*

Riccoboni's second novel, *Histoire du marquis de Cressy,* features a woman's despair and her remedy of last resort. The novel is infused with pathos not only by virtue of its somber themes, but through its economy of expression, suggesting how language falls short in expressing emotion.[37] For eighteenth-century readers, the work was also high in shock value. But its more philosophical message has gone largely unnoticed.

At the end of her first season at the Comédie Italienne, on March 14, 1735, Riccoboni performed the *compliment de clôture.* In it, she posed a series of questions: "Quelle est la fatale injustice / Qui préside à notre destin? / Dans quel temps vivons-nous? Sur quoi compter enfin?" [What is the fatal injustice / That presides over our destiny? / In what times do we live? What can we count on, in the end?]. She went on to acknowledge: "Je ne m'adresse qu'aux absents" [I address only those who are absent].[38] While the *compliment*'s principal theme was distress over small audiences, these lines are evocative of broader issues that resonate with *Histoire du marquis de Cressy:* fatalism, tragedy, and appeals that fall on deaf ears.

Of herself as an actress, Riccoboni wrote: "Mon talent était le tragique, les comédiens français me voulaient avoir, mon mari s'obstina contre eux . . . il me voulut à la Comédie-Italienne" [My talent was tragedy; the Comédiens Français wanted me, but my husband argued against them . . . he wanted me at the Comédie Italienne].[39] And so she performed exclusively in comedic roles with the *Italiens.* Denied the opportunity to play tragic roles onstage, Riccoboni included a bracing dose of the tragic in some of her literary creations. These include *Histoire de Cressy*, a philosophical tale focused quite explicitly on remedy, culminating with the motif of the cup. In it, the author turns her critical lens toward the stage of the world and the human drama unfolding there.

A tale of one man and four women narrated in the third person, *Histoire du marquis de Cressy* turns on love and betrayal. Quite unlike the gender-enigmatic narrator of *L'Abeille,* the narrator of *Histoire de Cressy* discloses that she is female, albeit subtly, sometimes employing an "us" versus "them" contrast between women and men. Noble and somber in atmosphere, the work is infused with a fatalist foreshadowing of ruined lives to come. The novel's marquis attempts to seduce an inexperienced sixteen-year-old named Adélaïde du Bugei, and subsequently marries a young, wealthy widow, Mme de Raisel. The Cressy couple enjoys one year of happiness, until the arrival in their home of an orphaned adolescent, Hortense de Berneil, whom Mme de Cressy has agreed to care for. The marquis has an affair with Hortense, and ultimately also with the scheming Mme d'Elmont. *Histoire de Cressy* closes with Mme de Cressy's dramatic response to her husband's deception, a response that she explicitly identifies as a remedy.

Olga Cragg rightly notes that the third-person narration used in *Histoire de Cressy* was not the norm in the eighteenth century, particularly in female-authored works; the *courant sensible* fostered the widespread use of first-person narration with its confessional tone.[40] If *Cressy* does not use the narrative technique that would best support the "sensitive trend," we may rightfully suggest that the novel's focus lies elsewhere.

To that end, it is instructive to examine the circumstances leading to the novel's bleak conclusion. Mme de Cressy learns the truth about her husband's calculated and deliberate deception: he had married her for money, after attempting to rape then abandoning Adélaïde. She also learns of his adulterous liaisons. Mme de Cressy "se repentit mille fois de s'être procuré ce fatal éclaircissement" [regretted a thousand times having procured this fatal Enlightenment].[41] She retreats to a country estate to ponder what has happened. Her decision follows a week of reasoned introspection: she does not want to wait for a slow, natural end to her life, but decides, as if speaking of a river, to "en abréger le cours" [shorten its course] (*HC* 104). Calmly and deliberately, she prepares gifts for her attendants and puts her affairs in order.

This chapter's opening section invoked the figure of Tragedy from the *Encyclopédie* frontispiece, who holds a cup of poison.

That image is an apt illustration for *Cressy*'s final scene, in which Mme de Cressy casts her husband in a fitting role, manipulating him as he had manipulated her.[42] The unsuspecting marquis de Cressy becomes an accomplice to his wife's dramatic suicide as he is made to hand her a poisoned cup of tea. Mme de Cressy says to her husband: "Je suis charmée, Monsieur, de tenir de vous-même ce remède salutaire" [I am charmed, Monsieur, to accept from you this salutary remedy] (*HC* 105).

Riccoboni once wrote to Liston: "je n'ai . . . jamais pris des poisons que la médecine prétend si *salutaires*" [I have . . . never taken the poisons that medicine claims are so *salutary*].[43] It would seem that poison and remedy are not facts but interpretations. While Monsieur de Cressy (along with most readers) interprets the tea as poison, Mme de Cressy calls it a remedy. Just as women and men are often interpreted differently, so too do they offer differing interpretations.

In the novel's last lines, we learn that the marquis lived on after his wife's suicide to gain wordly accolades, but that he was unhappy. He could not escape the terrible image of both Adélaïde and his wife sacrificed for him, a memory that "empoisonna le reste de ses jours" [poisoned the rest of his days] (*HC* 108). The marquis thus gets a taste of his own toxic medicine. In fact, it is his treachery that has led this otherwise honest woman to employ deceit, tricking him into helping her die. She contradicts how she may otherwise act, resorting to a lie in order to remain honest to herself. This is a relational problem: a woman's apparent failing actually results from her relation with a deceptive man.

The novel's theatrical dénouement shines a spotlight on two of the work's valences: one symbolic and the other philosophical. The symbolic valence revolves around temperature, which *Histoire de Cressy* uses to convey mood. *Ardemment,* "ardently," a favorite adverb in Riccoboni's letters, appears throughout *Cressy,* along with its adjective form, *ardent,* usually to refer to the heat of passion. Moods in the novel, which run both hot and cold, are often presented as conflictual. Flirting with the initially resistant Hortense, Monsieur de Cressy says: "soyez sûre que les réflexions que l'on fait de sang froid, ne se présentent pas à une âme attendrie" [you can be certain that cool-headed reflections do not present themselves to a tender soul] (*HC* 86–87). Here, he is counting on the heat of passion to melt the young woman's frosty response to his advances. Inversely, when his ardor for his wife has cooled, Monsieur de Cressy is often characterized using some variant of *froideur,* or "coldness." And after Mme de Cressy makes the final decision to end her life, she receives the duplicitous Hortense "d'un air froid" [with a cold air] (*HC* 104). Moreover, Mme de Cressy prepares the poisoned tea at midnight, but it is one o'clock when her husband returns. The tea has likely gone cold.

With hot passion and cold poison at the poles, the novel's symbolic valence of temperature is mediated by a third term: cool reason. For example, following her agony when faced with Monsieur de Cressy's betrayal, Adélaïde becomes calm; we learn that she has decided to retreat to a convent. This is a metaphorical death: she writes to the marquis, in her words, "du fond d'un asile" [from the depths of a refuge] in order to bid him "un éternel adieu" [an eternal good-bye]. She describes being buried and says it is the marquis de Cressy who has driven her into "cette espèce de tombeau" [this sort of tomb] (*HC* 84). Similarly, once Mme de Cressy decides to die, a deep calm overtakes her. She describes the lethal powder she puts into her tea as a *calmant,* or "tranquilizer" (*HC* 105). The adjective *calme* and its derivatives make several appearances in the novel's suicide scene. Passion is hot, death is cold. In the end, cool reason—the real remedy—prevails. The example of Mme de Cressy suggests that a calm decision to die can be infused with reason. But before turning in more detail to that philosphical valence, it will be helpful to situate Mme de Cressy's suicide within the eighteenth-century French context.

The Suicide in Context

Although death by poison was a popular topic of discussion during the French eighteenth century, readers were shocked to encounter in *Histoire de Cressy* a virtuous woman's suicide. The esteemed writer Stéphanie-Félicité de Genlis called it "révoltant" [revolting].[44] A reviewer for the *Année littéraire* attacked Mme de Cressy's suicide for its *invraisemblance:* "on lui trouve l'âme trop vertueuse et les passions trop douces pour la faire finir par ce genre de mort" [her soul is too virtuous and her passions too gentle to have her end in this type of death].[45] This condemnation seems rather misplaced, given the increasing tolerance of suicide among the *philosophes* at the time, not to mention the growing number of actual suicides occuring in France. As part of a broader trend toward secularization, the mid-century saw a proliferation of essays about suicide by authors including Montesquieu and Rousseau as well as Riccoboni's friends Diderot, d'Holbach, and Hume.[46] Public discourse hungrily dissected reported cases of poisonings, either self-inflicted or homicidal, suspected or real.[47] False stories circulated—and were even published in the *Correspondance littéraire* in 1749—according to which Mme Du Châtelet had killed herself by drinking poisoned bouillon that she had asked a certain M. de Guébriant to hand her.[48]

Riccoboni's own letters show that she stayed up to date on the macabre news of poisonings and suicides. One example, which, like the false Du Châtelet story, recalls the *Cressy* plot, involves a young girl who killed her sick mother with poisoned tea.[49] Riccoboni mentions several suicides, sometimes providing graphic descriptions. For example, she writes: "On recommence à se tuer ici. Deux dames ont donné l'exemple. Une s'est jetée par la fenêtre, l'autre s'est brûlé la cervelle" [Once again, people are killing themselves here. Two ladies set an example. One threw herself out a window; the other blew her brains out].[50] These letters were written some fifteen years after *Cressy,* but their rather cavalier tone suggests a less melodramatic point of view on the novel's conclusion. If the author could remain so unmoved in the face of real poisonings and suicides, perhaps she intended above all a symbolic significance for Mme de Cressy's suicide.

Jeffrey Merrick has studied the political meanings attributed to suicides in the 1770s and 1780s, that is, during the period when Riccoboni was writing these letters. He invokes the stereotype according to which male suicides were considered rational and endowed with "public significance," while female suicides were viewed as irrational and devoid of such significance.[51] Merrick concludes that contemporaries who reacted to suicide drew upon "gender-based assumptions about human nature and conduct," sometimes reading political meanings into male suicides—linking them to the upheavals in French society.[52]

The interpretation of suicide varied according to the gender of the victim—such a decisive, violent act was better tolerated when

committed by a man. Perhaps women were not considered free
to dispose of their own lives; as discussed in chapter 1, eighteenth-century laws made women the property of men. Perhaps
the threshold of tolerance was even lower when a woman, rather
than being pushed to suicide by her own despair, created, cool-
headed, a literary work in which a virtuous female character
takes her own life.

Such a plot element was highly unusual among women authors. A few eighteenth-century women playwrights—Marie-
Anne Barbier, Madeleine de Gomez, and Anne-Marie Fiquet Du
Boccage—composed plays that end with the heroine's suicide.[53]
Among the three focal authors of this study, Riccoboni is the only
one who actually depicts a woman's self-inflicted death, although
Graffigny's Zilia and Charrière's Mistress Henley both contemplate the idea. In Riccoboni's 1759 novel *Lettres de Milady Ju-
liette Catesby,* Lord Ossery marries Jenny Montfort (whom he
has impregnated through rape) after she threatens suicide; Jenny's death two years later is a kind of symbolic fulfillment of this
threat. But *Cressy* is the author's only work featuring a woman's
suicide.

Reading the conclusion back through the novel, we find that
there is a cadaver poisoning the narrative stream. That is, the
tale's unfolding leaves a woman dead. Nancy K. Miller, both in a
review of Pierre Fauchery's 1972 book *La Destinée féminine dans
le roman européen du dix-huitième siècle* entitled "Exquisite Cadavers" and in her own book *The Heroine's Plot* (1980), notes the
frequency with which eighteenth-century narratives end with a
woman's death. In the review, she asks: "What is the appeal of
the feminine death: if it is a literary strategy, what is its objective; if it is a code, what message does it transmit?"[54] Fauchery's
"autopsy" (Miller's word) implies that women are born to suffer,
and, most significantly, that the woman must die (literally or
figuratively) in order for men to bond through her. The lifeless
body at *Cressy's* end is no accident, but a sign of the poisonous
undercurrent bubbling throughout the narrative, indicative of
noxious social forces. At the same time, both Fauchery and Miller
focus on male-authored texts (such as Prévost's *Manon Lescaut*
or Rousseau's *Julie*). Riccoboni's text is different; for one thing,
we need to consider the plot from which this conclusion flows,
and the deliberateness of Mme de Cressy's death. Unlike other

novelistic heroines who meet their end through some accident or illness, Mme de Cressy chooses this remedy to end her troubles.

Madame de Cressy, Socratic Figure

It is instructive to read the *Cressy* conclusion with an eye to its philosophical valence. Doing so reveals that Mme de Cressy's fate bears a certain similarity to the trial and death of Socrates, as recounted in Plato's *Apology, Crito,* and *Phaedo.* At the most basic level, both figures are condemned by the ignorance of others. They both appeal to reason in self-defense. From a formal perspective, *Cressy's* third-person narrative technique, with quotation of dialogue among the characters, parallels the story of Socrates. But the resonances also go far beyond this structural similarity.

Riccoboni wrote at a time when the topic of Socrates was in the air. In a letter to Liston in January 1774, Riccoboni remarks cryptically that the victims of a recent double suicide did not need to read a treatise on immortality in order to realize that they fell short of that goal. James Nicholls, editor of her correspondence, speculates that this is a reference to Plato's *Phaedo.*[55]

Across centuries, Socrates has remained the quintessential representative of a life devoted to reason and virtue. In the minds of many eighteenth-century thinkers, Socrates was an ideal symbol for the French Enlightenment. This was true for two reasons: first, Socrates was a martyr to fanaticism and intolerance, perceived characteristics of the institutions of Church and State denounced by the *philosophes;* second, he conducted his life as a model of wisdom, virtue, and faithfulness to his principles.[56] Diderot explicitly drew the analogy, proclaiming: "Socrate au moment de sa mort était regardé à Athènes comme on nous regarde à Paris" [Socrates at the time of his death was regarded in Athens as we [*philosophes*] are regarded in Paris].[57]

In his 1758 *De la poésie dramatique,* Diderot spoke of bringing Socrates to the stage, though he never completed that project. Voltaire wrote a three-act *Socrate* in 1759. Rousseau made explicit appeals to Socrates, particularly in his *Discours sur les sciences et les arts.*[58] Several visual artists of the era took the theme of Socrates drinking the hemlock as a subject for painting, including Jean-François-Pierre Beyrou in his 1788 *The*

Death of Socrates. In that image, the philosopher reclines on a bed in in a stylized, stagelike space. Surrounded by friends in various states of emotional response to his impending death, Socrates is resolutely rational and impassive. His left hand is raised, as if to punctuate an argument, and his right hand holds the cup of poison. This cup, golden and bathed in light, appears roughly at the center of this painting. Its importance cannot be missed. Just as the painter chose the cup as the central symbol of Socrates' death, Riccoboni places the cup at the center of her novel's conclusion.

The comparison between the tale of Socrates and the tale of Mme de Cressy is compelling because it helps us to cast Riccoboni's thought in a new light. In terms of reception, of course, the two figures contrast sharply. While Socrates' suicide has often been celebrated, Riccoboni's heroine has been virtually forgotten. Readers are unused to viewing the lives and actions of women as having philosophical import. There is a tendency to view women's works, ideas, and problems as merely local, lacking a broader message or appeal. In death, Socrates rises to the great and public; a figure like Mme de Cressy is considered modest and personal. Socrates is condemned, but his sphere of influence is vast. He has reached a public who will keep and glorify his memory. Women like Mme de Cressy, by contrast, suffer privately and die without creating so much as a ripple in the still pool of men's public control. It thus seems troubling to follow those critics who read Mme de Cressy's death "as an act of empowerment."[59] We would do well to remember the words of Gayatri Spivak, who notes "[t]he profound irony in locating [a] woman's free will in self-immolation."[60]

Nevertheless, both characters possess the nobility of reasoned deliberation. While dying, they both seem almost superhuman in their virtue. Socrates "died nobly and without fear."[61] On her deathbed, Mme de Cressy asks her husband's forgiveness and even accepts the antidote (a remedy to her remedy) that he offers, though she knows it will be useless. This gesture is a nod to the *bienséances*, conveying Mme de Cressy's fundamental goodness despite her un-Christian decision. Amid all of the novel's references to appearances and dissimulation, her death is deeply, irrevocably real. Both characters—Socrates and

Mme de Cressy—die calmly even as bystanders are overtaken by emotion.

The conclusion to Riccoboni's tale may be read in light of the Socratic tradition according to which philosophy is a preparation for dying and death.[62] Put another way, as the Stoics and others would claim, life is an illness for which death is the cure. In *Cressy,* the cup of tea provides a remedy to an impossible situation. It is emblematic of the larger context: the unfulfilled promise of Enlightenment for women, who continue to face unjust social conditions even while men proclaim faith in equality.

In each case, who is really on trial? Socrates transgressed, and was put to death. M. de Cressy transgressed, and his wife was put to death. Both Socrates and Riccoboni's heroine were condemned by their contemporaries. But we are to understand that the two characters who die in their respective narratives are not really the guilty parties. In the case of Socrates, it is Athenian society that is put on trial and found culpable: the men of Athens are unable to appreciate Socrates' gifts, his appeals to reason and philosophy. In the case of Riccoboni's novel, it is French society that is put on trial: men are unable to relate to women equitably. In both cases, the expiation is misplaced but the blame finds its mark.

From a more positive perspective, Mme de Cressy does challenge the double standard according to which men repay women's virtue and fidelity with unkindness and deception. By determining the time, place, and manner of her death, and by symbolically involving her husband, Mme de Cressy refuses to remain simply a passive victim. Although the woman dies, her tale lives on. Unlike the unfortunate suicide victims that Riccoboni mentioned in her letter, then, Mme de Cressy gains a measure of immortality. Thus a more nuanced reading of this suicide seems appropriate, one that is neither wholly negative nor entirely positive. As Antoinette Sol has observed, Riccoboni's novels tend to eschew a simple either/or, instead exploring the fundamental ambiguities with which eighteenth-century women had to live.[63] This is neither pure oppression nor clear empowerment. Rather, Riccoboni depicts the complexity of a poisonous situation, calling to mind the fate of a famous philosopher, and in so doing extracts a remedy from it for her readers.

4. Engraving of Riccoboni as Erato accompanied by Socrates, from
Restif de la Bretonne, *Les Contemporaines.* Courtesy of Special
Collections Research Center, The University of Chicago Library

At least one late-eighteenth-century writer made the connection between Riccoboni and Socrates. In a chapter of *Les Contemporaines* on women authors, Restif de la Bretonne condemns these women in general, but simultaneously describes some of Riccoboni's novels in positive terms. Accompanying that chapter, which includes a fictionalized biography of Riccoboni, is an engraving that depicts the nine Muses, the three Graces, and the seven Sages, in a parlor along with Restif himself. One of the Muses—Erato, Muse of romantic poetry—represents Riccoboni, being crowned by Virtue. The sage standing behind Erato/Riccoboni is none other than Socrates.[64] The brief explanation that accompanies the engraving reads, in part: "Cleobule regardant Erato: 'Remuant tes lauriers, je crains de les flétrir'!" [Cleobulus [one of the Sages] looks at Erato: "Touching your laurels, I am afraid to wilt them!"].[65] A virtually identical phrase was used by Riccoboni in a letter to Garrick in 1765, on the topic of malicious attacks against the Comédie Française actress Clairon: "C'est assurément de quoi flétrir ses lauriers, les entrelasser d'absinthe" [That is assuredly enough to wilt her laurels, to intertwine them with absinthe].[66] This evocation of a toxic drink recollects *Cressy*'s key motif.

The engraving's polysemic image merits a closer look. True, Riccoboni is represented in the rather stereotypical guise of a Muse devoted to romantic love. And it is the case that Riccoboni wrote of love. But it can scarcely be called unphilosophical to do so. From its early beginnings with the pre-Socratics, philosophy has been understood as closely connected to love. In fact, love lies at the heart of philosophy, as the word's etymology ("love of wisdom") implies. And Plato, through the figure of Socrates, provides a preeminent model for this link in texts like the *Phaedrus* and the *Symposium,* to which I return below. The presence of Socrates in the image of this engraving, placed next to Riccoboni, suggests that we may also read her as a lover of wisdom—that is, as a philosopher. It is Riccoboni herself, just as much as Mme de Cressy, who is the Socratic figure. While *Histoire de Cressy* illustrates the limited remedy available to a woman trapped by a manipulative man, *Lettres de Mylord Rivers*, by contrast, offers a distinctly positive perspective on experience and relation, reason and remedy.

LETTRES DE MYLORD RIVERS:
"AS MUCH REASON AS A WOMAN
IS PERMITTED TO SHOW"

When *Lettres de Mylord Rivers* was set for publication, Riccoboni confessed that she feared bad reviews: "Mon livre va paraître. Je le vois tombé, hué, sifflé, mis en pièces et traîné dans les boues" [My book is going to appear. I picture it failed, booed, hissed at, torn to pieces, and dragged through the mud].[67] Her fears were allayed when the book was well received; Riccoboni told Liston that even Jean-François de La Harpe, a reviewer for the *Mercure de France,* "le plus judicieux de nos critiques, mais si hargneux qu'on le nomme *la harpie,* s'est fort étendu sur la *noblesse* et *l'élégance* du style" [the most judicious of our critics, but so surly that people call him *the harpy,* wrote at length about the *nobility* and the *elegance* of the style].[68] Note, however, the reviewer's emphasis on style over substance; what Riccoboni's contemporaries (including not only La Harpe, but Mercier and Grimm, mentioned above) did not seem to notice was the work's treatment of reason and its philosophical message.

Riccoboni's last novel, *Lettres de Mylord Rivers* was published in late 1776 or early 1777.[69] It seems to be the fruit of years of reflection. Granted a royal pension in 1772, Riccoboni no longer needed to publish in order to support herself. Thus *Mylord Rivers* was composed under conditions relatively free from financial constraint, perhaps to satisfy a need more personal than external. In 1769, Riccoboni had written to Garrick: "Faire encore des romans, toujours parler d'amour, de sentiment, de passion! Je suis bien grande pour m'occuper de ces propos enfantins; le temps où j'aimais est si loin de moi!" [To continue writing novels, always speaking of love, of sentiment, of passion! I am too grown up to occupy myself with these childish topics; the time when I loved is so far from me now!].[70] The scene was set for her to compose a less conventional work. And she wrote to Liston about *Mylord Rivers* in September 1774: "Je ne fais pas un roman, mais . . . je poursuis les lettres de cet Anglais" [I am not writing a novel, but . . . I am pursuing the letters of that Englishman].[71] She may have called the work "letters" rather than a "novel" because the latter genre has traditionally been associated with love and disassociated from philosophy (although, as I have already sug-

gested and will discuss again below, those two topics are not as
far apart as we often assume). Letters, on the other hand, enjoy
a venerable philosophical past.

Compared with *Histoire de Cressy, Mylord Rivers*'s tone is
moderated and conversational, as befits the epistolary form.
Nearly twenty years separate the two novels, and yet they share
a philosophical emphasis on reason, relation, and experience.
Mylord Rivers revolves around English characters. The title
character is staying in France, and from there he corresponds
with various friends, recalling Riccoboni's own correspondence
with her English acquaintances. Mylord Rivers is a traveler
abroad, in the lineage of Voltaire's Candide, Montesquieu's Per-
sians, and Graffigny's Peruvian princess. The ostensible reason
for Rivers's departure from England was what he considered his
impossible love for his young pupil, Adeline Rutland. Their
shared stubbornness and unacknowledged mutual attraction
combine to create dramatic tension. In the novel's succinct conclusion, contained within the last letter of this collection of forty-
six, we learn from a third party that Mylord Rivers and Miss
Rutland have finally realized their love for one another, obstacles are cleared from their path, and marriage is on the horizon.
As Grimm wrote in his review of *Rivers,* "le dénouement est
prévu [dès] que l'action commence" [the outcome is predictable as
soon as the action begins].[72] The rapidity of this dénouement
demonstrates that the love story is not the primary arc around
which the narrative is organized.

The novel is driven by analysis rather than action. *Mylord
Rivers*'s love plot and resultant separation are a thin premise for
the need to write letters, allowing Rivers and his acquaintances
to engage in discussions about reason, happiness, books, philosophy, and relations between the sexes. The work repeatedly invokes *raison* and *raisonnable*, as when Rivers explains his stay
in France as necessary for his reason, or when characters offer
advice, praise another's behavior, or approach a decision in terms
of it being reasonable, as in Adeline Rutland's speculations on
marriage.

Particularly significant is a terse yet revealing statement
about the novel that Riccoboni wrote to Garrick: "Peut-être trou-
verez-vous dans ce petit livre autant de raison qu'il est permis à
une femme d'en montrer" [Perhaps you will find in this little

book as much reason as a woman is permitted to show].[73] She does not write that a woman cannot *possess* too much reason, but rather that a woman must be careful not to *show* excessive reason. So there is a tension of modalities, between *being* and *appearing,* centered on that perennial question of women's reputation.

It is true that most of the letters in *Mylord Rivers* are written either by or to a man. This characteristic leads Susan Lanser to describe the novel as "entirely an affair between men."[74] But in fact, of the six characters engaged in correspondence, only two (including Rivers himself) are men. Women play a key role, and their letters are among the most memorable of the collection. As explained at the beginning of this chapter, critics have repeatedly claimed that Riccoboni's works focus on the ways in which men hurt women. Yet this idea sits uneasily with the many sympathetic male characters in the Riccobonian corpus, of which Mylord Rivers is perhaps the most striking example.

Women of Reason in Mylord Rivers

Like the Count of Lipari in *L'Abeille,* Rivers is a sympathetic man who acts as a spokesperson for women's plight. But he is not the only admirable philosopher here. Simply put, Riccoboni's own views are variously reflected in many of this novel's likable characters, of both genders. Several women in the novel demonstrate their own philosophical skills. They tell philosophical tales and invoke reason as a guide. For instance, Adeline's sister, Lady Lesley, writes to her, asking rhetorically if wit is an advantage "quand la raison ne le règle pas" [when it is not ruled by reason].[75]

Mylady Orrery, the sister of Rivers's close friend and correspondent Charles Cardigan, has been subjected to social norms that have made her unhappy. She fell in love with a man considered too young for her, so she broke off the relationship. Critics have seen in this episode an allusion to Riccoboni's own bond with the young Robert Liston. But more generally, the example of Mylady Orrery illustrates how a woman must struggle against sexist conventions. Rivers calls her "raisonnable" [reasonable] and counsels her: "Croyez-en l'expérience et la vérité. On ne fait point de sacrifice à la raison, qui ne coûte un effort pénible" [Believe in experience and truth. One makes no sacrifice to reason that does not cost a painful effort] (*MR* 59). Mylady Orrery offers explicit meditations on reason. After describing her angst and solitude, she reports that, happily, "un coup de vent souffle sur ce flambeau presque éteint; rallume cette lumière vacillante, appelée raison. Je rassemble mes petites idées philosophiques [et] je reprends ma petite portion de courage" [a gust of wind blows on this almost-extinguished torch; rekindles this flickering light called reason. I gather up my little philosophical ideas [and] I recover my small portion of courage] (*MR* 54). She complains to Rivers that men have suppressed women's rights, and protests against the norm that allows older men to marry younger women but that forbids the inverse. She summarizes eighteenth-century gender politics with a powerful message: "Eh pourquoi cette différence? parce que je suis femme, obligée par état d'être raisonnable" [So, what explains this difference? Because *I am a woman, obliged by my status to be reasonable*] (*MR* 61, emphasis added). Here, being reasonable for a woman means internalizing social convention, an idea reminiscent of the *Encyclopédie*'s restrictive definition of the *femme raisonnable*. This harsh truth is the poison from which Riccoboni's bold narrative extracts a remedy: education.

Lady Mary Courteney Cardigan, married to Charles, is another of Rivers's correspondents. In a letter to Rivers, she iterates Mylady Orrery's remarks, ringing a variation on reason: "On ne sait comment traiter votre sexe, il est si déraisonnable!" [No one knows how to treat your sex, it is so unreasonable!] (*MR* 95). She critiques the French books Mylord Rivers has sent her on the grounds that they evince "la raison immolée sans cesse à l'esprit" [reason constantly sacrificed to wit] (*MR* 174). Similarly, complaining about the low quality of current books, Riccoboni wrote to Liston: "Les Français se sont mis à courir après l'esprit et le sens commun se perd dans leurs sublimes réflexions" [The French have set about running after wit, and common sense gets lost in their sublime reflections].[76] Lady Mary instructs Rivers:

> Surtout ne vous avisez pas de me répéter, *vous aurez toujours raison avec moi.* De ma vie je n'entendis un homme dire à une femme, *vous avez raison,* sans lire sur le visage de l'impertinent qu'il n'en croyais rien.

[Above all, don't you dare repeat to me, *you will always be right* [literally, "have reason"] *with me.* In my whole life I have never heard a man say to a woman, *you are right,* without reading on his impertinent face that he didn't believe a word of it]. (*MR* 138)

That is, no man—whether Mylord Rivers or members of the reading public as a whole—ever really thinks that a woman is right, that her words convey reason.

Overall, the novel employs several gender strategies. It features a central male character, it has female characters who invoke reason in philosophical tales and commentary, and it introduces gender complementarity through male/female pairings. Choosing a male protagonist allows Riccoboni to avoid the rhetorical problem described by Lady Cardigan: coming from a man, the novel's message may find a more generous reception. The novel's central reasonable women are both linked to Rivers's friend, Charles: Mylady Orrery is his sister and Lady Mary Cardigan his wife. As in the case of the pair formed by Adeline Rutland and Mylord Rivers, this is an implicit appeal to the idea of complementarity between the sexes. Feminine and masculine principles combine in fruitful relations. In fact, Rivers and Rutland, tutor and pupil, are like two complementary aspects of the same character, one older and wiser thanks to a greater range of experience. Here as elsewhere, Riccoboni highlights the relational aspect of reason and women's place in society. This is another example of the author's propensity toward a logic of "both/and" rather than "either/or."

Mylord Rivers *and Philosophy*

Riccoboni wrote to Garrick in February 1777 that he would enjoy reading *Mylord Rivers* under the following conditions: "si vous pouvez vous amuser d'une critique douce sur le changement actuel de nos moeurs, sur la fausse philosophie d'une troupe d'imbéciles qui nous inondent de plats écrits dictés par l'enthousiasme et la folie" [if you can laugh at a gentle critique of the current shift in our customs, of the false philosophy of a troop of imbeciles who inundate us with dull texts dictated by enthusiasm and madness].[77] Perhaps in part due to a misunderstanding of this letter, *Mylord Rivers* has been called one long satire of the *philosophes.*[78] In fact, it is nothing of the kind. Riccoboni was friendly with many philosophers of the *Encyclopédie* group, and shared with them an allegiance to Enlightenment values like tolerance, equality, and the power of reasoned discourse. At the same time, *Mylord Rivers* does satirize narrow-minded rationalists.

Rivers describes one of the novel's ridiculous philosophers, his uncle Sir Henry Montford, as follows: "Studieux et mélancolique, il ne parlait guère, écrivait beaucoup" [Studious and melancholy, he rarely spoke, and wrote a lot] (*MR* 41). Rivers says that he once had to restrain Henry from beating a black servant boy who spilled a little water on one of his manuscripts. When Rivers asked the subject of the manuscript, Henry replied, without irony, that it was about the happiness of the few and the tyranny of slave-owning European planters. Equally ridiculous is Sir George, about whom Rivers writes to Charles: "Je reçus hier le plus maussade essai critique, ou philosophique, qui soit encore sorti de sa lourde plume" [I received yesterday the most sullen critical, or philosophical, essay ever to come from his heavy pen] (*MR* 51). Rivers continues: "ses raisonnements prouvent bien peu de connaissance de ce monde dont il entreprend la *réformation*" [his reasoning proves he has little knowledge of this world whose *reformation* he is undertaking] (*MR* 52). Sir George is kin to the ignorant men of *L'Abeille's* first embedded story. Commenting on George's professed philosophical love for humanity, Rivers asks: "Si tous les hommes lui sont si chers, pourquoi méprise-t-il, pourquoi hait-il ceux qui ne pensent pas comme lui?" [If all men are dear to him, why does he suspect and hate those who do not think like he does?] (*MR* 41). Intolerant, George is no philosopher of the Enlightenment. For Rivers, and implicitly for Riccoboni, the performative contradictions enacted by Henry and George epitomize too many self-styled rationalist philosophers. Such false philosophers are ridiculous precisely because they disregard experience. Their actions do not match their theories. They are the pedantic authors, as described in *L'Abeille,* of dull books no one reads.

The satire of ridiculous philosophers in *Rivers* harmonizes with other Riccobonian ideals. In the author's letters to Garrick and especially to Liston, one often finds *orgueil,* "pride," used along with references to philosophy. In a letter to Garrick dated

August 12, 1766, Riccoboni remarks: "A la honte de la philosophie, de l'esprit, du savoir, nos académies sont remplies d'extravagants. Tous ces sublimes raisonneurs n'ont pas le sens commun.
L'orgueil les guide et les égare" [To the shame of philosophy, of
intellect, of knowledge, our academies are full of extravagants.
All of these sublime reasoners lack common sense. Pride guides
them and misleads them].[79] And she writes to Liston in 1772 that
she hopes a "petit orgueil philosophique" [petty philosophical
pride] is not the source of his happiness.[80] A few years later, she
complains that his diplomatic career has changed him, that before studying politics he was a "moraliste sans humeur, philosophe sans orgueil" [a moralist without ill temper, a philosopher
without arrogance].[81]

Mylord Rivers strives to be the exact opposite of ridiculous
philosophers like George and Henry. In response to George's
praise of pursuing renown, Mylord Rivers writes that he has
"beaucoup de respect pour ceux qui s'immortalisent, et pas la
moindre envie de les imiter" [a lot of respect for those who gain
immortality, without the slightest desire to emulate them]. He
continues: "Passager sur ce globe, . . . je n'y élèverai point de monument. Jamais je ne désirai l'admiration des hommes, heureux
d'espérer leur amitié" [A passenger on this globe, . . . I will raise
no monument. I never desired the admiration of men, [but am]
happy to hope for their friendship] (MR 52). This idea precisely
echoes a passage from one of Riccoboni's own letters: "Mon passage sur ce globe ne peut exciter ni satisfaire la curiosité de personne. . . . J'ai vécu dans un petit cercle" [My passage on this
globe can neither excite nor satisfy anyone's curiosity. . . . I have
lived in a small circle of acquaintances].[82] Social status is secondary to virtue and to relations with those near at hand.

Rivers takes his distance from philosophers, and not just ridiculous examples. Though he is eminently philosophical, he rejects the label, writing to Lady Mary: "je vous en prie, ne me
nommez jamais ni *sage,* ni *philosophe*" [please, never call me either a *sage* or a *philosopher*]. Such names, he says, in the lineage
of Riccoboni's *L'Abeille,* usually designate a "pédant" [pedant] or
an "ennuyeux" [bore] (MR 50). This is a retort to critics who
point to some eighteenth-century women's rejection of the title
"philosopher" as proof of their lack of philosophical thought. His
avowed allergy to the term notwithstanding, Mylord Rivers is

clearly a philosopher. In an example of cool reason reminiscent of *Histoire de Cressy*, Mylord Rivers writes to Charles: "moi, dont la bienveillance raisonnée manque d'*ardeur*, je suis moins blessé des fautes de mes semblables" [I, whose reasoned benevolence lacks *ardor,* am less wounded by the faults of my fellow human beings] (*MR* 129). Rivers writes to his young friend James Morgan: "J'approuve . . . votre amour pour la philosophie" [I approve . . . your love of philosophy]. But Rivers warns him not to "errer" [go astray] reading certain authors. Specifically: "Gardez-vous d'adopter leurs suppositions, de voir un monde qui n'est pas, des hommes qui ne peuvent pas être" [Refrain from adopting their suppositions, from seeing a world that does not exist, men who cannot exist]. By contrast, Rivers describes "[l]es règles de la saine morale, de l'utile philosophie" [the rules of good morality, of useful philosophy] as follows: "Étudier la nature et son propre coeur, chercher à diminuer les peines attachées à la vie, à notre position dans le monde; étendre les ressources que la raison nous présente pour les adoucir" [Studying nature and one's own heart, seeking to diminish the sorrows attached to life, to our position in the world; extending the resources that reason offers us for allaying them] (*MR* 86). Terms like "diminuer" and "adoucir" suggest a remedy, as does Rivers's reference in this same passage to the resources of reason. This evocation of reason bears no resemblance to the accounts of Enlightenment by the caricaturists described in chapter 1. Rivers adheres to a practical reason deeply rooted in, and relevant to, one's lived experience.

He describes himself as follows: "Je suis assez dans le monde, comme sont au théâtre ces paisibles spectateurs qui, cherchant à s'amuser de la pièce, l'écoutent sans s'embarrasser si elle pouvait être mieux faite" [I am in society like those quiet spectators at the theater who, seeking to be amused by the play, listen to it without worrying whether it could be better done], although he does acknowledge that "la déraison" [the unreason] one witnesses there may "révolte" [becom[e] revolting] (*MR* 37, 147–48). Here, Riccoboni aligns Rivers with the French moralist tradition of the seventeenth century, including writers like La Rochefoucauld and La Bruyère as well as Molière. These writers, inheritors of Montaigne, saw themselves as "spectators of life," the title of Louis Van Delft's comprehensive study on the subject.[83] This understanding of the moralist was reflected in the title of Addison and Steele's *Spectator,* which Riccoboni so admired. Reading any of these moralists' texts, which offer observations rather than making pronouncements, we the readers are invited to judge the players on the stage of society and, in so doing, to judge ourselves.

A useful and positive counterpoint to *Histoire de Cressy, Lettres de Mylord Rivers* presents a number of eminently reasonable women characters. They critique social prejudice but simultaneously maintain peaceable relationships with men. Satirizing ridiculous philosophers, the novel endorses a reasoned, introspective mode of existence. It will be helpful now to return to a level of greater generality in order to discern some broad tendencies in Riccoboni's thought.

LOVE AND REASON

Riccoboni's work highlights the interface between the relational and the rational, and, more specifically, between love and reason. Although she gives this theme a unique twist, it appeared among the received ideas of her era. For example, an anonymous 1715 text entitled *Tablettes de l'homme du monde* affirms that "[l]'amour et la [r]aison sont les sources des deux plus grands plaisirs de la vie. Ils sont tellement incompatibles qu'il est impossible d'en pouvoir goûter en même temps le souverain degré de la perfection de l'un et de l'autre" [love and reason are the two sources of life's greatest pleasures. They are so incompatible that it is impossible to enjoy simultaneously the sovereign degree of perfection of both of them]. The solution, according to the *Tablettes*, is to strive for alternation between the two, "se donn[ant] tour à tour au charmant abandon d'un parfait amour et au plaisir céleste d'une raison triomphante" [giv[ing] oneself over by turns to the charming abandon of a perfect love and to the celestial pleasure of a triumphant reason].[84] Beyond incompatibility, other texts trace an outright conflict between love and reason, including some eighteenth-century plays performed at the Comédie Italienne, Riccoboni's former milieu. For example, a play called *L'Impromptu des acteurs* staged in 1745 proposed the following among its many maxims: "Trop d'amour trouble la raison, Trop de remords est poison" [Too much love troubles reason, Too much remorse is poison].[85] While Riccoboni was certainly not the first to note a tension between love and reason, she made original contributions to this debate. Sometimes—as in the conclusion to *Cressy*—her texts suggest that love as it exists in society is a poison for which reason is the remedy.

In a related but distinct vein, there is a recurring discussion in Riccoboni's works and in her letters about love's capacity to overpower reason. She wrote to Liston that "quand le coeur est vivement touché, la raison est sans force" [when the heart is deeply touched, reason is powerless] and that "la raison . . . a bien peu de pouvoir sur les mouvements du coeur" [reason . . . has very little power over the movements of the heart].[86] Riccoboni often described the interference between love and reason in toxic terms of drunkenness, enchantment, or poison. In her first novel, *Lettres de Mistriss Fanni Butlerd* (1757), poison is invoked in a context of sensuousness when the female protagonist describes her beloved's lips as "la coupe enchanteresse où le plaisir presse le doux poison dont il se sert pour enivrer la raison" [the enchanting cup where pleasure presses the sweet poison it uses to intoxicate reason].[87] Likewise, in *Histoire de Cressy*, Adélaïde laments that men "se plaisent à voir fermenter dans nos coeurs le poison qu'ils y versent eux-mêmes" [enjoy fermenting in women's hearts the poison that they themselves have poured into them] (*HC* 59). But there are limits. For example, as the marquis de Cressy tries to seduce Adélaïde, his "témérité" [temerity] awakens her from her "ivresse dangereuse" [dangerous drunkenness] and "lui ren[d] sa raison" [gives her back her reason] (*HC* 71).

I would suggest that these invocations of love's ability to overpower reason function on a double register. First, they are an acknowledgment of the power of love in human relations. Second, they often question what kind of resource women's reason can be, given the social context of women's lesser power and influence.

Riccoboni's attitude toward the nexus of women, love, and reason has so often been misunderstood that it will be helpful here to examine some of the critical commentary on that issue. Olga Cragg cites the following line from the narrator in *Histoire de Cressy:* "Mais que peut la raison contre une passion qui nous maîtrise, qui tient à nous, qui est en nous, qui fixe et absorbe toutes nos idées?" [But what can reason do against a passion that overtakes us, that depends upon us, that is in us, that focuses and absorbs all of our ideas?] (*HC* 74). By way of analysis, Cragg writes: "This weakness associated with the impotence of reason, which the author attributes to feminine nature, is . . . inherent. . . . [T]he Riccobonian female slave resigns herself stoically to the inferiority of her own nature."[88] This claim is simply untenable, for at least two reasons. First, Riccoboni's works illustrate that when reason proves to be impotent for women, it is due not to their inherent failing but to social conditions. Second, men in Riccoboni's work, including Mylord Rivers, share the same opinion. He writes to Lady Cardigan, speaking of himself in the third person: "Un *homme raisonnable!* eh, l'est-on quand on aime?" [A *reasonable man!* Is one reasonable when one is in love?] (*MR* 161). He describes his early love affairs as a time when he saw "[s]es jours s'écouler dans cette ivresse qui charme les sens, assoupit la raison" [his days flow by in that drunkenness that charms the senses and makes reason drowsy] (*MR* 165). Clearly, Riccoboni did not view women as the only ones susceptible to having their reason affected by the overwhelming power of love. Instead, this is a relational phenomenon, with specific effects for women.

Furthermore, note Cragg's assumption that *nous* here equals "we women." Implicitly, she suggests that a woman cannot speak with an authoritative voice in which "we" could mean "humanity" in general.[89] True, the narrator of *Histoire de Cressy* is female. This does not mean, however, that everything this narrator says is meant to apply only to women. I would suggest that many readers—including Cragg—are still unused to the idea of women assuming the authority entailed in authorship. And, as I have already mentioned, it is often supposed that women authors only treat issues of limited, local importance. Cragg is not alone in the kinds of assumptions she makes about women. James C. Nicholls writes in his introduction to Riccoboni's correspondence that the author's "feminism" sometimes affected her "customary objectivity."[90] The subtext here is that when men address men's concerns, they are objective and philosophical; when women address women's concerns, they are neither.

And what happens when men write of love? Let us turn briefly to a text invoked above: Plato's *Symposium*. It is comprised largely of speeches by various characters, each of whom articulates a different view of love. Two are especially pertinent here. First, Aristophanes says that the god of love "supports us and heals precisely those ills whose alleviation constitutes the deepest human happiness."[91] In short, he describes love as a remedy. Second, Diotima explains that the goal of all love is knowledge.[92] She alludes, thus, to the etymology of "philosophy": the love of wisdom. Love between two people may not be identical to the love of wisdom but, on Diotima's account, all love shares the same goal. I invoke these examples to erase any doubt that love is a topic worthy of philosophy. Historically, when men write of love, their text is called philosophical, a treatise. When women write of love, their text is called personal, a romance. Taking women's ideas more seriously is a crucial step in expanding our understanding of Enlightenment.

RICCOBONI AS AUTHOR AND PHILOSOPHER

The question bears repeating: Given social arrangements in which men hold the power, what kind of a resource is women's reason? This is perhaps the most crucial issue posed by Riccoboni's work. And so we return to the question of women and philosophy, of Riccoboni as a philosopher, that is, as a thinker who addressed crucial issues of her time (and ours). The analysis in this chapter has demonstrated Riccoboni's Enlightenment critique of inequality, her reliance on reason, her emphasis on experience, and her focus on relation. Here, I would like to consider the question of "stoicism," which Riccoboni invoked on numerous occasions, as well as the author's famous quarrel with Choderlos de Laclos and what it can tell us about reason.

Riccoboni understood stoicism as a coldhearted, passionless reason. She took her distance from such a narrow definition. At the same time, it is important to remember that critique does not entail rejection. Riccoboni's letters and other works contain frequent references to stoicism. In *Mylord Rivers,* Mylady Orrery writes about men: "Le sexe qui se prétend fort, sait maîtriser ses passions" [The sex that claims to be strong, knows how to master its passions] (*MR* 55). But this is not her own opinion; she is only repeating "ce qu'un stoïque a le front de me soutenir" [what a stoic has the impudence to argue to me] (*MR* 55). Mylord Rivers responds by saying that both men and women draw upon the same strengths to moderate their passions, adding that a stoic would have a "coeur froid" [cold heart] and thus "n'existe pas, ne saurait exister" [does not exist, could not exist] (*MR* 59).

Prefiguring Rivers's remark just mentioned, Riccoboni wrote to Liston in March 1771: "je vous crois très courageux, très *philosophe,* mais je vous estime trop pour vous mettre dans la classe des stoïques, l'homme qui ne sent rien n'existe pas, et s'il existait, ce serait un stupide!" [I think you are very courageous, very *philosophical,* but I esteem you too much to put you in the class of stoics; he who does not feel does not exist, and if he did exist, he would be an idiot!].[93] Riccoboni finds that joyful sense experience is more philosophical than stoicism: "En vérité, mon ami, je vous crois plus philosophe en dansant des contredanses anglaises, que vous ne me le paraîtriez en vous livrant à l'austérité stoïque" [Truthfully, my friend, I think you'd be more philosophical dancing English quadrilles, than you appear to me giving yourself over to stoic austerity].[94] Notwithstanding Diderot's praise for the philosopher in his *Essai sur la vie de Sénèque,* reading a text by Seneca (in French translation) confirms Riccoboni's dislike of the Stoics.[95]

But what, exactly, does *stoïque* signify here? According to the *Dictionnaire de l'Académie française* (1762), the term and its variants could mean not only "[q]ui tient de l'insensibilité et de la fermeté qu'affectaient les Stoïciens" [what relates to the insensibility and the resoluteness assumed by the Stoics] but also, and more generally, what is "austère et sévère" [austere and severe]. Riccoboni rails against stoicism because of a desire to justify, to herself and her interlocutors, deep passions and feelings—both her own and others'. As she wrote to Liston on December 22, 1776: "Vous parlez comme un stoïque, mais vous sentez comme un homme naturellement tendre et compatissant. La résignation, la philosophie ne détruisent pas la sensibilité" [You talk like a stoic, but you feel like a man who is naturally tender and compassionate. Resignation and philosophy do not destroy sensibility].[96] Because she equates "stoicism" with "lack of feeling," she rejects it.

At the same time, Riccoboni did not endorse the expression of feeling in every imaginable guise. Riccoboni wrote to Liston that she regretted her *sensibilité*.[97] Similarly, Mylord Rivers writes to Miss Rutland: "je commence à douter si la sensibilité est un bien. Peut-être avez-vous raison de la redouter" [I am beginning to doubt that sensibility is a good thing. Perhaps you are right to fear it] (*MR* 142). To better understand the plots of sensibility driving *Histoire de Cressy* and framing *Lettres de Mylord Rivers,* it is helpful to remember that there were market forces at work. Then as now, love sells—especially when it breeds misery. Riccoboni's letters show that she was aware of this fad and skeptical of it. Writing to Garrick on May 3, 1769, she complains that French playwrights seek only to "faire pleurer" [make the audience cry] and that the cult of *sensibilité* is part of a "fantaisie universelle" [universal fancy]. Even Molière had fallen out of favor, so great was the taste for all things serious and melancholy.[98] Three years later, the tendency persisted: "Nous sommes actuellement dans une fureur de *sensibilité* qui passe toute imagination, nos dames veulent pleurer, crier, étouffer aux spectacles" [We are currently living in a furor for *sensibility* that surpasses all imagination; our ladies want to weep, cry out, get choked up at the theater].[99] Mirroring Riccoboni's own attitude, Mylord Rivers calls *sensibilité* the "universelle manie" [universal mania]. He writes: "Les spectacles sont fort tristes, je te l'assure. On pleure à tous les théâtres" [Plays are very sad, I assure you. They cry at all of the theaters].[100]

Despite her avowed "anti-stoic" bent, Riccoboni actually embraced some stoic principles (without, of course, labeling them as such). Citing her calm in the face of a conflict with her bookseller, Riccoboni wrote to Liston: "je puis me compter au nombre des philosophes pratiques" [I can count myself among the practical philosophers].[101] The following year, she noted: "Mon esprit est calme, mon coeur me semble tranquille, je m'applaudis fort de ma raison, je la crois grande, inaltérable même" [My mind is calm, my heart seems tranquil, I congratulate myself on my reason, I believe it is large, even unalterable] and "[l]es événements ne sont rien. Notre façon de les envisager est tout" [Events are nothing. Our way of viewing them is everything].[102] Similarly, Mylord Rivers writes to James Morgan: "Le bonheur ne me paraît point attaché à une situation, mais à l'idée qu'on se forme de la sienne et de celle des autres" [Happiness does not seem to me attached to a situation, but to the idea one forms about one's

own situation and that of others] (*MR* 84). Like the Stoics, Riccoboni often invokes tranquility; in a letter to Garrick she calls it
the "source véritable du bonheur" [the real source of happi-
ness].[103] Mylord Rivers characterizes this same idea as a need for
"repos" [rest] (*MR* 35). Mme de Cressy exemplifies this ideal as
she faces her death with composure. The Stoics were among the
inheritors of Socrates, emphasizing cool reason and equanimity.
Riccoboni is an inheritor of this tradition too, insofar as she endorses ideals like the tranquility of the soul. To the Stoic tradition, though, Riccoboni adds an emphasis on relation and circumstances, which she experienced with special urgency thanks to
her identity as a woman.

That gender identity played a role in Riccoboni's critique of a
certain type of calculating reason. In 1782, she undertook a brief
yet famous epistolary quarrel with Choderlos de Laclos about the
notorious Marquise de Merteuil, a central character in his smash
success *Les Liaisons dangereuses*, which was published that year.
Riccoboni's objections could be understood as a moralist's defense
of virtuous women's reason against the poisonous Merteuil, who
uses her diabolical reason to treacherous ends.[104] Note that M. de
Cressy engages in a kind of scheming similar to that of the Marquise de Merteuil; apparently the author found it more believable
in male characters. In any case, the author's critique of a certain
kind of reason does not equal a wholesale rejection of reason. Perhaps we could apply to Laclos a remark that Riccoboni made in a
letter to Liston a few years earlier: "Tous nous écrivains
s'éloignent de la vérité, ils se perdent dans les nues, il semble que
la fin du siècle suit aussi celle de la raison" [All of our writers
stray from the truth, they get lost in the clouds; it seems that the
end of the century is following the end of reason].[105]

CONCLUSION: RICCOBONI ON
REASON AS REMEDY

The traditional view of Riccoboni as a sentimental novelist sin-
gle-mindedly focused on critiquing men and their deceptive behavior does not stand up to scrutiny. Riccoboni wrote to Liston a
phrase that serves as a retort to critics who claim otherwise: "Si
c'est votre idée, ni vous ne me connaissez, ni vous ne lisez ce que

j'écris dans son véritable sens" [If that is your idea, you neither know me nor read what I write in its true meaning].[106] As I have suggested, women authors in particular are often understood in ways that conform to stereotypes rather than to what they actually wrote. A more careful interpretation shows that Riccoboni's texts operate in both a critical and a constructive vein: identifying the sexual double standard and proposing reason—both education and introspection—as a remedy to it.

Elizabeth Heckendorn Cook suggests that Riccoboni believed participation in the public sphere through authorship was the answer to women's woes.[107] But Cook stops short of calling Riccoboni an Enlightenment thinker. And it is not clear that Riccoboni prescribed authorship as a cure-all for women. Rather, her works suggest that education—awareness of women's social situation, a turn to the evidence of experience—and reasoned analysis will prove to be surer remedies.

Riccoboni's works show that reason is an especially potent remedy for the social ills that women face. L'Abeille appeared in a self-consciously "philosophical" publication, as Bastide's description suggests, and introduced the concerns of women—education, marriage, everyday sexism, and so on—as major themes. By doing so it elevated these concerns as worthy of philosophical investigation. Recall that the bee does not simply gather honey but transforms it and makes it useful. Similarly, Riccoboni and her protagonists do not simply compile and report stories about women. Rather, these gleanings from experience and observations about relation are meant to be remedial: they call readers' attention to women's plight, but they also advocate change. And all the while, they show that a woman author can perform philosophy, use reason, extract a remedy from the most poisonous experiences, and complicate our understanding of eighteenth-century women's struggles and triumphs.

The Cressy narrator speaks with the voice of reason, as do female characters in L'Abeille and Mylord Rivers. Like several of her characters, Riccoboni espouses a practical reason rooted in lived experience. She rejects a reason incapable of change, devoid of attention to the world and to experience. She suggests that reason is a positive quality and a trustworthy guide. Her works also show that it is good, though sometimes difficult, to listen to reason—it can inform our lives and lead us toward equanimity.

She offers a thoughtful response to men's denial of women's reason. The remedy that Riccoboni proposes may be called *polyvalent,* as is said of a vaccine that is effective against more than one ailment.

At the beginning of this chapter, I noted that the cup is an apt motif for the idea of remedy in the works treated here. This is all the more true because all three works play upon liquid imagery. In *Cressy,* it could not be more explicit: the protagonist drinks tea from a cup in the novel's pivotal scene. In *L'Abeille,* the narrator advocates making and drinking nectar, as well as extracting beneficial sap. Sounding a ringing note of humility, the *Abeille* narrator writes that even the person of genius must recognize that his or her knowledge is "un bien recueilli dans la société" [a good gathered in society] comparable to a great river formed from many small streams. This great river, in turn, waters the ground, making it fertile (*L'Abeille* 235). That is, our triumphs as well as our challenges may be traced back to our relations with others. And *Mylord Rivers* highlights the watery metaphor in the title character's very name. There is a narrative stream linking the image of the river with the nectar in *L'Abeille,* the liquid poison in *Cressy,* and the protagonist named Mylord Rivers.

In Riccoboni's works, we see that when women are in relation to men (in a love relationship, for example), reason is often denied them. In light of unequal social arrangements, women can ill afford to forget about relationality. All three narratives highlight social structures and relations between the sexes designed to women's detriment. But relation—including love—can also become a positive remedy when it is cultivated under equitable conditions.

Above, I discussed the reception of men's and women's works on the topic of love, suggesting that men's ideas are granted a more universal application while women's ideas are considered to be limited and local. Now, I do not claim that the philosophical voice has to be "universal." Indeed, it never is. There is always a perspective from which an idea comes forth. Witness Riccoboni's comment in a 1775 letter to Liston that "[a]ucun voyageur ne peut voir exactement, ni juger juste" [no traveler can see exactly, or judge fairly]. She goes on to explain that one's "habitudes" [habits], "préjugés" [prejudices], "usages" [customs], and "opinions" [opinions] "influeront sans cesse sur sa raison" [will always influence one's reason].[108] The relativism expressed here is a response to caricaturists today who define "Enlightenment reason" as a belief in the "view from nowhere." But let us add to what Riccoboni writes in this passage that we can still claim for women writers, as for men, the ability to say something beyond the strictly local and personal.

Mylord Rivers writes to Charles Cardigan:

> [L]a société forme un tribunal où tous les membres sont forcés de comparaître, de subir un rigoureux examen: qu'ils répondent ou se taisent, ils n'en sont pas moins jugés, et l'estime publique, ou le mépris général résulte de l'arrêt qu'elle prononce.

> [Society forms a tribunal before which all members are forced to appear, to submit to a rigorous examination: whether they respond or remain silent, they are nonetheless judged, and public esteem or general scorn results from the decision handed down] (*MR* 53).

Applicable also to the judgment on Socrates, this is a near-perfect example of Roger Chartier's formulation of the eighteenth-century "tribunal of opinion," or the idea that the birth of the oppositional bourgeois public sphere gave rise to the new role of the public as judge.[109] Rivers's statement has special resonance for women, especially if we are mindful of the importance placed on women's reputation. If Riccoboni has not been considered a philosopher, this is because of the way she is judged rather than the way she was.

One cannot help but compare the counsel of *L'Abeille*'s narrator to read the book of the world with the trials of many of Riccoboni's female protagonists (including Adélaïde and Mme de Cressy): experience yields difficult lessons. The key is learning to read the signs in the book of the world, adopting reason as a remedy. Through her writings, Riccoboni proposes to readers a variety of remedies: forging relations, learning from experience, and relying upon reason as solace and guide. Riccoboni's works offer a remedy that her readers, unlike the unfortunate Mme de Cressy, can drink without dying.

Reading the Riccoboni/Laclos correspondence, Janie Vanpée argues that Riccoboni bases her indignation about la Merteuil specifically on her identity as a woman. And, indeed, in her second letter to Laclos, Riccoboni insists: "C'est en qualité de femme, Monsieur, de Française" [It is as a woman, Monsieur, as a French woman] that she writes.[110] This question of reading as a woman is a crucial complement to this study's focus on writing as a woman. It helpfully forecasts the next chapter's discussion. There, I turn to the work of Isabelle de Charrière and engage the topics of books, reading, and literacy. Of the three authors, Charrière offers the most hopeful account. She suggests a fresh understanding of literacy that informs and supports women's claim to reason and participation in Enlightenment.

4

Reading Reason:
Isabelle de Charrière's
Portrait de Zélide,
Élise ou l'université, and
"Des Auteurs et des livres"

ISABELLE DE CHARRIÈRE EXPLORED WOMEN'S ENLIGHTENED LITERACY
in three works spanning thirty years of her writing life: a literary self-portrait (*Portrait de Zélide,* 1762), a comedy (*Élise ou
l'université,* 1794), and an essay ("Des Auteurs et des livres" [Of
authors and books], 1796 or 1797). These works address gender,
reason, and Enlightenment through reading and writing practices, social norms, and spaces of reflection and relation, including the library. This chapter engages the motif of the book and
the trope of reading to illuminate a central facet of Charrière's
thought.

The two previous chapters proposed imagery from the *Encyclopédie*'s frontispiece to illustrate the motifs of mask and cup.
Here, for the book, the *Encyclopédie* itself serves as a fitting
image. It represents at least two distinct functions of eighteenth-
century books: on the one hand, they are possessions, luxury
goods, and decorative objects. On the other hand, they are com-
pendia of information, routes to introspection, and keys to learning. As the *Encyclopédie* article "Livre" reminds us about books,
"c'est par eux que nous acquérons des connaissances" [it is
through them that we acquire knowledge].[1] The three works at
the core of this chapter approach the question of literacy from
different perspectives: *Zélide* centers on writing the self, *Élise* on

5. Charrière's room and replica desk in her family home, Zuylen Castle, near Utrecht. Photograph Zuylen Castle, Oud-Zuilen, Netherlands

reading the social world, and "Des Auteurs" on the more general question of why one reads and writes.

In this analysis, "literacy" exceeds the basic ability to read and write. Following scholars in literacy studies such as Brian Street, Ellen Cushman, and members of the New London Group, the term is intended here to encompass identites, social and cultural practices, and understandings related to reading, writing, and learning.[2] Within this general framework, Charrière's works illuminate a dual perspective on reading: the ways in which women are read by others as well as the literacies that women must develop in order to read and succeed in the social world. Historian Roger Chartier explains that in the early modern period, growth in literacy along with the increased production of portable books created new practices of silent, individual reading and writing. These practices in turn fostered the development of different understandings of the self.[3] That is, the space opened up by changing literacy practices encouraged the growth of a new and richer conception of the individual's interior life. It also contributed to the bourgeois oppositional public sphere, the space for public debate, fueled by writing and reading, at the heart of Enlightenment sociality. Charrière's works illuminate this broad understanding of literacy—which, as I will discuss below, belongs to the same lineage as the Kantian definition of Enlightenment— and illustrate the close link between reason, literacy, and women's participation in Enlightenment.

Belle van Zuylen, the future Isabelle de Charrière, was born in Holland in 1740 to a French-speaking aristocratic family. While scholars have debated which national tradition may most legitimately claim her, the consensus places this cosmopolitan writer among other French-language authors of the eighteenth century. Like Graffigny and Riccoboni, she composed in various genres; indeed, Charrière's range as a writer is the most expansive of the three, encompassing novels, poetry, letters, plays, political pamphlets, and opera libretti. She did not write to earn her living, but solely to satisfy other needs: self-expression, communication with others, and participation in the world of ideas.

In 2005, an international conference in Utrecht commemorated Charrière's life and work on the two-hundredth anniversary of her death. At that time, visitors to nearby Zuylen Castle discovered an exhibit on display throughout the castle gardens, a self-paced tour guided by numbered markers and a pamphlet several pages long, entitled "Une Promenade avec Belle et les Hommes dans sa jeune vie" [A walk with Belle and the men of her youth]. As the title suggests, it tells Charrière's story through her relationships with men. It instructs visitors to imagine the young Belle standing near a certain tree or rosebush, thinking of one or another of the young men she had met. The tour creates a purely fanciful link between these relationships and the garden. The pamphlet quotes Belle's remark, written in a piece of personal correspondence, that she is not a "grand philosophe." As we have seen in previous chapters, the insistence that a certain woman writer was not really a philosopher—often bolstered by such decontextualized quotations—is common yet frequently ill-founded. Such remarks often say more about the *convenances,* or social rules, than they do about a woman's real distance from philosophy. In fact, that Belle would have felt it necessary to say anything at all with regard to being a philosopher suggests she was aware of possibly meriting this label.[4]

The pamphlet's concluding paragraph focuses on the future author's eventual marriage to her brothers' former tutor, Charles-Emmanuel de Charrière, with whom she moved to his native Switzerland. Subtly but significantly, this text reinforces the idea that a woman exists primarily for and through her relation with men. That is, it emphasizes the relational in a circumscribed way. It follows a stereotypical reading protocol according to which "woman" equals "love object." It disregards the fact that the young woman was already an author when she lived at Zuylen Castle: her first work, the satirical tale *Le Noble,* published in 1762, scandalized her family with its bold challenge to class hierarchy. Ignoring the intellectual biography, the pamphlet directs us to read Charrière's life along the familiar lines of a romantic plot. To put it another way, the pamphlet reinforces a narrow literacy. Similar to the situations described in chapters 1 and 2, the woman of reason in this example is read as a coquette.

But we should not be surprised that a tourist text reflects this stereotype, as even scholars for years spoke of Isabelle de Charrière—if at all—strictly in terms of the men she knew. One contributing factor is the future author's fifteen-year correspondence—initially clandestine and later notorious—with the military officer David-Louis Constant d'Hermenches, which she initiated in 1760. Their relationship was not physical, but the letters do not always sound chaste. This passionate correspondence has sometimes overshadowed her other writings, contributing to Charrière's eclipse behind her relation to men.

One episode in their correspondence evokes this chapter's central themes. In a letter to Belle dated August 7, 1762, in which he famously likens her talent as a writer to that of Voltaire, Constant d'Hermenches goes on to complain that she has not been paying enough attention to him, describing himself as follows: "rangé dans votre mémoire comme ces livres que l'on a voulu acquérir à tout prix et que l'on n'a fait que parcourir le sont dans une bibliothèque" [shelved in your memory rather as certain books—books that one wanted to acquire at any price and then merely skimmed—get shelved in a library] (*OC* 1:125).[5] Belle responds: "jamais ce ne sera là votre sort" [that will never be your fate].[6] The book and the library function here as a cipher of the affectionate link between Belle and her correspondent, just as they will between the heroine of *Élise* and her suitor. The metaphor of the long-forgotten yet valuable book is also a reminder to read works too long stored and forgotten, including *Élise* and "Des Auteurs et des livres."

Charrière scholar and biographer Cecil Courtney has identified four stages in the reception of Charrière's work since her death in 1805.[7] The first was near-complete oblivion, while the next two demonstrate the author being read in terms of her relation to various men. The second stage was her "discovery" by Charles-Augustin Sainte-Beuve following the critic's visit to Switzerland in the 1830s. His interest focused on Charrière's relation to literary author Benjamin Constant. The third stage came in the early twentieth century with three important studies: Philippe Godet's 1906 biography, which tended to bury Charrière in the history of Switzerland; a 1909 study on Constant by Gustave Rudler with chapters on Isabelle de Charrière; and Geoffrey Scott's 1925 *Portrait of Zélide*, focusing on Belle's relation to the Scottish writer James Boswell, which was widely published, translated, and distributed. It was thanks to Scott that the French public discovered Charrière (including Simone de Beauvoir, who mentioned the author in the section on marriage in *Le deuxième sexe*).[8] Scott had a low opinion of Charrière as a literary writer, and described her life as gloomy. A turning point finally came with the fourth stage, beginning in 1974 when a team of scholars undertook the preparation and publication of a ten-volume edition of Charrière's *Oeuvres complètes*. Thanks to the accessibility of this edition, coupled with efforts such as the creation of the Belle van Zuylen Chair for visiting scholars at the University of Utrecht, scholarly and popular interest in Charrière has continued to grow. All of this critical energy has created an opportune moment to examine and interpret Charrière's underread texts. Scholarship on Charrière has centered almost exclusively on her role as *épistolière* and novelist. This chapter highlights instead some relatively neglected genres: the literary portrait, the play, and the essay. To contextualize those readings, it will be helpful to consider briefly the treatment of reason in her novels.

Recent evidence suggests growing attention to Charrière as a philosopher. A chapter devoted to her appears in the anthology *Hypatia's Daughters: Fifteen Hundred Years of Women Philosophers*.[9] Two of her post-Revolutionary novels have garnered scholarly studies on the themes of reason or philosophy. *Lettres trouvées dans des porte-feuilles d'émigrés* (1793) offers, according to Marie-Hélène Chabut, a new kind of male character, one that unites reason and sensibility, representing what Chabut calls a *raison sensible,* or "sensitive reason."[10] Emma Rooksby published an article in the feminist philosophy journal *Hypatia* using Charrière's novel *Trois femmes* (1795) to explore moral questions.[11] That novel is a literary response to Immanuel Kant's categorical imperative, or the idea that moral dictates must be universally valid and applicable. It centers on three women—Émilie, Constance, and Joséphine—who must make moral choices that challenge the dictates of Kantian morality. In addition to Rooksby, several literary critics and historians have studied the novel and its philosophical messages.[12] Charrière was introduced to Kant's work in 1794 by her friend Ludwig Ferdinand Huber, and she discussed the philosopher's thought in an exchange of letters with Benjamin Constant. In fact, some of the key themes about Enlightenment expressed most famously in Kant's 1784 essay "What is Enlightenment?" appear throughout Charrière's corpus. As explained in chapter 1, that essay emphasizes having the courage to break free from the tutelage of authority and to exercise one's reason in the public sphere. It highlights the importance of presenting ideas in written form to the reading public. From one perspective, Kant's essay is merely the best-known articulation of a number of Enlightenment themes that also appear in the work of other writers, including Charrière. These themes include a broad understanding of literacy and an emphasis on the individual's role as reader and writer in the public sphere of ideas. Whereas critics have examined the Kant/Charrière link through *Trois femmes*, this more general perspective— the transition from tutelage to enlightened maturity as a form of literacy—remains unexplored.

more general

READING REASON IN CHARRIÈRE'S NOVELS:
THE CASE OF *LETTRES DE MISTRISS HENLEY*

Belle van Zuylen's indomitable wit and keen intelligence scared away many potential suitors—to whom she referred disparagingly as *les épouseurs*—until she finally settled with her even-tempered if somewhat dull husband, whom she marrried in 1771. The couple lived together on his estate near Neuchâtel. The marriage was not stormy like those endured by Graffigny and Riccoboni, and yet it was not happy. Charrière wrote in part to quell the boredom of her new domestic situation.

Charrière's richest novelistic treatment of reason appears in a brief text widely considered to bear reflections of her own marriage. Its genesis may be traced to a trip to Geneva in 1784, when Charrière found the city's readers in an uproar over a recent novel by Samuel de Constant (uncle to Benjamin Constant and brother to Constant d'Hermenches). Entitled *Le Mari sentimental, ou le mariage comme il y en a quelques-uns* [The sentimental husband, or marriage as it sometimes is], that novel consists of letters from a Swiss country gentleman and sworn bachelor named Bompré, who impulsively marries a thirty-five-year-old woman from Geneva. The relationship promptly turns sour and the novel ends with the sentimental husband's suicide.

Taking up her pen in response, Charrière wrote *Lettres de Mistriss Henley publiées par son amie [Letters of Mistress Henley Published by Her Friend]* (1784), today one of her best-known

Henley

France

works. In the novel, a young, sensitive Englishwoman writes sorrowful letters to a female friend in Switzerland, recounting the tale of her courtship and marriage to a widower. This was a *mariage de raison,* or marriage of convenience, the result of pressure the young woman felt to select this spouse over a younger and more exciting suitor.

Joan Hinde Stewart accurately notes that *Lettres de Mistriss Henley* offers a "continual nuancing of notions of reason, right, and wrong."[13] But Stewart makes this remark as an aside and does not elaborate. In fact, many readers of this novel have suggested that Mistress Henley rejects reason or lacks it altogether. This interpretation may be attributed to three factors. First, as I have suggested previously, readers often just assume that women authors will privilege sentiment over reason. Second, Charrière employs a subtle narrative technique that tempers and partially conceals her critique. Third, critics tend to treat "reason" as if its meaning were both self-evident and univocal, and thus unwittingly collapse the distinct senses of reason at work in Charrière's novel.

Stewart herself claims that Mistress Henley's happiness "depends on renouncing the female principles of vivacity and change and accepting reason."[14] Thus Stewart treats "reason" as something that men regulate and possess, indeed as something antithetical to "female principles." Similarly, Susan K. Jackson writes that "it is a given of the Henley marriage that *he* enjoys a monopoly on reason," an interpretation echoed more recently by Claire Jaquier and Monique Moser-Verrey.[15] But is that really the direction indicated by Charrière's text? What we know of Charrière and her work does not suggest that she would simply give reason over to men. Across many of her texts, Charrière offered a nuanced account of gender relations and affirmed women's ability to reason—including her own.

In the introduction to *Lettres de Mistriss Henley* in Charrière's *Oeuvres complètes,* the editors remark that Monsieur Henley "shares with the sentimental husband an essential character trait: both of them are eminently reasonable beings."[16] Critics are quick to label the men—any and all men, it would seem—as reasonable. "Reason" is frequently invoked in Charrière's novel; Mistress Henley often says to her husband *Vous avez raison,* or "you are right"—literally, "you have reason." But rather than indicating that the husband has a monopoly on reason, in fact this refrain, along with other evidence, suggests two things: that Monsieur Henley, as a man, is invested with social power; and that he is ruled by a sort of Cartesian rationalism, devoid of affect and impervious to sense experience.

Mistress Henley's refrain to her husband is an excellent example of Charrière's understated rhetorical technique, which has been variously described as tacking, tactics, double text, and *metis* (or "cunning wisdom").[17] This technique averts disapproval or censorship by permitting the author to advance a view opposite to the one the text seems to endorse. On the surface, Charrière's heroine continues to say "he is right, I am wrong," but the reader can see through this double text to the implicit critique underlying it. When Mistress Henley alludes to "les gens qui passent pour raisonnables" [those who are reputed to be reasonable],[18] she subtly undermines their authority.

Furthermore, Charrière's novel points out the type of "reasonable" behavior expected of women, illustrating the constraints advocated by Rousseau and outlined in the *Encyclopédie* article "Raisonnable." For instance, Monsieur Henley proclaims that girls should be raised to be "modestes, douces, *raisonnables*, femmes complaisantes et mères vigilantes" [modest, kind, *reasonable*, obliging women and vigilant mothers] (*OC* 8:121, *Letters* 39, emphasis added). And Charrière's novel subtly indicates the husband's lack of feeling; disappointed by his characteristically insensitive response to a concern she raised, Mistress Henley laments: "De moi, de ma santé, de mon plaisir, pas un mot" [Of me, my health, my pleasure, not a word] (*OC* 8:120, *Letters* 38). Throughout the novel, Monsieur Henley's "reason" becomes a code word for patriarchy and power, highlighting the heroine's struggles.

Mistress Henley issues an ultimatum at the novel's end. In ill health due both to pregnancy and to her domestic struggles, she writes a farewell letter to her friend, stating: "Dans un an, dans deux ans, vous apprendrez, je l'espère, que je suis raisonnable et heureuse, ou que je ne suis plus" [In a year, in two years, you will learn, I trust, that I am reasonable and contented, or that I am no more] (*OC* 8:122, *Letters* 42). Not to be confused with a desire for conformity, her words instead describe the terrible dilemma she confronts. The least acceptable option is to be unhappy and alive—that is, to continue as she is. The "you" in her remark is not just her epistolary correspondent, but the reading public as a whole, to whom she seems to be saying: you will learn to see women like me as reasonable.

Reading the novel requires a literacy that is cognizant of the social realities faced by eighteenth-century women and the wider context of Charrière's life and works. It also suggests a reading protocol for her other texts, one attuned to shades of meaning and subtle suggestion. Such a literacy and a reading protocol will guide the interpretations that follow: of *Portrait de Zélide,* focused on writing, and *Élise ou l'université,* focused on reading.

PORTRAIT DE ZÉLIDE:
WRITING THE SELF

In marked contrast to the traditional interpretations of Isabelle de Charrière in terms of men—reflected in tourist pamphlets, popular biographies, and scholarly works—stands her own literary self-presentation, called *Portrait de Mlle de Z . . . sous le nom de Zélide* or, more simply, *Portrait de Zélide.* The use of the pseudonym Zélide promotes a distancing from the self, almost as if the author is reading herself as one reader among others. Extremely popular in the seventeenth century, literary portraits were often used to pay compliments. Enthusiasm for the genre waned somewhat during the eighteenth century, but persisted nonetheless. Belle van Zuylen composed, as far as we know, a total of three literary portraits including the *Portrait de Zélide:* the other two describe female friends. The latter texts fit the traditional pattern of compliment.[19] The self-portrait, however, is quite unusual, for three primary reasons: it is realistic rather than idealized, it is metanarrative (that is, it demonstrates the author's conscious reflection upon its content), and it is funny. In these ways, the *Portrait* sets its author apart from her contemporaries who wrote in the genre. It offers a complex, ironic, and philosophical meditation on the identity of a young woman coming to terms with her relation to the social order. In so doing, it gives readers a framework for reading the author. The *Portrait* was never published during the author's lifetime, but it circulated widely in manuscript form.

Zélide Iconoclast: A Reading Protocol

The *Portrait de Zélide* was composed in autumn 1762, soon after *Le Noble* and during the early years of the correspondence with Constant d'Hermenches. It consists of a first section followed by a longer "Addition au portrait." The text starts by announcing that "Zélide n'est bonne que par principe" [Zélide is good only on principle]. It is "un effort" [an effort] for her to be "douce et facile" [sweet and easygoing]; when she has to keep this up for a long time, "c'est un martyre" [it's an agony]. And, the narrator continues, Zélide is endowed with "vanité . . . sans bornes" [boundless . . . vanity] (*OC* 10:36, 37). These were shocking claims for a young woman of the Dutch noblility. We can guess why so many suitors were scared away. In a letter to Constant d'Hermenches composed around the same time as the *Portrait,* Belle describes herself by writing:

> quand je m'amuse je dis presqu'au hasard ce qui me vient dans l'idée . . . , quand je m'ennuie j'ai la malheureuse franchise de bâiller et de m'endormir, cela mortifie et désoblige, on dit que je dédaigne toute conversation commune et que je crois mon esprit au-dessus de tout.

> [when I am amused I say almost at random whatever comes into my head. . . . When I'm bored I am unfortunately frank enough to yawn and fall asleep, which is humiliating and unkind. People say that I disdain all ordinary conversation, and that I think my intellect is superior to everything].[20]

This description of unvarnished honesty and disdain for social convention closely resembles the self depicted in *Zélide.*

Recalling the first part of Riccoboni's *L'Abeille* in both style and content, the *Portrait* evinces a strong philosophical flavor. For example, the key theme of *bonheur* appears early and recurs throughout. We learn of Zélide that "[s]e voyant trop sensible pour être heureuse, elle a presque cessé de prétendre au bonheur, elle s'attache à la vertu, elle fuit les repentirs et cherche les amusements. Les plaisirs sont rares pour elle, mais ils sont vifs" [finding herself too sensitive to be happy, she almost stopped striving for happiness; she seeks virtue, she flees regret and pursues amusement. Pleasures for her are rare, but they are intense]

(*OC* 10:37). Such ideas suggest familiarity with the philosophical traditions of Epicureanism—which say that humans should
seize happiness whenever possible—and Stoicism—according to
which happiness does not last.[21] Such familiarity is not surprising, given that Isabelle de Charrière read widely and had bene-
fitted from an unusually good education, including mathematics
and letters. As she wrote to Constant d'Hermenches:

> On trouve . . . mauvais que je veuille savoir plus que la plupart
> des femmes, et on ne sait pas que . . . je n'ai de santé ni pour
> ainsi dire de vie qu'au moyen d'une occupation d'esprit conti-
> nuelle. . . . [J]e ne puis me passer d'apprendre.

> [People . . . take it amiss that I want to know more than most
> women; they do not know that . . . I have no health—nor, so to
> speak, life—except by a continual occupation of my mind. . . . I
> cannot do without learning things].[22]

The *Portrait*'s philosophical tone continues on the Epicurean
theme of carpe diem: "Connaissant la vanité des projets, et l'in-
certitude de l'avenir, elle veut surtout rendre heureux le moment
qui s'écoule" [Recognizing the vanity of projects and the uncertainty of the future, above all she wants to make the fleeting
moment happy] (*OC* 10:37). The *Portrait* thus portrays Zélide as
a philosopher, an unusual woman, left to her own devices yet
called upon to negotiate others' judgments of her.

The main section of the *Portrait* ends on a curious note: "Avec
des organes moins sensibles, Zélide eût eu l'âme d'un grand
homme, avec moins d'esprit et de raison, elle n'eût été qu'une
femme faible" [With less sensitive organs, Zélide would have had
the soul of a great man; with less intellect and reason, she would
have been only a weak woman] (*OC* 10:37). The suggestion is
that, when measured against gender norms, she is neither fully
a man nor fully a woman. And this statement is framed in an
original way. Rather than saying "Had Zélide been more . . . " or
"If Zélide had had this quality . . . ," it offers a subtractive logic.
Zélide's character is over-full: she is highly sensitive at the same
time that she is very witty and endowed with reason. It is sensitivity that means she lacks the soul of a great man, and it is intellect and reason that keep her from being a weak woman. She
combines strong doses of both sensitivity and reason. The gender

categories entail an ambiguity here—by invoking and playing upon the idea that sensitive organs belong to women, while intellect and reason belong to men, the author defamiliarizes the logic at work in these norms. We may usefully recall, as explained in chapter 1, that the *philosophes* themselves embraced sensibility and the passions along with reason, perfectly in line with eighteenth-century materialist anthropology. At the same time, a double standard assigned sensitivity to women. In a backward way, Zélide is praised here as possessing the height of all good human qualities. Blurring the distinctions between male and female, reason and sentiment, Zélide's identity as an iconoclast is solidly established. We must read her according to a protocol different from the norm.

Kees van Strien argues convincingly that the "Addition au portrait"—actually comprised of two short sections appended to the original text—was written in response to feedback from readers of the original *Portrait*.[23] The "Addition" begins by explaining that Zélide never meant for the original portrait to be released to the public; it was intended only for the eyes of a close female friend. Zélide's friends say it would be possible to create twenty different portraits of her, "tous ressemblants à l'original, tous différents entre eux" [all of them resembling the original, all of them different from the others] (*OC* 10:38). That is, interpretation always occurs as a function of perspective.

The "Addition" returns to the impertinent claim made in the first section, that Zélide "n'est bonne que par principe" [is good only on principle] (*OC* 10:38). According to the narrator, Zélide herself is no longer so sure about this claim. At the same time, if being good means "dissimuler ses mécontentements et ses dégoûts, se taire quand on a raison" [hiding one's dissatisfactions and disgust, remaining silent when one is right] (*OC* 10:38), then Zélide strives to be good in those ways. Such qualities seem to reflect social pressures that particularly affect women.

The "Addition" returns to the theme of happiness. The narrator reiterates that Zélide's sensitivity means she cannot always be happy, and emphasizes that Zélide tries to make her existence of use to others. Nevertheless, Zélide stands accused of "se moquer de tout le monde" [mocking everyone] (*OC* 10:38). Here we sense that her reputation is certainly linked to her gender: she is judged more harshly by virtue of being a woman. But Zélide continues to like those who make her laugh, and would never have expected to find humans without weaknesses. She is a realist: "C'est trait pour trait qu'il faut voir les hommes" [We must view human beings in all of their traits] (*OC* 10:38). Although Zélide keeps others' secrets scrupulously, she will sometimes tell her own secrets in order to "s'amuser et . . . surprendre" [have fun and . . . cause surprise] (*OC* 10:39). Thus: "L'avenir est toujours sacrifié au présent" [The future is always sacrificed to the present] and she commits "mille imprudences" [a thousand imprudences] (*OC* 10:39). The narrator alludes to a passage from La Bruyère's *Les Caractères* according to which women cannot keep secrets, and remarks: "en ceci, Zélide n'est point femme" [in this, Zélide is not a woman] (*OC* 10:38–39). Here, the "Addition" returns to the gender-bending theme with which the main section of the *Portrait* concludes.

Some of the misanthropic flavor of seventeenth-century French moralists such as La Bruyère reappears in other key passages. For example:

> Si elle eut réfléchi un instant, son portrait ne courrait pas le monde, elle aurait bien senti, que la moitié des hommes sont méchants, et que cette moitié fait parler l'autre *qui ne sait pas lire*. Par bonheur le blâme de mille sots, et de dix mille prudes ne vaut pas un regret. Tous les jours Zélide est moins sensible au jugement d'une aveugle multitude.

> [If [Zélide] had reflected an instant, her portrait would not be circulating in the world, she would certainly have realized one half of humanity is mean, and that half instructs the other, which *does not know how to read*. Happily, the reprimand of a thousand fools and of two thousand prudes is not worth one regret. Every day Zélide becomes less sensitive to the judgment of a blind multitude] (*OC* 10:39, emphasis added).

Crucially here, Charrière introduces the topic of reading. The narrator not only acknowledges the role of the reading public as judge, but emphasizes that reading entails interpretation and sometimes a lack of accuracy. Moreover, for all of the apparent harshness in the narrator's statement, Zélide is not utterly indifferent to others; she would be sad if, knowing her well, someone could leave her without chagrin, see her without pleasure, or speak of her without esteem. On the other hand, she does not care if those far away from her, "sur des ouï-dire, sur de vagues rapports" [on hearsay, on vague reports] admire or blame her: "qu'importe à son bonheur?" [what does it matter for her happiness?] (*OC* 10:39). The reader today may feel directly interpellated by this passage. We are in several important senses (including temporally and culturally) far away from Belle van Zuylen. Critical response to her and her work has indeed too often relied upon hearsay. Is the writer suggesting something about the immediacy of experience, of knowing her in person? Given our own lack of immediacy, can we know how to read her? Are we ultimately unable to judge her? The "Addition" concludes with an apostrophe to sensitivity:

> Zélide ne vous désavouera pas, unique compensation du malheur d'un discernement fin et d'un goût difficile. Heureuse sensibilité au plaisir qui lui faites chérir les dons de la nature et qui l'attachez aux arts, bien plus qu'à la folle vanité. Vous êtes bien dangereuse peut-être, mais vous êtes toujours un bien!

> [Zélide will not disavow you, unique compensation for the unhappiness of fine discernment and demanding taste. Oh fortunate sensitivity to pleasure that makes her cherish the gifts of nature and that attaches her to the arts, much more than to foolish vanity. You are perhaps very dangerous, but you are always good!] (*OC* 10:39).

Here, we learn that Zélide affirms the value of feeling, the source of art and of true happiness. In the end, self-satisfaction seems to triumph over public reputation.

Readers of Portrait de Zélide, *Then and Now*

Nearly as intriguing as the *Portrait* itself is the critical response that it has elicited, both during the author's lifetime and today. The *Portrait* caused a minor scandal among Belle van Zuylen's acquaintances. Extant letters and responses express readers' surprise about the author's candor and self-assessment, which is by turns harsh or egotistical. A Dutch journalist, Cornelis van Engelen, wrote snidely of the *Portrait* that "Zélide, wishing to pass for a *savante,* says things about herself that she would never allow others to say."[24] He suggests that Belle van Zuylen aimed to be provocative in order to gain status as an intellectual. The review thus not only questions the young woman's modesty, but actually pays her a sort of backhanded compliment by taking notice of the portrait.

Another reaction is recorded in an anonymous *Analyse du Portrait de Zélide*, composed by a contemporary of Charrière's.[25] It begins by claiming that Zélide depicted herself as she would like to be, a strange assertion given that the portrait is not wholly flattering. The claim is also in tension with the published review cited above. At the same time, the author, like the published reviewer, accuses Zélide of wanting to "prendre le vol audessus de son sexe" [soar above her sex].[26] The author of the *Analyse* accuses Zélide of being "en contradiction avec elle-même" [in contradiction with herself];[27] he or she seems not to realize, first, that tensions exist in any human being and, second, that the embrace of these tensions is what lends the portrait its authenticity. That is, the *Portrait* strives for realism rather than idealism. At the end of the *Analyse,* the author turns to Zélide's comments that less intellect and reason would have made her just a weak woman, that less sensitive organs would have afforded her the soul of a great man, and writes: "Il n'est nullement prouvé que la délicatesse des organes influe sur le nerf de l'âme" [It has in no way been proven that the delicacy of organs influences the vigor of the soul].[28] The *Analyse* author quibbles about the details and misses the point.

Recent reception of the *Portrait* yields commonplaces similar to those noted above and analyzed in previous chapters. For example, the *Portrait* is said to reflect Belle van Zuylen's fundamental feminine sensibility. Or, there is the suggestion that the author borrowed her ideas from a man. Here, I would like to focus on Kees van Strien's assertion that the *Portrait* "draws heavily on the portrait of Sophie from Rousseau's *Émile*." For evidence, van Strien points to the text's attention to happiness and virtue. It is true that these themes appear in Book 5 of *Émile,* but they also recur across a wide spectrum of eighteenth-century texts. Of Sophie and Zélide, van Strien writes: "Both girls [sic] are fully determined to devote themselves to virtue." Again, the same could be said of most any sympathetic eighteenth-century protagonist. He sidesteps the problem of Sophie being passive and submissive, and speculates that Belle "recognized much of herself in the highly sensitive Sophie." On van Strien's reading, the future Isabelle de Charrière's autonomy and creativity are obfuscated. She dissimulates ("hiding behind" a pseudonym) and borrows (from a man).[29] This allegation of borrowing further reinforces the tendency described at the beginning of this chapter, that is, to interpret Charrière in terms of her relations to men.

How can we justify equating an intelligent young woman's self-portrait with Rousseau's infamous description of the ignorant, submissive Sophie? Van Strien acknowledges that "in the way they behave in company the difference could hardly have been greater": Zélide has to force herself to be polite, while "Sophie does not find this difficult at all."[30] In fact, the similarities are very slight, as is evident in the sparkling wit, sly self-deprecation, and unconventional, even shocking, statements of the *Portrait*. Nothing could be farther from Rousseau's Sophie. Whereas Sophie appears as a kind of accessory for a man, Zélide is resolutely independent; her self-portrait makes no mention of finding or pleasing a man. And so, what motive could underlie comparing Zélide to Sophie? I return to two possibilities mentioned in the introduction: legitimation and limitation. The first means trying to make Charrière seem more significant by linking her text to that of a canonical male author. The second means trying to make Charrière seem less significant by calling her text derivative. Both perspectives de-emphasize the creative, original act involved in writing the *Portrait*.

We do know that Belle was reading Rousseau's *Émile,* which had recently been published, around the time that she composed the *Portrait*. Aside from that fact, one thread connects the two texts and seems to form the basis for a claim of similarity between them. In the final lines of the "Addition au portrait," Belle van Zuylen, having just stated her disregard for readers who would judge her based upon partial evidence, adds: "Ce n'est pas pour eux, comme dit l'auteur d'*Emile;* Non, ce n'est pas pour eux que j'écris" [It is not for them, as the author of *Émile* says; No, it is not for them that I write] (*OC* 10:39). It is worth taking a closer look at the passage to which the author alludes here. In the preface to *Émile*, Rousseau writes: "Ce n'est pas sur les idées d'autrui que j'écris; c'est sur les miennes" [It is not about others' ideas that I write, it is about my own].[31] The difference between the two formulations is important: while Rousseau emphasizes the originality of his ideas with respect to other writers, the future Isabelle de Charrière emphasizes the *readers* of her text. She explains that she disregards the kind of readers who would judge her hastily based upon sparse evidence; rather, she writes for another, more thoughtful audience.

As careful readers, we must recognize that the *Portrait* is both satirical and enigmatic. It will remain forever slightly out of reach. The *Portrait* is an exercise in self-knowledge that explicitly distances its subject from many of the constraints of convention. It is disarming in its purported honesty. If we are able to read it free of the gender stereotypes that lead to hasty assumptions about its message, the text can reveal much about the thoughts and self-perception of the young woman who would become Isabelle de Charrière.

What is most extraordinary is that this *Portrait* exists at all. It was created under a pseudonym, which demonstrates an awareness of eventual readers. In her reformulation of Rousseau's remark at the end of the *Portrait,* Charrière overtly refers to these readers. She thus self-consciously seeks to participate in the public sphere of ideas, reaching out to the reading public that Kant described as the hallmark of Enlightenment. The text promotes a kind of literacy that encourages readers to rethink rigid boundaries between genders and to reconsider their preconceived ideas about women. Through it, the author reads herself complexly, inviting readers to witness her self-creation through words.

ÉLISE OU L'UNIVERSITÉ:
COQUETRY AND LITERACY

Charrière's novels and letters have earned increasing attention in recent years. Even her iconoclastic *Portrait de Zélide* has attracted more readers. By contrast, Charrière's works for the stage remain virtually unknown. And yet this body of work, rich in insight, merits a wider audience. Notable among the few scholars who have studied these texts is Guillemette Samson, author of the first book-length study on Charrière's work as a dramatist.[32] Charrière completed a total of seventeen works for the stage—of which twelve were comedies—in addition to several other drafts of theatrical works left unfinished. The plays were written between 1784 and 1800, with the greatest output occurring in 1793 and 1794.

L'Émigré (1794), a tale of French émigrés set in Switzerland, is the one play composed by Isabelle de Charrière that has not languished in total oblivion. For example, it was performed in Neuchâtel on January 15, 1906, to commemorate the hundredth anniversary of Charrière's death. In that play's first act, the otherwise unlikable Mme Vogel makes an astute remark that echoes throughout Charrière's work for the theater: "On s'instruit par l'expérience" [One learns from experience] (*OC* 7:279).

Guillemette Samson observes that Charrière often centered her plays on a young female character in an effort to counteract the cultural tendency toward the *bel-esprit* and to emphasize the importance of cultivating reason in young women. She adds that "[t]he female characters who have [Charrière's] sympathy use their reason."[33] At the same time, Samson begins her book on Charrière's theater by suggesting that feminist approaches to Charrière have ignored the theatrical works in part because, unlike Charrière's narrative works, they do not fit feminist goals.[34] In what follows, I offer a different interpretation.

Charrière was proud of her plays; she wrote to her friend Jean-Pierre de Chambrier d'Oleyres on June 14, 1794, that she found her comedies "comme de raison, fort belles" [as they should be, quite lovely] (*OC* 4:460). She placed special importance on a handful of these works, including both *L'Émigré* and *Élise ou l'université*. She wrote to Benjamin Constant on October 4, 1794, about what she had included in her comedies:

> presque toutes mes idées sur les rangs de la société, les besoins des hommes . . . ainsi que sur le courage, l'industrie, et l'impartialité que je veux qu'on ait . . . relativement à soi. Quiconque lirait *L'Émigré, L'Inconsolable, Brusquet,* et *Élise* me lirait moi à peu de choses près sur tous ces points.

> [almost all of my ideas about social classes, the needs of human beings . . . as well as about courage, industry, and the impartiality that I want people to have toward themselves. Whoever reads The émigré, The unconsolable, Brusquet, and Élise would actually be reading me, on all of these topics.] (*OC* 4:593)

She describes herself here as a social critic and philosopher. What Charrière offers the reader (or spectator) is a theater of ideas. While the link may not be self-evident, the text of a work for the stage bears a particularly close relationship to the reader. As Samson explains, theatrical works have representation as their objective; although narrative works "entail no direct confrontation with the reader," the text of a play speaks directly to he or she who reads, creating a kind of reality.[35]

The focus in this section is Charrière's three-act play *Élise ou l'université,* composed and published in 1794. *Élise,* with its coquettish protagonist, may seem an unlikely choice for analysis. But I will suggest that this play offers a new perspective on gender, reason, and Enlightenment, a perspective that is illuminated through the motif of the book. The reading of *Élise ou l'université* that I offer cuts against the grain, in a spirit similar to Jacqueline Letzter's interpretation of Charrière's novel *Sainte-Anne* (1799). Letzter shows that the character Babet d'Estival's inability to read is actually meant as a subtle condemnation of illiteracy among women. Indeed, Letzter suggests that Charrière had to *louvoyer,* or engage in the indirect strategy of "tacking," in order to express her pro-woman views.[36] Not only is the heroine of *Élise* literate (unlike Babet), but her literacy sets her apart from the norm and makes her a target of criticism. At the same time, the play invites us to witness this character's apprenticeship in a literacy of social norms.

One of the particularities of *Élise* is that it was conceived to be presented to a German-speaking audience. Charrière wrote it in French and then asked for her friend Ludwig Ferdinand Huber's help translating it into German. In the course of this process, the heroine's name was Germanized from Eugénie to Élise. Although the play's established title is *Élise ou l'université,* the heroine's name in the original French text is Eugénie. It is crucial to remember that this play was intended as a quintessentially *French* play for this audience, in some sense meant to be more French than the French themselves. As the editors of the *Oeuvres complètes* write: "We should not be fooled. . . . Isabelle de Charrière did indeed write a French comedy, in which the only German element is suggested by characters' names and a few allusions to facts and events."[37] And the numerous changes and corrections found in the French manuscript testify to the importance Charrière assigned to the French version of the play.[38] A general eighteenth-century association of Germans with books and libraries may help to explain the play's setting. For example, the *Encyclopédie*'s articles on "Bibliothèque" and "Livre" praise German libraries and attribute to Germans the invention of literary history.

Yvette Went-Daoust speculates that the German setting afforded Charrière a certain freedom to break away from the rules of classical French theater. In May 1794, Charrière wrote to Huber that she was working on the play that would become *Élise ou l'université*. She explains setting the action at a German university as follows: "je voudrais pouvoir dire des vérités passablement hardies et rire sans façon des ridicules que mon sujet m'offrirait" [I would like to be able to state rather bold truths and to laugh simply about the absurdities that my subject offers me].[39] Citing this passage, Went-Daoust remarks that *Élise* may be the comedy in which Charrière "most dares to be herself."[40]

The basic plot of *Élise ou l'université* revolves around love. In the play, Walter and Eugénie, the daughter of a university professor, love each other. Walter admires Eugénie's intelligence; he defends her when his friend the Count de Rhynberg invokes her coquettish reputation. Nevertheless, Walter reluctantly agrees to participate in a test devised by his friend: to hide Walter's social rank and thus discern whether Eugénie truly loves him for who he is. This stratagem recalls the test of Azor's fidelity undertaken in Graffigny's *Phaza*. Meanwhile, Walter's father arrives; he wants his son to marry Wilhelmine, the daughter of his friend the Baron de Schwartsheim. But a surprise awaits: Wilhelmine and the Count are in love. Some tension arises between the dictates of paternal authority and those of amorous inclination. In the end, everyone's true sentiments are declared and the play ends with the strong suggestion that the two couples will marry and live happily ever after. Woven into this rather canonical plot (reminiscent of Molière and Marivaux) is an inquiry about relations between the sexes, the value of experience, and what it means for a woman to become literate, broadly speaking. The young heroine becomes aware of her gender socialization, critiques the institutions associated with her father, and comes to a maturity combining love and intellect.

Eugénie as Coquette: Two Senses

As mentioned above, Eugénie may at first blush seem an unlikely choice for an analysis focused on reason and Enlightenment. The choice becomes clearer when we understand that Eugénie is reputed to be a coquette for two remarkably different
reasons. The first and most obvious is that she pays attention to
her appearance, presumably to attract the attention of men. But
there is also a second, quite different, sense in which Eugénie is
viewed as a coquette. She is the intelligent and educated daughter of a university professor. And so, joining the more evident
definition of a coquette—the flirt—is a second sense—the *savante*. Arguably, the first, in the realm of love, is considered
more excusable than the second, in the realm of learning.

The charge against Eugénie of being a coquette—communi-
cated first of all by her chambermaid, Caroline—is articulated
explicitly in terms of reputation. In fact, the question of reputation (an eighteenth-century obsession, as we have seen in previous chapters) becomes a principal axis around which the plot
turns. Eugénie is suspected of being inconstant, or fickle in love,
but she flatly dismisses the suggestion. Although Eugénie is reputed to have broken a young professor's heart, in fact she says
that she has never really loved. And so at least part of her identity as a coquette in the realm of love may be attributed to a
false rumor. Caroline warns Eugénie that her coquettish reputation may deprive her of a suitable marriage. Eugénie says she
does not care; she has inherited a large fortune and so marriage
is not a matter of survival.

Caroline tells Eugénie: "Je vous admire Mademoiselle, et ne
m'attendais guère à trouver chez la fille d'un professeur alle-
mand plus d'art et si j'ose dire plus de coquetterie que je n'ai vue
chez mes maîtresses françaises" [I admire you, Mademoiselle,
and I was scarely expecting to find, in the daughter of a German
professor, more art and I daresay more coquetry than I had seen
in my French mistresses]. In other words, Eugénie is more
French than the French. These women have included "une comé-
dienne, une financière, et une femme de la Cour" [an actress, the
wife of a financier, and a woman of the Court]. And, Caroline
tells Eugénie: "aucune d'elles ne vous égalait en désir de plaire
et de briller" [none of them was your equal in the desire to please

and to shine] (*OC* 7:413). This is, of course, an implicit commentary on the coquetry of French women. And this definition of *coquettrie*—a perceived wish to "please" and to "shine" —turns not so much on what a woman actually is, but rather on others' perception of her, particularly regarding her desires.

COQUETRY OF DRESS, APPEARANCE, AND FLIRTATION

Eugénie's coquetry differs from the kind described in the *Portrait de Zélide*. The *Portrait* defines being a "coquette" as "rendre un homme malheureux, et cela pour s'amuser, pour se procurer une espèce de gloire, qui même ne flatte pas sa raison et ne touche qu'un instant sa vanité" [making a man unhappy, and doing so to have fun, to attain a kind of glory, which does not even flatter one's reason and touches one's vanity only for a moment] (*OC* 10:37). Eugénie expressly denies engaging in coquetry in this sense. When Zélide succeeds in coquetry, she immediately regrets it. The *Portrait*'s narrator asks: "Quand est-ce que les lumières de l'esprit commanderont au penchant du coeur[?] Alors Zélide cessera d'être coquette. Triste contradiction!" [When will the mind's lights command the heart's penchant? Then Zélide will cease being a coquette. What a sad contradiction!] (*OC* 10:37). Kees van Strien describes this tension as "the conflict between [Zélide's] heart and her head."[41] But if we read the first phrase of the passage in another way, it seems to describe a social problem, or even a universal human one, rather than the fault of an individual. The formulation refers to some future time when minds will rule hearts, or, we could say, when people will live in a philosophical age.

Eugénie is reputed to be a coquette because she is a pretty and charming young woman who devotes time to her *toilette*. And indeed, the play's opening scene finds her in front of the mirror, arranging her accessories with help from her chambermaid, Caroline. This setting contrasts with that from an earlier manuscript version in which Eugénie and Caroline are returning from a walk (*OC* 7:750). The final version presents the women in a more static and staged pose, Eugénie at her dressing table, the two women in a private space within the home.

In fact, several of Charrière's theatrical works begin with a similar scene, including her comic opera *Les Femmes* (1790), in

which the character Albert complains of women: "J'ai tant souf-
fert de leur coquetterie" [I have suffered so much from their co-
quetry] (*OC* 7:214). This setting suggests intimacy and a space of
between-women. But it also emphasizes that a woman must pay
attention to appearances. The *toilette* depicted onstage denotes
not only coquetry, but an awareness of reputation.

The opening scene of *Élise* also introduces a leitmotiv: *bleuets,*
or cornflowers. Eugénie attaches artificial cornflowers to her
bonnet—the real ones are currently in bloom, she says—to
achieve an "air touchant d'innocente simplicité" [touching air of
innocent simplicity] (*OC* 7:413). The stage directions in act 2,
scene 6 will indicate that Eugénie is dressed "simplement et no-
blement sans rouge ni diamants ni d'autres fleurs que les
bleuets" [simply and nobly, without rouge or diamonds or other
flowers besides the cornflowers] she had worn in the first scene
(*OC* 7:441). The *bleuets* are a symbol of Eugénie's natural beauty.
But, artificial rather than natural, they also symbolize her coquetry. And as such, she will eventually throw them away.

What makes Eugénie unique is certainly not her display of
coquettish behavior. Rather, like the lady in the second embedded story from Riccoboni's *L'Abeille,* Eugénie explains that the
coquetry of dress and appearance fulfills a larger goal. Caroline
boldly tells Eugénie: "Je ne vous cèle pas que vous n'ayez la réputation d'être un peu coquette et un peu légère" [I won't hide from
you that you have the reputation of being coquettish and a bit
frivolous] (*OC* 7:415). To which Eugénie responds: "Coquette oui
si c'est l'être que d'occuper un insipide loisir à apprendre un art
dont on peut faire un jour le plus doux et le plus noble usage"
[Coquettish, yes, if that means filling an insipid leisure time
learning an art that one day can be put to the sweetest and no-
blest use] (*OC* 7:415). That is to say, in due time, coquetry will
become subsumed in the art of love, which Eugénie defines as
"sortir d'un sec et stérile égoïsme pour se charger du bonheur
d'un autre être" [leaving behind a dry and sterile egotism in
order to care for another being's happiness] (*OC* 7:415). Similarly, in a discussion with the Count, Walter comes to Eugénie's
defense by invoking a logic resembling her own: "On voit très
souvent la coquetterie finir quand une jeune personne devient
femme et mère" [Very often, coquetry ends when a young person
becomes a wife and mother] (*OC* 7:424).[42]

In Eugénie's conversation with Caroline, the coquetry of dress and appearance is also discussed in terms reminiscent of the second type of coquetry, related to book learning. The two types of coquetry—that of the flirt and that of the *femme savante*—are explicitly intertwined through the theme of love. Eugénie describes coquetry as a sort of training period on the way to real love, during which one learns to please one's romantic partner. But Caroline remarks: "Les hommes n'aiment pas les femmes savantes sur ce point" [Men do not like women who are *savantes* (knowledgeable) in that respect] (*OC* 7:415). Eugénie locates the solution in skillfulness (recall the metis, or cunning wisdom, with which Charrière has been credited), replying that "si une femme y est vraiment savante elle entraîne et séduit si bien" [if a woman is truly *savante* in this regard, she leads and seduces so well] that the man targeted by the coquetry is unaware of it (*OC* 7:415). Caroline asks rhetorically whether this procedure can victimize its target and perhaps even the coquette herself. Eugénie replies, "*très sérieusement:* Je ne sais. Peut-être" [*very seriously:* I do not know. Perhaps]. Caroline observes: "de pareils *peut-être* son hazardeux" [such *perhaps* are hazardous] (*OC* 7:415, 416).

The type of coquetry defended by Eugénie recalls the "good" variety of coquetry—the hidden kind that leads to love—advocated in Rousseau's *Émile*. More significant, though, is its link in this scene to the idea of a *savante*. This term is usually associated with scholarly activities in the eighteenth century; its feminine form was most always pejorative. But Charrière's play makes the use of *savante* in this discussion of coquetry seem logical when we learn more about the second reason for which Eugénie is labeled a coquette. That is, as happened to other women characters we have encountered, her knowledge is called coquetry. Here we may usefully return to the anonymous *Analyse* of the *Portrait de Zélide;* its author writes that Zélide "place dans son coeur une coquetterie qui n'existe que dans son esprit" [locates in her heart a coquetry that only exists in her mind].[43] In fact, the examples of both Zélide and Eugénie challenge this supposed division between heart and mind, between coquetry and reason. They offer a new reading protocol, a new way to understand women's identities that moves beyond simplistic opposition.

Coquetry of the *Femme Savante*

A distinct but equally important source of Eugénie's coquettish
reputation is her unusual intelligence and exceptional education.
This aspect of Eugénie's coquetry clearly lies in the eye of the
beholder. For example, Walter admires Eugénie's mind: "Elle a
de l'esprit et de l'instruction" [She has intellect and instruction]
(*OC* 7:424). But the Count adds: "Avec un grain de pédanterie"
[With a hint of pedantry] (*OC* 7:425). The two positions represent distinct readings of Eugénie's character. A review of the
play in a German newspaper, the *Allgemeine Literatur-Zeitung,*
notes: "Most of the characters [in this play] reason [*räsonniren*]
more than they act."[44] The verb *räsonieren* again calls to mind
Descartes's complaint against the endlessly debating scholastic
philosophers, as well as Bayle's Penelope and Restif's *épouse raisonneuse.* It is also, as discussed previously, used in Kant's
"What is Enlightenment?," where it means reasoning for reason's
sake, the freedom accorded to participants in the public sphere
of Enlightenment society. Like most of the male characters in
Charrière's play, Eugénie uses her reason to engage in debate.
But she is the only one labeled a coquette.

Eugénie is considered a *femme savante* and therefore a coquette in part because she has read so many books. That is, her
coquetry is linked to her literacy. But these books include novels.
In which type of coquetry shall we categorize novel-reading—
that of the flirt or that of the *savante?* The always-wry Caroline
remarks, during her discussion with Eugénie about love and coquetry: "J'ai lu quelques romans, vous en aurez lu beaucoup, est-
ce là uniquement que vous avez puisé ces belles idées?" [I have
read some novels; you are presumed to have read a lot of them,
is that where you got these lovely ideas?]. Later, in response to
Eugénie's fantasy (unfounded, as it happens) that Walter is a
disguised nobleman, Caroline retorts: "non je n'ai pas la tête
assez remplie de romans pour cela" [No, my head isn't sufficiently full of novels to believe that] (*OC* 7:415, 416). The terms
roman, novel, and *romanesque,* romantic, appear often when the
conversation turns to Eugénie. For example, Caroline invokes
Eugénie's "imagination romanesque et exaltée" [romantic and
excitable imagination] (*OC* 7:449). The Count describes Eugénie
as "[a]ssez belle, très polie, passablement coquette, pas mal ro-

manesque et un peu ridicule" [[b]eautiful enough, very polite, rather coquettish, quite romantic and a bit ridiculous] (*OC* 7:423). Novels were indeed often associated with the heart. As we have seen, however, a love plot often accompanies, yields, or conceals other meanings.

Education and the University

Eugénie's bookish reputation as well as her characterization as a flirt may be blamed on her education. Eugénie's mother died when Eugénie was very young, leaving her alone with her father, the quintessential absentminded professor. He attends to books rather than to life. Their family name, "Wits," echoes the German noun *Witz,* meaning either wit or joke. The father's amusing absentmindedness, however, makes him no less a symbol of knowledge.

The Baron de Schwartsheim says to Eugénie's father, Professor Wits:

> Une jeune fille n'est pas bien entre les mains de son père. Notre surveillance n'aperçoit pas tout et mille travers peuvent se prendre et s'enraciner avant que nous nous en doutions. Tantôt c'est de la toilette, tantôt c'est des romans . . . j'ai vu des demoiselles de qualité sortir du manoir paternel les unes si fières les autres si ignorantes les autres si romanesquement sensibles que cela me fait peur.

> [A young girl is not safe in her father's hands. Our oversight does not perceive everything, and a thousand failings can take root before we suspect anything. Sometimes it's the *toilette,* sometimes it's novels . . . I have seen young girls of quality leave the paternal manor either so arrogant or so ignorant or so romantically sensitive that it scares me] (*OC* 7:433).

A father figure's lack of effort, or useless attempts, to guide his daughter's upbringing is a recurrent theme (inherited from seventeenth-century playwrights including Molière) in eighteenth-century literature.

In the absence of a mother figure, it is the chambermaid Caroline who assumes the role of counselor and protector. Recalling the conversation between the two fathers—Professor Wits and the Baron de Schwartsheim—Caroline ironizes: "M. votre père

est trop savant pour savoir ce qui se passe chez lui de sorte que
vous avez été livrée à vous-même" [your father is too learned
[*savant*] to know what's happening in his house, and so you've
been thrown back on your own devices] (*OC* 7:416). Caroline jus-
tifies the frank tone she has adopted by adding: "c'est que vous
m'intéressez extrêmement" [I care deeply about you] (*OC* 7:416).
And, as we have seen, it is Caroline rather than Professor Wits
who is concerned about Eugénie's reputation. The play asks what
it means to be a *savant(e)* from the university and what it means
to possess practical knowledge. The theme, so common in seventeenth-century comedy, of the servant who is more clever than
the master is explicitly drawn out here. Eugénie says to her father about Caroline: "Elle a assurément de l'esprit et je la crois
aussi propre à se faire des idées justes de toutes choses que le
plus grand savant de l'université" [She certainly is intelligent,
and I think she is as able to judge anything as the greatest *savant* of the university] (*OC* 7:418).

The university milieu inflects the entire play, opening up discussions of education, books, libraries, and literacy. When Eugénie meets the Count de Rhynberg, she says to him: "On vous
aura peint le séjour d'une université comme quelque chose d'assez triste et dans le fond on n'a pas eu tout le tort du monde" [I
imagine that the university setting has been described to you as
something rather sad; and in the end, that is not entirely incor-
rect]. She adds that, compared to life in big cities and at court,
the university must seem like an "étoite sphère" [narrow space]
(*OC* 7:420). Eugénie comes across as bolder than her brainy father; indeed, her vigor is crucial here. The Count de Rhynberg
urges Professor Wits, as a man of learning, to "éclaire[r] les
autres hommes, attaque[r] de funestes préjugés, proclame[r] des
vérités utiles" [enlighten others, attack fatal prejudices, and proclaim useful truths] (*OC* 7:422). The professor responds that his
uncertainty on many questions makes him hesitant to speak. To
which the Count replies eloquently: "A quoi bon se taire. . . . Pen-
sons et parlons et faisons penser les autres" [What good is it to
remain silent? Let us think and speak and get others to think].
He notes that they have the right to express themselves: "On
peut raisonner et même déraisonner sans crainte" [We may reason and even talk nonsense without fear] (*OC* 7:422). This is a
Kantian defense of reasoning for reason's sake.

The preceding discussion of *Portrait de Zélide* raised doubts about borrowings from Rousseau's Sophie to create the persona of Zélide. But this is certainly not to suggest that Charrière and Rousseau share nothing in common. For example, through her description of Eugénie's less-than-perfect education, Charrière joins many other women in agreeing with Rousseau that women are unfortunately educated to become coquettes. On this topic, Charrière wrote to her friend Henriette L'Hardy: "Quoique je maintienne que les facultés sont originairement les mêmes je ne puis disconvenir que la faculté raisonnante ne soit bien plus perfectionnée chez les hommes et cela par l'étude et rien que par l'étude" [Although I maintain that the faculties are by their origins the same, I cannot deny the reasoning faculty is more perfected in men, and that happens through study, solely through study].[45]

Near the end of the play, with the dénouement in sight, Eugénie observes that everyone in her house is troubled, "[e]xcepté mon pere qui est seul avec ses livres" [except my father, who is alone with his books] (*OC* 7:454). Professor Wits resembles Charles, the title character of Charrière's play *L'Extravagant* (1795), who spends an inordinate amount of time locked away in his room studying. In an addition to the German text, Professor Wits announces that he can keep a secret; in fact, it is easy because he forgets everything else when he reads his books. He even forgot the time of his own wedding (*OC* 7:755). Samson writes: "The ineptitude of the professor is manifested through 'doubt,' inattention, and contradictions." She argues that Charrière's play highlights the dramatic contrast between Professor Wits's good reputation and the reality of his failings, writing that he "is a celebrity recognized throughout Germany whose weak character no one suspects; the author reveals to us his hidden side. . . . His weakness is paternal, political, and intellectual."[46] That Professor Wits studies his books so intently only serves to highlight his inattention, or illiteracy, on a larger scale. Charrière's critique of the father is emblematic of her more general critique of established convention. She embodies the Kantian motto of Enlightenment: *Sapere aude,* or "dare to know." Charrière puts in the mouth of Professor Wits a remark that could have come from Eugénie or several of her other heroines: "On ne ressemble pas toujours à son père" [One does not always resemble one's father] (*OC* 7:434).

The Count says to Walter: "Quant au père [d'Eugénie] j'en aurais été fort content sans la timidité d'esprit qu'il nous a laissé entrevoir" [As for [Eugénie's] father, I would have been very happy with him, without the timidity of mind that he allowed us to glimpse] (*OC* 7:423). The Count exclaims that he is exasperated by "la timidité parmi les chefs parmi l'état major de la science!" [the timidity among our leaders, among the highest rank of science!]. . . . "[T]out cela doit être prêt à boire la ciguë au besoin comme Socrate" [All of them should be ready to drink hemlock as needed, like Socrates] (*OC* 7:423). As explained in chapter 3, Socrates was an iconic image for eighteenth-century thinkers; in the *Phaedo,* Plato writes that philosophers should be ready and willing to die to defend their ideals.[47] Professor Wits, representative of the academic establishment, pales in comparison with his spirited, philosophical daughter.

The Book, the Library, and Love

In an episode of striking psychological realism, Walter undertakes to find Eugénie without appearing to search for her, though Caroline immediately recognizes the subterfuge. In response to Walter's conjecture that Eugénie is perhaps in the garden, Caroline says that if he doesn't find her there, "elle sera peut-être dans la bibliothèque de son père" [she may be in her father's library] (*OC* 7: 450). The rich symbolism of the father's library is an idea to which I will return shortly. Walter immediately invents a pretext for visiting the library: "A propos je voulais y aller prendre un livre. J'irai et par hasard je pourrai rencontrer Eugénie" [Oh by the way, I wanted to go there to get a book. I will go and perhaps by accident I will meet Eugénie]. Amused, Caroline observes: "Oui par hasard! Il est plus amoureux, c'est à dire plus fou, que je ne pensais" [By accident indeed! He's more in love, that is to say crazier, than I thought] (*OC* 7:450). And so a book (even if it is a fictitious one) will bring Walter and Eugénie together.

Meanwhile, about the two fathers, Caroline says to Wilhelmine and the Count: "Je les ai vu prendre ensemble le chemin de la bibliothèque publique" [I saw them heading in the direction of the public library] (*OC* 7:451). Everyone, it would seem, is converging upon a library. Books are distracting the fathers from the amorous intrigues of their children. The fathers, in fact, lack the literacy to read the situation.

The play's climax—the long-awaited confession of love, a meeting of hearts and minds—occurs in act 2, scene 5, when Walter and Eugénie meet in the library. There, in a refreshing variation on the more typical courtship dialogue, Walter praises Eugénie's education and knowledge, but at every turn she modestly plays down her accomplishments. For example, when Walter extols her mind and her *lumières,* she replies: "Le moindre apprenti savant me surpasse en connaissances acquises" [The least apprentice scholar surpasses me in knowledge] (*OC* 7:457). To funny and ironic effect, Eugénie completes several of Walter's sentences about her. Walter begins: "Vous avez lu . . . " [You have read . . .] and Eugénie adds: "Beaucoup de romans. Que ne puis-je les brûler et les oublier tous" [Many novels. If only I could burn them and forget them all]. Walter tries another tack with the sentence: "Vous avez fait . . . " [You have created . . .], which Eugénie completes with "[d]e petits vers" [little verses] (*OC* 7:457). At this point, according to the stage directions, Eugénie tears up her manuscripts and drawings. She pulls the cornflowers from her hat and stuffs them, along with the papers, in a sack, which she throws into a corner. She declares: "Tout cela appartenait à une personne qui n'est plus moi qui n'existe plus" [All of that belonged to a person who is no longer I, who no longer exists] (*OC* 7:457). She does this despite Walter's professed admiration for her creative talents. She tells him: "je veux vivre raisonnable et estimée" [I want to live reasonable and esteemed]. This phrase again raises the issue of reputation, as does another remark by Eugénie: "Après une jeunesse folle . . . j'aspire à une maturité estimable" [After a crazy youth, . . . I aspire to an estimable maturity] (*OC* 7:458). In this scene, Eugénie separates herself from both types of coquetry. Denying her achievements, she takes her distance from the role of *savante.* Removing her flowers, she refuses the role of flirt.

So, is Eugénie or is she not a *coquette?* We must remember that her coquettish ways are implicitly blamed on the absence of a mother's guidance. Due to that absence, she has been educated by society to play the coquette. Eugénie herself never accepts the label. But eighteenth-century critics took her coquetry for granted. The review in *Allgemeine Literatur-Zeitung* noted: "the

principal character, a refined coquette, changes in the end in an
unlikely way."[48] Characterizing her transformation as "unlikely"
is of course a question of perspective. What matters is discern-
ing what Eugénie has learned, how she has changed, and what
it all may mean.

Unlikely or not, Eugénie does resolve to turn over a new leaf.
The play's third and final act represents a further significant
change with respect to coquetry. Eugénie describes the reputation of coquette as a "triste lot" [sad fate], leading a woman to be
"dédaignée" [scorned] and "délaissée" [forsaken] (*OC* 7:448). She
declares: "le temps n'est plus où ma parure m'intéressait" [the
time when finery interested me is over] (*OC* 7:448). So her coquetry—the flirtatious variety—has disappeared. In the second
scene of the third act, Caroline says to Walter: "Vis-à-vis de vous
du moins Mlle Wits me paraissait avoir autre chose que de la
coquetterie" [With respect to you, at least, Mademoiselle Wits
seemed to me to possess something other than coquetry] (*OC*
7:449). She refers here to genuine love. And Charrière wrote of
her protagonist that "non seulement Élise [a.k.a. Eugénie] se
montre mais *devient* meilleure" [not only does Élise (a.k.a. Eugénie) appear better, she *becomes* better].[49] Eugénie fulfills her
own prediction as coquetry gives way to lasting commitment.

What of the father's library? Various readers of Charrière's
narrative works have emphasized the importance of place. For
example, Monique Moser-Verrey argues that the topography of
Charrière's family home, Zuylen Castle, informs the author's
works.[50] And in her book *Through the Reading Glass,* Suellen
Diaconoff examines "[t]he architecture of space" in Charrière's
fiction, arguing that the author's use of liminal spaces "testifies
to her belief that women exist on the borders in eighteenth-century society."[51] Diaconoff discusses, separately, the space of the
library and fictional works by Charrière. Reading *Élise* encourages us to connect the two topics. Diaconoff studies eighteenth-
century representations of women reading in two spaces—the
boudoir and the library—as symbolic of the body and the mind,
respectively.[52] She suggests that whereas women reading within
the boudoir were linked to desire, women reading in the library
enjoyed a higher status, linked to intellect. Congruent with these
ideas, *Élise ou l'université* demonstrates a spatial evolution. The
play begins with Eugénie at her *toilette* and ends with her in the

library. The final scene, then, emphasizes the protagonist's intellect. Even while Eugénie pledges her love to Walter, she is not called upon to abandon her intellectual identity. Once labeled as coquetry, it is redeemed as maturity.

Reminiscent of Zélide's self-critique, Eugénie renounces her "prétentions" [pretentions] and her "vanité" [vanity]. She says to Walter: "Si c'est de bon sens que j'ai jusqu'ici manqué à votre avis, vous avez raison, nous sommes d'accord" [If it is good sense that I've been lacking, according to you, then you are right, we agree] (*OC* 7:457). But Walter holds firm in his admiration for her: "Non, ébloui, charmé, j'ai admiré un esprit et des talents que vous méprisez trop. Tantôt sérieuse tantôt enjouée vous m'avez toujours paru riche de belles idées" [No. Dazzled and charmed, I admired a mind and talents that you scorn too much. Sometimes serious and sometimes playful, you have always seemed rich with beautiful ideas] (*OC* 7:457). In essence, the more Eugénie tries to conform to a social ideal of feminine modesty, the more Walter insists that he loves her mind. She is wealthy and lovely, but also, as he says here, rich with beautiful ideas. As Samson remarks, Walter acknowledges that Eugénie is "capable of reason."[53] Eugénie, while renouncing her past as a flirt, could also seem to renounce her role as *savante*. But Walter implicitly keeps separate these two quite distinct meanings of *coquette*. And indeed, the coquettish behavior of the flirt can be willfully modified; however, by what means does one undo one's identity as a *savante*? Learnedness can go underground, but it will not go away. The flirt is defined by action, the *savante* by knowledge. Secure in her relationship with Walter, Eugénie no longer needs to flirt. His praise of her mind suggests that she can go on cultivating her thought. In fact, with Walter's encouragement, perhaps Eugénie will stop viewing learnedness as coquetry. It is not some internal, personal failing that she must overcome, but rather what society has taught her. Her literacy, then, involves some reeducation.

Walter describes Eugénie in terms that recall the cornflowers as well as the definition of *coquetterie:* "Nulle affectation, nul artifice. C'est comme une belle fleur des champs, elle n'a pas eu besoin de culture. Elle est née ce qu'elle devait être elle brille de sa propre native beauté" [No affectation and no artifice. She is like a beautiful wildflower, she has not needed cultivation. She was born as she was supposed to be and she shines with her own native beauty] (*OC* 7:455). Included in this description is the verb *briller,* to shine, previously used by Caroline in defining the coquette. Walter is effectively creating a literary portrait of Eugénie, in the lineage of works like Charrière's. Eugénie is in many ways more conventional than Zélide. But we would certainly expect as much in a character destined for public performance on the stage, as opposed to a characterization that circulated only in manuscript form among acquaintances. Samson explains of Charrière's theatrical works that the female characters "agree to conform to the *bienséances* as long as the stakes do not go beyond *bienséance.*"[54] When something larger is at issue, however, these characters assert their right to strike out on a new path.

Rereading the Coquette

In the play's final scene, Eugénie appears to secure her father's consent to her marriage of inclination. Walter is likewise freed from the *mariage de raison* that his father had envisioned for him. Eugénie's father says to her: "Je n'avais pas trop songé à te marier. Libre, riche, entourée de livres de savants d'artistes que te manquait-il chez ton père ?" [I had not given any thought to marrying you off. Free, rich, surrounded by books, *savants,* artists, what were you lacking in your father's house?] (*OC* 7:459). He points out that she could have married someone else: "tu te verrais comme une autre Aspasie" [you would see yourself as another Aspasia] (*OC* 7:459). This is a subtle reference to Socrates—Aspasia frequented his circle—echoing the Count's call for courage worthy of the great philosopher. But this is not exactly the future that Eugénie has in mind. And in the end, Professor Wits seems to relent. A marriage of inclination thus wins out over a marriage of convenience, in marked contrast to *Mistriss Henley.* The reputed coquette finds a man who loves all aspects of her, including her intellect. The solution here is a relational one, forged between Eugénie and Walter. Earlier, both Eugénie and Walter had remarked that coquetry can blossom into love. That is what seems to happen in their relationship. Significantly, the other valence of Eugénie's supposed coquetry disappears too: as a *femme savante,* she had been the target of charges of coquetry. Those charges were based entirely upon her reputation, upon others' poor opinion of her. Now that Eugénie's intelligence has been affirmed, the sting of coquetry is soothed, replaced by esteem. Thus, both types of coquetry disappear.

In Charrière's play *L'Extravagant*, Monsieur de Malmont declares that his daughter Sophie should be allowed to choose a husband for herself (even though, in fact, each parent tries to steer her toward the spouse of his or her choosing). By contrast, the chambermaid Lucile's last line in *L'Extravagant* affirms the link between reason and marriage. She declares that, instead of "une insensée et romanesque flamme" [an unthinking and romantic flame], one should prefer a marriage "par la raison chaque jour confirmé" [each day confirmed by reason] (*OC* 7:524). Blending these ideas with the conclusion to *Élise,* we may suggest that Charrière's ideal of marriage is one both freely chosen and suffused with reason.

Is Eugénie resigned to fall more in line with convention, in preparation for marriage? Such a reading would match the standard interpretation of *Mistriss Henley*. One could propose a conservative reading of the play: the learned young woman forsakes her youthful love of sparkle and appearance in favor of matrimony. However, in a more progressive vein, this is a play featuring a well-educated and likable young woman; a play in which the marriage chosen between lovers wins out over the arrangement envisioned by the father. And the young man loves his future wife for her mind. But this conclusion should not surprise a careful reader. From the play's beginning, Eugénie describes flirtatious coquetry as taking a backseat to love and as existing in its service.

The play's progressive aspect is reinforced by its characters' critique of the nobility and allegiance to democracy. In fact, the work's critique of class distinctions rejoins that found in Charrière's work dating back to *Le Noble* and appearing in several of her comedies.[55] Professor Wits has obviously democratic sympathies, though when faced with this description of himself, he denies it to save face among his peers. Caroline says that she hopes Eugénie is wrong in her suspicion that Walter is a disguised nobleman, because if he is, he will not be able to marry her. Eugénie responds: "Les lumières s'étendent. La noblesse doit devenir plus traitable plus raisonnable de jour en jour" [Enlightenment is spreading. The nobility is becoming more tractable and more reasonable with each passing day] (*OC* 7:417). We need to remember that the play, while it does not explicitly refer to particular political events, was composed in 1794. Charrière was living in Switzerland and had helped a number of French émigrés fleeing the Revolution. In Paris, politicians and everyday citizens alike were sorting out the aftermath of the fall of Robespierre and the end of the Terror. This context inflects the play's political message. Walter explains that in the Count de Rhynberg's opinion, it should be "l'application et des lumières acquises" [effort and acquired knowledge] that earn people a post, not their noble birth (*OC* 7:421). The Baron de Schwartsheim tells Professor Wits that he is thinking of marrying his daughter to a commoner. The play ends with Professor Wits recalling the democratic implications of his tolerance toward Eugénie's choice of spouse:

> Je ne m'oppose pas précisément à ton mariage. Mais si avec le temps je le permets c'est bien qu'on criera au Démocrate qu'on dira que je méprise les usages reçus, le respect qu'on doit aux lois de la société. C'est bien alors qu'on m'appellera un sectateur des opinions nouvelles.

> [I am not exactly opposed to your marriage. But if, with the passing of time, I allow it, people will call me a Democrat and will say that I scorn accepted practices and the respect owed to society's laws. It is certainly then that I will be called a partisan of the new opinions.] (*OC* 7:460)

In sum, Eugénie goes from arranging cornflowers to organizing a partnership for herself. During the era when arranged marriages were giving way to companionate matches, Charrière's protagonist found her own mate; perhaps, if we emphasize its boldness, this maneuver has no name other than "coquetry"? The democratic strain thus inflects not only relations at the level of society, but relations within the family. The daughter asserts herself over the father, composing her own future.

It is instructive to return once more to the idea that one does not always resemble one's father, and to the setting of the play's climax: the father's library. The epigraph to the author's first published work, *Le Noble,* is a line from La Fontaine: "On ne suit pas toujours ses aïeux, ni son père" [One does not always follow one's elders, or one's father] (*OC* 8:19). In the end, Eugénie becomes a better reader of the social world. The kind of literacy she develops involves reading as well as acting—in marked contrast to her inept father, the man of inaction.

The title *Élise ou l'université,* thanks to its ambiguous conjunction and its combination of a woman's name with a place of learning, invites comment. Guillemette Samson interprets the title as an antinomy that Eugénie must resolve: "Her overly rich imagination 'works against' the reason that must direct the university." Samson continues: "It is thus necessary for Eugénie to become less romantic and more reasonable."[56] But the evidence and analysis that I have offered suggest a different conclusion. Eugénie was not truly lacking reason. Or, she was lacking reasonableness only according to a definition like that offered by the *Encyclopédie*—failing to ward off gallantry. She was intelligent *and* a flirt, learned *and* in love, perhaps inexcusably similar to a "real" woman with whom Charrière would have felt deep sympathy. Samson underscores Charrière's concern for verisimilitude, citing a letter to Caroline de Sandoz-Rollin in which Charrière says she cannot "bear an imitation that imitates nothing that exists."[57] A text like *Élise ou l'université* testifies to this concern with realism.

The play shows that being called a coquette is what happens when men judge women: it has to do with relation. It is according to an external judge that one is (or is not) proclaimed a coquette. The two perspectives are reflected by Walter and the Count. Others can have social authority over women through the mechanism of reputation. It is this authority—reading the social world and writing one's role within it—that Charrière claims for women through the characters of Zélide and Eugénie.

"DES AUTEURS ET DES LIVRES": WHAT TO WRITE, HOW TO READ

In *Portrait de Zélide,* Isabelle de Charrière draws her own representation; in *Élise ou l'université* she depicts the social conditions that young women face. Zélide writes the self; Eugénie reads the world. In other words, Charrrière is offering a dual lesson in literacy: first, how to read her, or at least her youthful persona; second, how to read society. In an unpublished manuscript entitled "Des Auteurs et des livres," or "Of Authors and Books," she offers guidance about reading other authors and counsels these authors about the types of books they should and should not write. It provides a fitting coda on the question of literacy.

The essay was likely composed in 1796 or 1797.[58] It was discovered, along with some other short works, as the editorial team was preparing the tenth and final volume of Charrière's *Oeuvres complètes*. The text was submitted to the publisher, but was mysteriously omitted from the printed volume.[59] Jeroom Vercruysse, one of seven editors responsible for the *Oeuvres complètes*, describes "Des Auteurs et des livres" as "a short essay that might easily pass as a newspaper article." He notes that "it consists of anecdotes, literary reviews, and ethical reflections that transcend the immediate Here and Now." As Vercruysse argues, it is in some of Charrière's shorter texts, including this one, that "the central message emerges most clearly." He continues: "I am inclined to believe that her true personality can best be found in those short and sketchy writings."[60]

The text's brevity belies its richness. It opens by describing a meeting with Denis Diderot in The Hague in 1774: "Diderot me dit un jour qu'il n'y avait point d'auteur qui eût un autre but en écrivant que d'acquérir de la réputation" [Diderot told me one day that there are no authors who have any goal in writing other than to acquire a reputation]. Charrière adds that she was young when she heard this and could not believe it. She writes: "Aujourd'hui . . . chacun ne parle guère que de soi" [Today . . . no one talks of anything else except him- or herself]. One author wants to "se faire mieux connaître" [become better known]; another, "accusé, veut se justifier" [accused, wants to justify himself]; and a third "a besoin de s'épancher dans le sein du public" [needs to open his heart to the public]. And this is not just true of literary texts: "Au lieu d'historiens nous n'avons plus que des biographes qui nous donnent leur propre vie à lire et leur propre coeur à étudier" [Instead of historians we have only biographers who give to us their own life to read and their own heart to study]. Here, Charrière is invoking the charge often leveled against women; she turns it around on all writers, mostly men. It would be different, she remarks, if the subjects of these texts were interesting, but "on n'est point curieux d'approfondir ce qui déjà au premier aspect nous lasse et nous ennuie" [we are not curious to know more about something that, at first glance, already tires and bores us].

She then goes searching for a cause: "A qui devons-nous ce débordement d'un loquace égoïsme?" [To whom do we owe this overflowing of a loquacious egotism?]. Rhetorically, she asks whether it may be due to the publication of Rousseau's confessions (which had appeared posthumously in 1782). Here is the piquant answer: "Oh! misérable effet d'une cause aimable! Il faut pardonner à Rousseau, mais c'est en gémissant que je lui pardonne" [Oh! Miserable effect of a likable cause! We must forgive Rousseau, but it is grudgingly that I forgive him]. Those authors who do not explicitly write about themselves "font des tableaux où ils se peignent tantôt *ex proposito;* tantôt et plus qu'il ne semble par le choix des sujets et surtout par leur style" [make paintings where they paint themselves sometimes by design; sometimes, and more than it seems, through the choice of subjects and above all by their style]. In other words, the writing style and choice of subjects will mirror an author's identity. A disingenuous complaint, perhaps, as most all authors, including Charrière herself, customarily create texts that in some way reflect them (*Portrait de Zélide* is only the most evident example).

In "Des Auteurs et des livres," Charrière interpellates several authors directly. In the background is an emphasis on reputation: she invites one unnamed author to correct the way in which his life has been read. Targeted apostrophe shades into a general appeal to authors as a group. The basic theme at the end of the essay is a desire to learn the sources and causes of "nos désastres" [our disasters], in other words, the upheavals of the Revolutionary period. The text's final paragraph is truly striking. It starts by urging authors to stay anonymous if they wish, suggesting that they may publish their works translated into another language. Charrière herself had followed something like this route with *Élise ou l'université,* intended for dissemination in German. This passage continues: "Mais, de manière ou d'autre, instruisez-nous" [But in one way or another, instruct us].

The essay ends with these powerful lines:

Hommes, femmes, vous tous qui savez écrire, laissez là un vain amour-propre, n'écrivez plus que pour nous instruire de ce qu'il nous importe tant de savoir. Vos noms si vous nous les faites connaître ou s'ils sont un jour découverts seront bénis pour quelques lignes intéressantes plus qu'ils ne pourraient l'être pour mille volumes que l'amour-propre vous aurait dictés.

[Men, women, all of you who know how to write, leave aside your empty vanity, write only to teach us about what it is so important for us to know. Your names, if you let us know them, or if they are one day discovered, will be blessed for a few interesting lines [you have written] more than they could be for a thousand volumes that vanity would dictate to you].

The essay thus emphasizes the crucial role of writers in the project of Enlightenment. Throughout this short text, Charrière returns to the key idea that authors have the responsibility to inform, to explain, and to edify. These perspectives will support an assessment of Charrière's contribution as a writer, as a philosopher, and as a reader of the social world.

CHARRIÈRE AS PHILOSOPHER

Valérie Cossy identifies two questions in Charrière's work that inflect all of her texts but that she never answered definitively: "why read, why write?"[61] The three principal works analyzed in this chapter go part of the way toward answering these questions, with particular emphasis on reading. The *Portrait de Zélide* is a reading of the self, a response to readers (through the "Addition"), and in its final lines an explicit if ambiguous invocation of those for whom the author writes. In *Élise ou l'université*, books and libraries are highlighted to emphasize the kind of reading practice, or literacy, that Eugénie must learn in order to be a better interpreter of her social world and a better actor within it. And "Des Auteurs et des livres" is a commentary on what authors write, what they *should* write, and what the public wants to read. In these texts, Charrière expands upon one aspect of Kant's meditation in "What is Enlightenment?," focusing more specifically on an author's interactions with and responsibilities toward the reading public.

Cecil Courtney observes that for Charrière, "anything that is not acceptable to reason is to be rejected; thus, she shocks her contemporaries by her somewhat ostentatious flouting of social conventions and her contempt for whatever is based on opinion, tradition or custom."[62] Unlike Graffigny and Riccoboni, Charrière has sometimes been described by scholars as an Enlightenment thinker. But the possibility of Charrière's place in Enlightenment is more often than not broached in less than respectful terms. Henri Coulet, for example, entertains this possibility through the language of passive receptivity. He asks to what extent the author "assimilated Enlightenment thought," invokes the names of "a few 'philosophes' of the Enlightenment who managed to help her think," and concludes the article from which I quote here with the puzzling assertion that Charrière was "above all a woman."[63]

Charrière proposes an enlightened literacy that involves not only reading and writing, but acting as well. She wrote to Constant d'Hermenches on July 25, 1764: "vous avez pu voir peut-être que je savais raisonner juste, mais vous ignorez si j'agis raisonnablement" [you have been able to see, perhaps, that I knew how to reason soundly, but you do not know whether I act reasonably].[64] She then speaks of her admiration for virtue and reason, while admitting that she does not always manage to follow their dictates. The extraordinary pronouncement that follows has made this one of her most famous letters: "Si je n'avais ni père ni mère je serais Ninon peut-être" [If I had neither a father nor a mother I would be a Ninon, perhaps].[65] This is a reference to the notorious seventeenth-century courtesan and intellect Ninon de Lenclos. However, she writes that she is aware of social convention (represented here by her parents), which in this case she more or less obeys. The letter emphasizes the tensions that coexist in Belle's personality. She describes herself as follows: "Tantôt musicienne, tantôt géomètre, tantôt soi-disant poète, tantôt femme frivole, tantôt femme passionnée, tantôt froide et paisible philosophe" [Sometimes a musician, sometimes a geometer, sometimes a self-styled poet, now a frivolous woman, now a passionate woman, then a cool and tranquil philosopher].[66] These tensions are equally suggestive of the persona expressed through Zélide and Eugénie.

On January 10, 1764, Belle wrote to Constant d'Hermenches: "je n'ai point de système; ils ne servent selon moi qu'à égarer méthodiquement" [I have no system—all that systems do, I think, is lead us methodically astray].[67] More than thirty years later, in a letter to her friend Caroline de Sandoz-Rollin, Charrière expresses a dislike of grand generalizations: "Il n'y a rien de général pour les individus et . . . il faut toujours faire des applications particulières si l'on veut connaître la vérité" [There is nothing general for individuals, and . . . we must always make individual applications if we wish to know the truth]. She adds: "Jamais, soit bien soit mal, je ne raisonne que sur des donnés simples et palpables. Si je m'égare c'est en marchant à terre non en cherchant mon chemin du haut des airs" [Never, whether well or badly, do I reason about anything except simple and palpable facts. If I go astray, it is walking with my feet on the ground rather than wandering in the ether].[68] Courtney remarks that Charrière was interested in "relating philosophical ideas to lived experience."[69] She emphasized experience over abstract philosophical systems.

We may draw two conclusions with regard to Charrière's status as a philosopher. She extends the boundaries of what may be considered "philosophical" through her suspicion of abstract principles and her emphasis on the mundane details of women's lives. She shows how a woman's journey toward literacy and toward being read fairly may be considered part of Enlightenment. In certain ways, Charrière is a philosopher in a rather canonical sense. In other ways, she challenges us to rethink the limits of philosophy.

CONCLUSION: GENDER, ENLIGHTENMENT, AND NEW HABITS OF LITERACY

Boldness could be what most unites Zélide, Eugénie, and the Charrière who speaks in "Des Auteurs et des livres." All three are unorthodox and iconoclastic. They ask questions about women's situation within the social world. They challenge the limits placed upon them. Thus they rise to the challenge of Kant's Enlightenment dictum *Sapere aude*. Professor Wits of *Élise ou l'université* observes, quite correctly, that "la pensée est un animal d'habitude" [thought is a creature of habit] (*OC* 7:434). As such, some unvarnished critique and bold interrogation are re-

quired to shake thought loose from its customary restraints.
When Professor Wits says that he has nothing but doubts to offer,
the Count de Rhynberg responds:

> Les doutes d'un sage atténuent les vieux édits des préjugés et les
> modernes arrêts de la présomption. Dites-nous ce que vous sau-
> rez ce que vous croirez ce que vous soupçonnerez ou bien brûlez
> vos livres et démolissez vos chaires, car les livres et les leçons
> n'ont rien de plus respectable que ce que vous pourrez nous dire
> de vive voix.

> [The doubts of a sage mitigate the old edicts of prejudice and the
> modern decrees of presumption. Tell us what you know, what you
> believe, what you suspect, or else burn your books and demolish
> your rostra, for books and lessons have nothing more respectable
> than what you can tell us out loud] (*OC* 7:423).

The injunction here reflects Charrière's message: books can inform us, but we must dare to challenge received wisdom. As Kant
reminds us in "What is Enlightenment?," it is not enough for "a
book to have understanding in place of me."[70] The courage of Enlightenment means the courage to think for oneself, a quality
that Isabelle de Charrière herself evinced from a young age. She
remarked to Constant d'Hermenches on January 10, 1764, just
two years after composing *Portrait de Zélide:* "on s'accoutume à
me voir secouer un peu l'esclavage de la coutume" [people are
used to seeing me slip the shackles of custom].[71] This is a humorous play on words: others are becoming accustomed to her challenge to their customs. That same year, she wrote to James Boswell: "Je n'ai pas les talents subalternes" [I don't have any
subaltern talents].[72]

The preceding analysis has sought to propose a new way to
read some of Charrière's most philosophical yet underread works.
Across the literary portrait, play, and essay, Charrière engages
issues of gender, literacy, and Enlightenment. She claims the prerogative of self-representation. But what of the dictates outlined
in "Des Auteurs et des livres"—does she follow her own advice to
authors? Paradoxically, she does. It is true that *Portrait de Zélide*
is a self-examination. And neither *Zélide* nor *Élise ou l'université*
focuses specifically on political matters in a narrow sense, which
is the primary example invoked in "Des Auteurs." Even so, both

texts respect the fundamental advice offered in that essay. Beyond the Horatian dictates to both please and instruct the reader, these texts offer a new reading protocol for Charrière and other women of her time. They scrutinize gender roles and suggest the kind of greatness that women may achieve if they are afforded the education to achieve literacy and the respect and opportunity to put that literacy into practice.

Conclusion

This study opened with visual examples reflecting the status of eighteenth-century women writers. Here, it seems appropriate to consider two additional images. They come from the February 2006 issue of *Le Magazine littéraire,* which contained a special section devoted to the Enlightenment. That issue's cover, beneath the heading "Le Siècle des Lumières," displays a curious image: a naked woman. This is not even a period piece selected for its historical interest, but rather a new (and not particularly skillful) pastel drawing, reminiscent of paintings by François Boucher such as *Diane sortant du bain* (1742). Just a glance at this cover image reinforces the age-old dichotomy between men's minds and women's bodies.[1] On the opening page of the special section we find an eighteenth-century engraving that features two female nudes. It is *Les Espiègles (The Pranksters)* by Charles-Melchoir Descourtis, after a painting by Jean Frédéric Schall. The two female figures are seated in the foreground on a riverbank; apparently they have been bathing. One of them is reading a printed page; the other is next to her, in an attentive pose, gazing into the middle distance. The pranksters of the painting's title are two boys in the background. High on a bank above the river, unobserved by the women, they are using a fishing pole to snare the women's clothing.

These illustrations of Enlightenment in terms of men's ideas and women's bodies reflect a bias that persists throughout the magazine's special section. The section offers article upon article devoted to *les grands*—Voltaire, Rousseau, Diderot—as well as, predictably, an essay about "Le roman libertin," in which one of the issue's numerous naked ladies appears as illustration. There is no mention of women's contributions to Enlightenment and no reference to women writers. We can interpret this exclusion through comments made by Michèle Le Doeuff about an earlier issue of *Le Magazine littéraire* devoted to French philosophy. Lamenting the lack of women represented in that issue, Le Doeuff observes wryly: "Thought is male in our country—the function of this type of special issue is not to inform people or to incite them to read, but to produce precisely this image."[2] The eighteenth-century notion that only men create ideas persists in philosophical circles today, both within the French context and beyond.

The publication of this magazine issue on Enlightenment coincided with an exhibition at the Bibliothèque Nationale de France on the eighteenth century, entitled "Lumières! Un héritage pour demain" ("Enlightenment! A Heritage for Tomorrow"). That exhibition provided the magazine images. We need to ask: just exactly what kind of heritage does this exhibit pass along to the future? Both the exhibit and the magazine issue call to mind a 1989 billboard by the Guerrilla Girls, a feminist art activist group, in which the body of Ingres's famously languorous Odalisque is joined with the head of a gorilla. The billboard text reads: "Do Women Have to Be Naked to Get into the Met. Museum? Less than 5% of the Artists in the Modern Art sections are women, but 85% of the Nudes are Female."[3] Inspired by the Guerrilla Girls' impertinent question, we may ask, in turn: Do women have to be naked to get into the Enlightenment? Readers today are called upon to craft a new legacy that moves beyond the idea of women as bodily adornment, to the fact that women, too, have been participants in the history of ideas.

But let us come back to the Descourtis engraving and its pranksters. What if we read the title another way? Perhaps the boys in the background are not really the interesting pranksters, but rather the young women, who have retired to the woods not only to bathe, but to read, converse, and contemplate. The boys' antics seem clumsy and predictable by comparison. Such a subversive reading of the image suggests a way of understanding Enlightenment otherwise. The women may be the mischief makers: reading, thinking, and questioning. We could place these female figures in a lineage that includes Graffigny, Riccoboni, and Charrière.

EIGHTEENTH-CENTURY WOMEN
OF REASON AND THEIR LEGACY

In the *Discourse on Method,* Descartes tells the story of his education and travels. There, he remarks:

> Et comme, en abattant un vieux logis, on en réserve ordinairement les démolitions pour servir à en bâtir un nouveau, ainsi, en détruisant toutes celles de mes opinions que je jugeais être mal fondées, je faisais diverses observations et acquérais plusieurs expériences, qui m'ont servi depuis à en établir de plus certaines.

> [Just as in tearing down an old house, one usually *saves the wreckage* for use in building a new one, similarly, in destroying all those opinions of mine that I judged to be poorly founded, I made various observations and acquired many experiences that have since served me in establishing more certain opinions].[4]

metaphore

This metaphor is helpful for thinking about eighteenth-century women of reason: how shall we save the wreckage of Enlightenment? The question may be addressed in three parts. First, the old house to be torn down is the idea of Enlightenment as an affair exclusively among men. Second, the wreckage to be saved is the basic definition of Enlightenment in terms of its core values: relying on reason to question tradition and authority, asserting rights and freedoms. This is the Enlightenment that gave rise to progressive social movements, of which feminism is a prominent example. Third is the new house to be built, in which women's contributions to Enlightenment are fully acknowledged. This ongoing task returns to the tripartite definition of Enlightenment advanced in chapter 1: a historical revision, a critical project, and the ways in which this historical revision can inform our ongoing project of Enlightenment.

Eighteenth-century women did not simply leave the philosophizing to men. And relations between the sexes are less peripheral to the philosophical quest of Enlightenment than has sometimes been supposed. The works of Graffigny, Riccoboni, and Charrière expose a double standard: when men address men's concerns, they are considered objective and philosophical. When women address women's concerns, they are considered neither. Enlightenment for women must include an awakening to the ways in which men may use their social power to women's detriment.

Graffigny, Riccoboni, and Charrière are in some ways undeniably distinct from one another: they represent different moments, different milieux, different styles and strategies. Graffigny injected a comedic and playful spirit into gender roles, claiming women's right to the privileges that men have enjoyed. Riccoboni is, by contrast, realistic and even melancholy, emphasizing women's tragic fate in playing out the gender roles handed to them by society. And Charrière, possessing the wisdom of one who lived across cultures at the end of an era, adopts a stance both light-hearted and serious, exploring what women can achieve thanks to and in spite of their material conditions. But these three authors are united by their central concerns. They all recognized the limitations placed upon women and simultaneously worked to transcend them. They all participated in the movement of Enlightenment.

The three motifs that organized the preceding chapters elucidate ways in which these writers help us to revise our ordinary understandings of reason and Enlightenment. The mask illuminates Graffigny's appeal to masquerade as a way to uncouple bodily identity from philosophical role. The cup symbolizes Riccoboni's faith in reason as remedy and in the possibility of a peaceable mixed-gender sociality. The motif of the book underlines Charrière's support of a new kind of literacy, showing women's efforts to write their self-identity and to read the social world of the public sphere to which they aspire.

As the previous chapters have shown, Graffigny, Riccoboni, and Charrière turned the *philosophes'* own methods back upon them. They submitted gender bias to the same scrutiny that men applied when denouncing other traditional sources of arbitrary authority. As noted in the introduction, in a sense these women embraced the ethos of Enlightenment more fully than their male contemporaries. They critiqued sexism, showing its link to inequality and unfreedom—that is, a core prejudice that these men largely ignored. Sexism, too, is *l'infâme*.

Some strong thematic links exist among the three writers. They each call gender roles into question, even if they maintained somewhat differing attitudes about their own gender identity. Recall Graffigny's remark to Devaux that she wanted to "être homme à la barbe des gens" [be a man right under people's noses]. Riccoboni chose to narrate under an ambiguous gender in *L'Abeille* and to engage men as allies both there and in *Mylord Rivers*. At the same time, she insisted in a letter to Garrick: "je m'honore d[u] nom de *femme*, à la barbe de toute l'impertinente trib[u] de votre espèce; je ne voudrais pas changer de sexe" [I am honored to be called a *woman*, under the nose of the whole impertinent tribe of your species; I do not want to change my sex].[5] Charrière herself published some narrative works, including *Trois Femmes*, under a male pseudonym, l'Abbé de la Tour. The young Belle wrote to Constant d'Hermenches in 1762: "Vous n'êtes pas le premier qui ait des regrets que je ne sois pas un homme, j'en ai eu moi-même bien souvent . . . je serais apparemment une créature moins déplacée que je ne le parais à présent, ma situation donnerait plus de liberté à mes goûts" [You are not the first to regret that I am not a man; I have regretted it myself very often. . . . I would probably be a less misplaced creature than I seem to be at present; my situation would give me more freedom to pursue my interests].[6] In Charrière's autobiographical *Portrait de Zélide*, the protagonist explicitly claims both female and male qualities. Charrière joins Graffigny and Riccoboni in challenging the strict division between male and female intellectual roles. Such gender ambiguity indicates the three authors' struggles to come to terms with their identity as women of reason in a society that resisted such an identity. The authors, especially Riccoboni and Charrière, explore gender complementarity. The relational element pervading their texts yields an exploration of love, reason, and their interplay.

All three authors critique a certain kind of dogmatic, rationalist philosopher. This tendency is perceptible in Graffigny's "La Réunion," Riccoboni's *L'Abeille* and *Mylord Rivers,* and Charrière's *Élise ou l'université.* These rationalist-philosopher characters have no real knowledge of the world, a key facet of which is unequal social conditions that women must face. These characters are critiqued through appeals to the authority of experience, legitimating women's perspective. In their denunciations of these characters' dogmatism, the three authors evince a key characteristic of eighteenth-century thought.[7]

Graffigny, Riccoboni, and Charrière either implicitly or explicitly ask the question of why one writes. They offer a range of answers, including edification, ethical guidance, and truth-telling. In addition to those factors, there are others: demonstrating the biases against women, showing that women are endowed with the ability to reason, and suggesting women's role in Enlightenment thought. Particularly helpful in this regard is the technique of accusation and response that they use; examples include Madame Reason in Graffigny's "La Réunion," the embedded stories of Riccoboni's *L'Abeille,* and the narrator of Charrière's *Portrait de Zélide.* As Riccoboni's Mylord Rivers reminds us, society is a tribunal that makes judgments and determines reputation. This mechanism generates labels such as *coquette* and *savante,* which all of these authors scrutinize. They displace the debate away from these stereotypes, toward a new image of the reasonable woman.

As the preceding analyses have suggested, texts by Graffigny, Riccoboni, and Charrière reflect a broader conception of reason than the strictly instrumental version that the caricaturists associate with Enlightenment. These authors—like many of their male contemporaries—endorse a reason quite distinct from the rationalism discovered in Descartes's solitary stove-heated room. Indeed, they demonstrate that reason imbricates with relation and experience. Their position as sometime designated outsiders to Enlightenment enabled them to illustrate this point persuasively. Against the caricaturists, they help us to see that sexism is not an integral part of Enlightenment. In fact, Enlightenment ideals not only bolster arguments against discrimination, but actually serve as the basis for many such arguments. An "Enlightenment reason" tainted with gender bias deserves neither the name of reason nor the qualification of Enlightenment. Connections between the eighteenth century and the twenty-first come into view when we recognize that feminist concerns are not peripheral but rather central to the Enlightenment project. Graffigny, Riccoboni, and Charrière did not simply give reason over to men. As their works help us to see, the Enlightenment still has much to teach us about our status as reasoning subjects in the world.

These writers' identity as women does not mean that everything they said about reason somehow applies only to women. And we should not assume that when a woman author critiques reason, she means to reject it. To make that assumption is to commit the error against which several contemporary feminist thinkers warn us: collapsing different senses of the "critique of reason," an idea to which I will return shortly. One does not have to be a naive apologist for reason in order to champion reason in these women's works. At the same time, the focus of the preceding chapters has been a reading of these writers' works with an eye to their social identities as women, to discover what we can learn about women and reason thanks to their unique standpoints.

Despite their many intellectual continuities, Graffigny, Riccoboni, and Charrière were not truly in dialogue with one another, either personally or through their works. As Michèle Le Doeuff remarks with respect to a sampling of French women intellectuals across the centuries, "[e]ach one seems to start from scratch and from her own present."[8] This, too, is one of the effects of the Salic law of reason: women are cut off from a tradition. Surely one of our tasks today—a task that the preceding chapters have endeavored to undertake—is to reconstitute that continuity.

1789 AND BEYOND

Some interpreters have sounded a pessimistic note about the legacy of eighteenth-century women intellectuals. Hilda L. Smith describes eighteenth-century women's claims for access to reason and education as "[s]eldom successful." Similarly, Timothy Reiss asserts in *The Meaning of Literature* that women writers of late-eighteenth-century France "achieved little or no effect."[9] But the foregoing chapters have provided evidence for a more positive interpretation. In fact, reception is fluid rather than fixed. Even if women failed to earn the respect they deserved during their lifetime, we can work to grant it to them now.

Graffigny's life ended some thirty years before the storming of the Bastille. The advent of the Revolution spelled ruin—the end of her royal pension—for Riccoboni, who died in 1792 in obscurity, her loyal companion Thérèse at her side. Charrière lived until 1805. She experienced the Revolution vicariously, from abroad. Her letters and other works reflect horror at its excesses as well as her efforts to help *émigrés* fleeing to Switzerland.

Today, the legacies of all three writers can complicate and enrich interpretations of the eighteenth century.

Lively debates have arisen about what the Revolution of 1789 really meant for women, with particular attention paid to public figures and authors. Prominent individuals like Marie-Jeanne Roland and Olympe de Gouges gained public notoriety and died as martyrs. They also left behind a significant body of writings. Historian Carla Hesse argues that women writers actually published more after the turn of the nineteenth century than before. This claim has been substantially and convincingly challenged by Aurora Wolfgang, who scrutinizes publications according to type—arguing that, for example, legal briefs are not equivalent to novels—and questions whether Hesse's method actually captures all appearances in print of works by women.[10] In any case, debates limited to numbers of works in print risk overlooking the content and impact of women's ideas.

Following the Revolution, Condorcet was perhaps the strongest male champion of women's rights. In 1790, he published his short text "Sur l'admission des femmes au droit de cité," arguing for a strict equality of rights between the sexes: he thought that women should have full citizenship and should be able to vote. In that essay, he makes the following observation:

> On a dit que les femmes, malgré beaucoup d'esprit, de sagacité, et la faculté de raisonner portée au même degré que chez de subtils dialecticiens, n'étaient jamais conduites par ce qu'on appelle la raison. Cette observation est fausse: elles ne sont pas conduites, il est vrai, par la raison des hommes, mais elles le sont par la leur.

> [It has been said that women, despite possessing much intelligence, sagacity, and the faculty of reasoning carried to the same degree as that of subtle dialecticians, were never guided by what is called reason. This observation is false: women are not guided, it is true, by the reason of men, but they are guided by a reason all their own].[11]

At the heart of Condorcet's argument for equality, then, lies the idea that women are different. Hence, for Condorcet, gender difference trumps equality. Despite his rather hedged claims in their favor, Condorcet long remained a symbol of women's rights.

As Le Doeuff reports, in July 1914 a group of women's suffragists in Paris laid flowers on the statue of Condorcet, acknowledging him as "a founding hero and father of the idea of women's right to vote."[12]

In autumn 1793, churches throughout France were converted to Temples of Reason as part of a Revolutionary de-Christianization campaign. Festivals were held in these converted churches, at which officials read aloud the Declaration of the Rights of Man and of the Citizen, among other legislative documents, and participants sang republican hymns. The question of women's relation to reason resurfaced during these events—such as the Festival of Reason at Notre Dame Cathedral in Paris on November 10, 1793—which often featured a live allegory of Reason portrayed by a beautiful young woman. Such female impersonation of reason drew sharp criticism, for example from Jean-Baptiste Salaville, editor of a patriotic periodical, who insisted that women possessed only a weak ability for reason, making them poor symbols of it. Salaville suggested that only a strong, mature man should play the part of Reason.[13] This controversy died out along with the short-lived Cult of Reason and the equally fleeting Cult of the Supreme Being, championed by Robespierre. Even during the tumult of the Revolution, this allegory in the flesh crossed a line about women's perceived incapacity for reason. This view of reason reinforces the fact that the slogan *liberté, égalité, fraternité*—with its gender-exclusive final term—remained an unreachable ideal for women.

There is near unanimity that the French nineteenth century saw a serious decline in women's rights, beginning with the establishment of the Napoleonic Code in 1804, which strengthened husbands' legal authority over their wives.[14] According to this interpretation, women actually enjoyed greater freedoms during the ancien régime than during the century following its overthrow. Indeed, it was not until 1944 that French women gained the right to vote and 1949 that Simone de Beauvoir's manifesto *Le Deuxième sexe* launched a new generation of feminism. But, as Pauline Johnson insists, "the failure of the historical Enlightenment to implement its own project does not mean that the project itself was abortive and doomed."[15] The eighteenth century did not end well legally or politically for women. Although the promise of Enlightenment may remain unfulfilled, it does not follow that the Enlightenment is at odds with women's emancipation.

   Critiques of Enlightenment have often been overstated, equating a complex phenomenon with one narrow conception or with a rationalist caricature, erasing rival strains within eighteenth-century thought. Graffigny, Riccoboni, and Charrière affirm reason, they question authority, and they believe in the possibility of progress. At the same time, they critique some of the categories and assumptions often associated with "Enlightenment" in ways that foreshadow the work of feminist theorists today.

Women and Enlightenment in the Twenty-First Century

What is the enduring significance of these eighteenth-century women's works? Do we accept, or even acknowledge, their contributions to Enlightenment? Current feminist theorists generally do not recognize what they have inherited from eighteenth-century women of reason (other than Wollstonecraft). They overlook what we could call, following Alison Jaggar, "the 'recessive' Western tradition."[16] But Graffigny, Riccoboni, and Charrière deserve a place in the broader history of ideas. Critics like Suellen Diaconoff have rightly questioned the tendency to read early modern women as our "direct precursors," as sharing our precise concerns and forecasting our struggles.[17] But we could reverse the argument and say instead that contemporary feminist theorists—feminist epistemologists in particular—need to recognize their lineage. With respect to eighteenth-century women, perhaps we should see less of ourselves in them, and more of them in us. These women should be recognized as part of a heritage to which feminists today lay claim. As Karen Offen writes from her perspective as a historian: "It is less a question of 'inventing a tradition' than of retrieving and reclaiming a well-buried but surprisingly well-documented aspect of the European past."[18]

   In an autobiographical essay, philosopher Alison Jaggar writes that her experiences as a woman in a predominantly male field have taught her that no philosopher is free from the effects of his or her particular location in time and place, that "philosophy is not an autonomous realm of pure reason; rather, it is continuous with the natural and social sciences, and with literature. Thus, it is best pursued through multidisciplinary approaches."[19] Drawing upon Jaggar's idea, I propose that the feminist tradition in the wake of Enlightenment appears most clearly when we read women's texts of various genres—from the literary to the traditionally philosophical—together. Enlightenment may usefully be understood as an ongoing conversation with the goal of human liberation. And we may understand ourselves, today, not only as inheritors of a tradition but as participants in these ongoing debates.

Twenty-first-century phenomena demonstrate the continuing relevance of this project's concerns. To illustrate this point, I will briefly invoke three categories of examples: theatrical, political, and intellectual. In 2007, the Odéon-Théâtre de l'Europe featured a widely discussed stage adaptation of the Marquis d'Argens' eighteenth-century novel *Thérèse philosophe,* a work already invoked in the introduction. The French do not have a reputation for prudery; even so, a reviewer for the newspaper *Le Monde* suggested that the play's eroticism and violence made it almost unwatchable.[20] The choice to stage *Thérèse philosophe,* while excellent theatrical works by women authors sink further into oblivion, demonstrates, alongside a host of other evidence, that the eighteenth century is still viewed as an affair among men. When women appear, it is as adornment, object, or eroticized sidekick. Even well-educated French people have generally never heard of any women writers between Madame de Lafayette and George Sand.

The political arena has yielded some especially pertinent examples. In April 2007, for the first time in French history, a woman stood a real chance of being elected president of the Republic. That woman, the Socialist Ségolène Royal, ultimately lost in the second round to the conservative male candidate. The smear campaign against Royal featured a slogan (not officially endorsed, of course, but heard on television and seen in graffiti): "Allure de Jeanne d'Arc, Tête de Bécassine." That is, she is pretty like Joan of Arc, but stupid like a stereotyped female cartoon character from the provinces. Such misogynous attacks were also frequent during the United States presidential campaign of Hillary Clinton leading up to the 2008 election.[21] Now, the mere fact that a woman became a leading party's candidate

in France (in the first round of the elections, there were also female candidates from three smaller parties, all left-leaning) suggests that the ideal of *parité*, or "equal representation of men and
women in politics,"[22] is gaining a foothold. At the same time,
however, the sexist attacks against both Royal and Clinton illustrate the continued threat posed by intelligent women in public
life.

   And there is no lack of examples in the intellectual arena.
The anti-Royal slogan cited above bears a trace of the old accusation of coquetry, suggesting once again the association of women
with the body rather than the mind. The attacks on Royal would
have been all too familiar to eighteenth-century women of reason. As would the notorious comments made in January 2005 by
then-president of Harvard University, Lawrence Summers, that
women may lack the innate ability to excel in science and mathematics on a par with men.[23] Unfortunately, Summers is not
alone in these views. His talk occurred at a time that also saw
the promulgation of neurological research according to which
women's brains are essentially different from men's (familiar
from eighteenth-century sensationalist anthropology and psychology). And around the same time, a university press published
Harvey C. Mansfield's *Manliness,* an encomium to the virtues of
macho comportment in the guise of scholarship, a directive for
men to combine rationality with stubbornness, the argument
cloaked in appeals to literary works (all by men) as well as to
popular icons like Tarzan.[24]

   Several years earlier, cognitive psychologist Virginia Valian
published a book documenting pervasive workplace discrimination against women, who are consistently evaluated less highly
than men for equivalent achievements. Valian coined the term
"gender schemas" to name the implicit hypotheses about sex differences that shape such biased judgments.[25] A study at the
Massachusetts Institute of Technology showed systemic gender
discrimination as reflected by the inequitable allocation of resources to MIT women faculty in science, including smaller sal-
aries and less lab space. A 2006 study documented the persistence of gender inequities at MIT.[26] By way of summary, across
these domains (theatrical, political, and intellectual), the Salic
law of reason is alive and well today, on both sides of the At-
lantic.

The Reason Debates: Feminist Theory
and the Enlightenment Heritage

Given this context, what of the eighteenth-century women of reason today? Some of their concerns and experiences continue to
be ours. The literary texts analyzed in the preceding chapters
can bring a fresh angle to the contemporary feminist critique of
reason, both culturally and philosophically. This "critique"
should be understood not just as criticism, but as an exploration
and expansion, testing the limits of our understandings of reason. For example, Graffigny, Riccoboni, and Charrière critique
the caricatured variety of instrumental reason in much the same
way as some theorists today do. The major difference is that the
caricaturists today label what they are doing as a criticism of
"Enlightenment." Graffigny, Riccoboni, and Charrière, by contrast, were engaging in the project of Enlightenment. Contemporary feminist theorists may take up the question of reason as a
way to approach the history of Western philosophy and the role
of women in that history.

Here, I will provide an overview of selected crucial and relevant dimensions of the ongoing reason debates, in order to connect the literary analyses in the preceding chapters to current
discussions, and to suggest why feminists today should read authors like Graffigny, Riccoboni, and Charrière. A fuller treatment of the various dimensions of feminist theory in the wake of
the "crisis of reason" and critiques of Enlightenment lies outside
the scope of this study. And some of these debates—those growing from the Anglo-analytic tradition, those focused on reason
as a specifically cognitive faculty, those seeking to create an in-
tricate ethical theory based upon reason, and so on—do not have
a great deal to do with reason as it is invoked in this study, that
is, as a historically and socially situated phenomenon susceptible
to exploration through literary texts. It is important here to
highlight feminist critiques of reason that harmonize much less
with a caricaturist approach, and much more with ideas put
forth during the eighteenth century.

In chapter 1, I advanced the basic division in responses to Enlightenment between apologists and caricaturists, and alluded
to the work of some pro-Enlightenment feminists. Keeping that
discussion in the background, here the focus will be somewhat

different: contemporary feminist theorists who grapple with the issue of reason (or rationality—the terms are often used interchangeably) and gender. As Karen Jones remarks, it should not surprise us that so many feminists deal—directly or indirectly—with the issue of reason, given that women's supposed deficiency in reason has been used throughout history to exclude them from full participation in society.[27]

Crucially, feminist theorists need not abandon reason or rationality as a ground for their thought. Several theorists, including Jones, Herta Nagl-Docekal, and Hilda Smith, have identified a seeming paradox. It arises when feminists critique reason, all the while clearly using reason to advance their arguments.[28] As both Jones and Nagl-Docekal explain, this apparent paradox rests upon a conflation of different meanings of "reason." Jones proposes a distinction between "the *concept* of rationality" on the one hand and "various substantive *conceptions* of rationality" on the other hand, while along similar lines Nagl-Docekal distinguishes "the capacity for thinking" from "the content of thought."[29] That is, critiquing the way in which reason has been defined or deployed does not entail a wholesale rejection of the faculty of reason.

Indeed, Nagl-Docekal notes that the Western philosophical tradition has embraced broader definitions of "reason" than those critiqued by feminists who espouse a blanket suspicion of *logos*. She notes moreover that battling a straw person—a narrow conception of reason—amounts to letting one's adversary set the terms of the debate.[30] Giving reason over to their opponents is precisely what eighteenth-century women did not do. Nagl-Docekal summarizes her overview of feminist critiques of reason by arguing that "the actual target of the critique is not the faculty of reason (in both its theoretical and practical use) per se; rather, it is the view that this faculty is part of the masculine character."[31] She adds: "I am not proposing that any traditional conception of reason be simply appropriated. . . . The central point of the feminist critique of reason lies not in the thesis of the irrevocably masculine character of the rational but in overcoming the traditional masculinization of reason."[32] This idea exemplifies the threefold task of Enlightenment: historical revision, contemporary engagement, and the intersection between the two.

Somewhat similarly, Geneviève Fraisse distinguishes the faculty of reason from the exercise of reason.[33] In keeping with this study's emphasis on the social functioning of reason, however, we must remain aware that the use and the faculty are not always so easily separated in debates about women's reason. The attempt to exclude women from the production and circulation of knowledge has not always been carried out in obvious ways. Karen Jones explains that what is at stake in discussions of reason is the granting or withholding of legitimacy, given that "norms of rationality underwrite discriminatory credibility practices."[34] Like Jones, Helen Longino emphasizes that reason is a normative concept. That is, reason can serve to legitimate experience. She calls attention to the rhetorical aspects and "historical baggage" of invocations of reason, distinguishing between two senses of reason: as a (universal human) capacity and as "rules for the proper exercise of that capacity."[35] During the eighteenth century, it was not merely a matter of attempting to limit women to the social spheres that seemed most appropriate to their sex. Rather, the very epistemological categories (including "reason") through which knowledge was formulated and debated were infected with gender bias. Despite these difficulties, it is clear that we can critique certain ways in which reason has been defined, ways that have contributed to discrimination against women, without in the process discounting reason as a whole. Reason itself is not the problem.

Longino draws upon the work of Miranda Fricker to suggest that postmodern concerns about the tyranny of reason have nothing to do with reason (the capacity) per se, but rather with the use of reason.[36] In the article to which Longino refers, "Feminism in Epistemology: Pluralism without Postmodernism," Fricker helpfully distinguishes between "authoritarian" uses of reason (the kind she identifies as the object of "anti-epistemological" or postmodernist critique) and "authoritative" uses of reason.[37] The pluralism reflected in her article's title "acknowledges the existence of many different perspectives on a shared world." She suggests that reasoning does not need to be a foundational, authoritarian system, but can be understood as something worked out at the "ground level," with an eye to actual situations and needs. We can thus acknowledge that "social differences" create a variety of perspectives, and furthermore that "power can be an

influence in whose perspectives seem rational."[38] Again, we see
that recent feminist theory reaches some of the same conclusions
advanced by this study's eighteenth-century focal authors. In
fact, if contemporary theorists read these eighteenth-century
writers, they would find further evidence to bolster some of their
claims.

Does it really advance women's cause to write them out of Enlightenment? Here it will be helpful to consider some views common to standpoint theorists. As these theorists have explained,
from Descartes onward, an epistemology based on the concept of
detachment, including separation from emotions, has informed
the modern scientific ideal of objectivity. Counter to this ideal,
and building on a critique of the Cartesian mind/body split, is
an acknowledgment of the sociohistorical situatedness of the
knower.[39] This recognition challenges the claim of philosophy to
be universal or objective, in the sense of being able to adopt a
"view from nowhere."[40] A critique of this God's-eye view has
been a cornerstone of recent thinking in feminist philosophy. As
Iris Young writes: "Impartial reason must judge from a point of
view outside the particular perspectives of persons involved in
interaction, able to totalize these perspectives into a whole or
general will. This is the point of view of a solitary transcendent
God."[41] In other words, the mere mortals that we are cannot
hope to access some kind of impartial reason. Seyla Benhabib
makes this point in her book *Situating the Self,* calling reason a
"contingent achievement" and writing that "the subjects of reason are finite, embodied and fragile creatures, and not disem-
bodied cogitos."[42]

It is out of similar concerns and ideas that standpoint theory
grew. Sandra Harding is perhaps the best-known theorist associated with feminist standpoint epistemology. The basic contention
of standpoint theorists is that all knowledge is socially situated.
Harding suggests that "outsiders"—those who are not members
of the dominant group—may be uniquely able to perceive how
knowledge is organized and symbolically distributed by those
who possess more power. Standpoint epistemology does not conflict with the goal of seeking objective knowledge. On the contrary, by embracing a methodology that includes a wider body of
informants, standpoint epistemology may actually produce a
more accurate description of a given situation.[43]

Chapter 1 cited an article on feminist standpoint theory by postmodernist Susan Hekman. That article, along with a cluster of response pieces by feminist standpoint theorists as well as a final response by Hekman, provide insight into what is at stake in standpoint theory, focusing on the central question: what is reality and who decides?[44] The scholars who respond to Hekman—Nancy Hartsock, Patricia Hill Collins, Sandra Harding, and Dorothy E. Smith—emphasize a central concern with justice, power relations, and the political implications of decisions regarding what is knowledge and who possesses it. Standpoint theorists regard knowledge as collective rather than individual. They do not claim that all women occupy an identical standpoint, but rather that we can trace out some similarities in women's experiences within a certain time and place and certain material conditions.

Hekman views standpoint theory—presumably thanks to its ambition to democratize knowledge—as deriving from what she calls the Enlightenment heritage. But she goes on to assert that standpoint theory ultimately destabilizes that heritage: "Women speaking their truth had the effect of transforming truth, knowledge, and power as the Enlightenment defined them."[45] In other words, for Hekman, as for so many other feminist theorists, Enlightenment is reducible to a limited and static characterization. As discussed in chapter 1, Hekman advances an understanding of "Enlightenment" that is narrow, universalizing, and instrumental.

In fact, "standpoint" and "Enlightenment" do not have to be understood as existing in tension. Further elaboration of this idea may help to clarify points of convergence not only between feminist thought of the eighteenth century and today, but also between feminist movements in the United States and in France. Judith Ezekiel explains that French feminists often rally around Republican universalism, which they identify as an Enlightenment ideal. In so doing, they cast doubt on what we could call the "standpoint" style of American feminism, with its emphasis on diversity and multiculturalism.[46] But as I have suggested throughout this study, a more generous understanding of Enlightenment makes room for a variety of perspectives within that tradition. Enlightenment ideals need not be understood as contrary to standpoint theory, an idea to which I return below under the guise of Enlightenment and difference.

Not all work in feminist epistemology falls neatly within the rubric of standpoint. The anthologies *Feminist Epistemologies* and *Engendering Rationalities* suggest some of the breadth of this work, including topics like embodiment, critiques of objectivity, the role of values, and the relevance of social identity to epistemic judgment.[47] As these collections attest, feminist epistemology is best understood not as some "specifically feminist or feminine logic of investigation," but rather as "a specific mode of questioning" that endeavors to expose, for example, the androcentric bias of current scientific practices.[48] At the same time, some of the contributors to this work retain a narrow, caricatured view of Enlightenment. For instance, Judith Richards refers to Enlightenment as one of several "theories of rational autonomy."[49] For all of their discussion of rationality, feminist epistemologists often elide the question of *what reason is* in historical perspective.

Attention to the writings of women from other periods in the Western tradition, particularly the eighteenth-century writers that have been the focus of this study, would add a richness of insight to such a question. It would highlight the manifold ways in which reason has been defined, particularly in ways that bear directly on social conditions for women. In fact, attention to these eighteenth-century women's testimonies would align with the stated goal of standpoint theory: to include more viewpoints, yielding a more accurate account. Such a strategy would link to other feminist concerns and identity categories, including race and class.

In her book *Feminism as Radical Humanism,* Pauline Johnson identifies feminism "as an episode in Enlightenment thinking," which she calls a "radically incomplete, open-ended project of cultural criticism." She continues by writing: "Feminism takes its vital and distinctive place in the project described by Kant as the future-directed optimism that people could emerge from their self-imposed minority to legislate for themselves."[50] Johnson concludes that feminism relates to Enlightenment in two distinct ways: first, feminism "preserves and extends the Enlightenment's emancipatory vision"; second, feminism "unmasks the failures of the various episodes in the Enlightenment tradition to fully interpret the meaning of the Enlightenment project."[51] I would add that attention to a broader range of eighteenth-century texts contributes crucially to this fuller interpretation of Enlightenment. As should by now be clear, "Enlightenment" is not a generic term for that which feminists should automatically critique.

"ENLIGHTENMENT" RECONSIDERED

Which brings us full circle, back to the question of defining Enlightenment. Pauline Johnson suggests that "current attempts to sever feminism's ideological ties with the Enlightenment rest on a basic misinterpretation of the character and spirit of the Enlightenment."[52] Historian Dena Goodman concurs, explaining the increased turn to postmodernism on the part of some feminists as based upon a mistaken claim that Enlightenment equals universalism. Against that claim, Goodman argues persuasively that an equally important Enlightenment value was difference. She notes that Enlightenment discourse about difference, including gender difference, was cultivated in spaces of mixed-gender sociability, especially the salon.[53] She argues that the importance of women in the salon kept alive an appreciation for the contributions of both sexes, an interpretation with which I engaged in chapter 1, questioning Goodman's emphasis on how women helped men. What I wish to retain of Goodman's argument is her emphasis on difference. I have suggested that in order to understand this key yet overlooked Enlightenment value, a rich resource is the literary works that women created.

As demonstrated in the preceding chapters, Graffigny, Riccoboni, and Charrière created works that show us how "the Enlightenment" as usually defined is a fiction. Their works also illustrate, through an emphasis on experience, relation, and the social function of reason, another side of the Enlightenment story. Their texts live on, and can be read and interpreted by successive generations. The texts' meanings are informed by the contexts of their readers, participating in an ongoing exploration of Enlightenment as both historical phenomenon and contemporary project.

The editors of the collection *What's Left of Enlightenment?* summarize Richard Rorty's answer to the question posed in the book's title by emphasizing the Enlightenment's "forward-looking aspiration to create a more decent human society."[54] This idea suggests why Graffigny, Riccoboni, and Charrière may rightly be considered Enlightenment thinkers whose relevance did not end with the eighteenth century: they worked to create a better society, beginning with the self while looking outward at social conditions and norms in need of change.

The idea of "Enlightenment as conversation" was mentioned in the introduction. In an essay by that name, Lawrence E. Klein describes Enlightenment thinkers as "engaged conversers rather than detached observers." He notes that the diversity of Enlightenment thought challenges the "simplistic grand narrative" that postmodern critics have constructed. Klein identifies a fundamental irony: "In searching for an alternative to the alleged legacy of the Enlightenment, postmodern writers have themselves often put a high value on conversation: condemning the Enlightenment, they identify remedies for its legacy in modes most favored in the Enlightenment itself."[55] This study's focal authors often invoke the pleasure they take in conversation. Consider, for instance, a letter from Isabelle de Charrière to Constant d'Hermenches about an afternoon she had spent with her friend Susanna Hasselaer: "nous causâmes quelques heures avec la tranquille volupté de l'amitié et de la raison" [we chatted for several hours with the tranquil, luxurious delight of friendship and reason].[56] For his part, Klein adds that "the Enlightenment was not one project but rather an array of projects."[57] The missing piece here is that, although several critics say something similar, none invokes the eighteenth-century texts or authors I study to help make this point. Although they are seldom invoked in defenses of the Enlightenment, women writers must be taken seriously as intellectual contributors to Enlightenment.

The Enlightenment represents a pivotal moment in Western intellectual and cultural history. As such, Daniel Gordon reminds us that "to be an insurgent, one must also be an heir. The Enlightenment is the inheritance one must accept in order to revolt against the present."[58] As an ongoing project of critical questioning, the Enlightenment remains with us. We inherit its ideals even when we question how they have been defined. I do not suggest that Enlightenment should be held immune to criticism. Instead, I urge that a well-informed critique must explain just what, exactly, is being critiqued. This study is one step on the way toward a different and richer approach to Enlightenment.

Toward a Post-Rationalist Reason

Narrow views of the eighteenth-century Enlightenment risk impoverishing our present and foreclosing certain possible futures. The broadened sense of Enlightenment to which I have appealed here speaks to our collective past as well as to the present and the future. If we view Enlightenment as an ongoing project, it is fitting to ask whether we accept and further these eighteenth-century women's Enlightenment. If we can view a luminary like Christine de Pizan as a foremother to eighteenth-century women writers, we may in turn view eighteenth-century writers as precursors to writers of the twentieth and twenty-first centuries, who continue this ongoing project and conversation across the centuries. By reclaiming the voices of those who affirmed the existence of women of reason in the eighteenth century, we not only create a clearer understanding of the elided aspects of the past but also uncover rich resources that can helpfully inform contemporary debates that are not so new after all.

I have suggested that if we can come to consider women like Graffigny, Riccoboni, and Charrière as Enlightenment thinkers, the resultant shift in perspective will significantly modify the formulation of "critiques of (Enlightenment) reason." These writers themselves cast suspicion on received ideas. They asserted women's right to reason. Their texts also point to the work that remains to be done. That work includes recuperating these women's voices not only for scholars of the eighteenth century, but for contemporary feminist theory. It includes opening up some new space for discussion and debate. It means providing a stage on which Graffigny, Riccoboni, and Charrière can speak. They call our attention to the work of reason, leading us to ask: to whom does that work fall today?

These women's texts seem to indicate emergent feminist epistemologies. Their works foreshadow the appearance of what I propose to call a "post-rationalist reason." While this idea awaits fuller development in a future project, it could be described as a conception of reason that does not endorse any of the caricaturists' depictions. It is a conception that draws ethics and epistemology closer together than they often have been in the history of philosophical thought. It is mindful of relation, experience, and the connections between them. It is a kind of reason that feminists today may find salutary.

Eighteenth-century women's literary works were not only aesthetic achievements but significant contributions to the production of knowledge. For these women, the first necessary step was an imaginative leap, beyond seeing structures as a "fact."[59] Their works show that the challenges eighteenth-century women faced were structural, not simply personal. It is in reading these women's texts together that we perceive the power of their contributions.

GRAFFIGNY, RICCOBONI, AND CHARRIÈRE, NOW AND INTO THE FUTURE

The monumental task of editing and publishing Graffigny's correspondence is projected for completion in 2010. The fruit of collaborative work by an international team of scholars, the correspondence runs to fifteen sizable volumes. An international scholarly association devoted to Riccoboni was formed in 2007. And a peer-reviewed journal called *Cahiers Isabelle de Charrière / Belle de Zuylen Papers,* sponsored by the Genootschap Belle van Zuylen, or Dutch Isabelle de Charrière Association, was launched in 2006. Bringing these authors to greater prominence will take all of this effort plus something more, however. As Ludwig Wittgenstein famously wrote, "knowledge is in the end based on acknowledgment."[60] That is, a first step is mere recognition that these women lived and wrote.

A brief tale will illustrate this idea. In 2007 I visited the Église Saint Eustache in Paris, the final resting place of Marie Jeanne Riccoboni. Others from her era who are likewise buried there—such as the composer Jean-Philippe Rameau or more obscure figures like the military officer François de Chevert—are honored with marble plaques. Of Riccoboni, however, there is no trace. Indeed, the *gardien* on duty during my visit not only did not know the location of her tomb, but had never heard of her. Of course, given that her death occurred in the midst of Revolutionary tumult, it is little surprise not to find a tangible commemoration. But the oblivion is poignant nonetheless. I am unaware of any public monument, however small, to Graffigny. Only Charrière garners some admiration from the general public, at least in the region of her native Utrecht. Whether or not these women will ever gain widespread acknowledgment remains an open question. More pertinent perhaps would be to ask how to communicate these authors' significance to those already interested in the historical and philosophical eighteenth century and to those who participate in feminist work. Anyone who takes an interest in these writers is called upon to become their ambassador to the future.

Throughout this study, I have emphasized that reason cannot be treated as a transhistorical constant. But this is not to say that there is an utter lack of continuity across time. As I suggested in this project's introduction, while it is important to place these writers in history, it is equally important not to abandon them there. Beyond historical curiosity or the aesthetic pleasure of reading a good story, these women's works offer something that can remain meaningful for us today. They are women demanding the right to be considered fully human by virtue of their intellectual capacities. Their works help us to chart the ethical results of certain social arrangements. The paired questions of women and reason have a role in most any discussion of social justice.

In a particularly philosophical letter to David Garrick in 1777, Marie Jeanne Riccoboni bemoans the fragility of human happiness, concluding that, in the face of pain and suffering, "on ne lui connaît encore de remède que le plus impatientant de tous, *la patience*" [the only remedy we know is the most irritating of all: *patience*].[61] Riccoboni's counsel is one we must take to heart: it would seem that only time can bring about fundamental change in an ancient institution like the Salic law of reason. But while this strategy is necessary, it is far from sufficient. We must devote our energies not only to waiting but also to working: committing ourselves to changing perspectives and creating a more just world for women.

Graffigny, Riccoboni, and Charrière laid the groundwork for subsequent thinking on women and reason. For example, in her 1823 novel *Ourika*, Claire de Duras asked: "Mais qui peut dire ce que c'est que la raison? est-elle la même pour tout le monde?" [But who can say what reason is? Is it the same for everyone?].[62] Questions like this continue to occupy feminist thinkers today, and will into the future. The eighteenth-century Enlightenment bespoke, perhaps as much as any period before or since, the value of public discourse, of conversation, of seeking to know and understand. Enlightenment thinkers explore differences, challenge assumptions, and rethink traditions. They endeavor to cut through the chaff of fanaticism in order to reach the core of human value. The eighteenth century is our century too. Graffigny, Riccoboni, and Charrière are our contemporaries in ways that matter. In keeping alive the memory and message of these women writers, we become worthy of calling ourselves their inheritors.

Notes

INTRODUCTION

1. Sergueï Karp, ed., *Être dix-huitiémiste* (Ferney-Voltaire: Centre international d'étude du XVIIIe siècle, 2003), v, vii, 71, 273.
2. A second volume was published in 2007. It was edited by a woman and includes essays by several women. It seems likely that this more inclusive volume was designed in response to critiques of the original book's gender bias. See Carol Blum, ed., *Être dix-huitiémiste II* (Ferney-Voltaire: Centre international d'étude du XVIIIe siècle, 2007).
3. Raymond Trousson, ed., *Romans libertins du XVIIIe siècle* (Paris: Laffont, 1993).
4. Nancy K. Miller, *French Dressing: Women, Men and Ancien Régime Fiction* (New York: Routledge, 1995), 9.
5. See the database project "The Reception of Women Writers" directed by Suzan van Dijk at the University of Utrecht. http://www.databasewomen writers.nl/.
6. Raymond Trousson, preface to *Romans de femmes du XVIIIe siècle,* ed. Trousson (Paris: Laffont, 1996), xxvii.
7. Lawrence E. Klein, "Enlightenment as Conversation," in *What's Left of Enlightenment? A Postmodern Question,* ed. Keith Michael Baker and Peter Hanns Reill (Stanford: Stanford University Press, 2001), 148–66; Dorinda Outram, *The Enlightenment,* 2nd ed. (Cambridge: Cambridge University Press, 2005).
8. Richard Rorty, "The Humanistic Intellectual: Eleven Theses," chapter 8 in *Philosophy and Social Hope* (New York: Penguin, 1999), 127.
9. Paul Ricoeur, *Time and Narrative,* trans. Kathleen McLaughlin and David Pellauer (Chicago: University of Chicago Press, 1984), 1:77 (see also 79–81); 2:20, 5.
10. Joan W. Scott, "Experience," in *Feminists Theorize the Political*, ed. Judith Butler and Joan W. Scott (New York and London: Routledge, 1992), 22–40.
11. Paula Moya, *Learning from Experience: Minority Identities, Multicultural Struggles* (Berkeley: University of California Press, 2002).
12. Elaine Showalter, "Feminist Criticism in the Wilderness," in *The New Feminist Criticism: Essays on Women, Literature, and Theory,* ed. Showalter (New York: Pantheon Books, 1985), 244; Dorothy Smith, "Comment on Hek-

man's 'Truth and Method: Feminist Standpoint Theory Revisited,'" in *The Feminist Standpoint Theory Reader: Intellectual and Political Controversies,* ed. Sandra Harding (New York: Routledge, 2004), 265; John C. O'Neal, *The Authority of Experience: Sensationist Theory in the French Enlightenment* (University Park: Pennsylvania State University Press, 1996).

13. Miller, *French Dressing,* 61–62, 71–79, 83–89.

14. Genevieve Lloyd, *The Man of Reason: "Male" and "Female" in Western Philosophy,* 2nd ed. (Minneapolis: University of Minnesota Press, 1993); Geneviève Fraisse, *Reason's Muse: Sexual Difference and the Birth of Democracy,* trans. Jane Marie Todd (Chicago: University of Chicago Press, 1994).

15. Jeffrey Ravel, "France," in *Encyclopedia of the Enlightenment,* ed. Alan Kors (New York: Oxford University Press, 2003), 2:64.

16. Erica Harth, *Cartesian Women: Versions and Subversions of Rational Discourse in the Old Regime* (Ithaca: Cornell University Press, 1992); Mary Trouille, *Sexual Politics in the Enlightenment: Women Writers Read Rousseau* (Albany: State University of New York Press, 2007).

1. WOMEN, ENLIGHTENMENT, AND THE SALIC LAW

1. See Lynn Hunt, *The Family Romance of the French Revolution* (Berkeley: University of California Press, 1993), 82–84; Marina Warner, *Monuments and Maidens: The Allegory of the Female Form* (Berkeley: University of California Press, 2001).

2. Mary Sheriff, "Decorating Knowledge: The Ornamental Book, the Philosophic Image and the Naked Truth," *Art History* 28.2 (April 2005): 161.

3. On historical precedent for portraying Reason in feminine guise, see Londa Schiebinger, *The Mind Has No Sex? Women in the Origins of Modern Science* (Cambridge: Harvard University Press, 1989), 144–50; Schiebinger, "Feminine Icons: The Face of Early Modern Science," *Critical Inquiry* 14 (Summer 1988): 673–74.

4. Schiebinger, "Feminine Icons," 663. Schiebinger takes up these same ideas in virtually identical terms in chapter 5, "Battles over Scholarly Style," of *The Mind Has No Sex?,* 119–59.

5. Sheriff, "Decorating Knowledge," 161.

6. Emphasis added. Desmahis, *Encyclopédie ou dictionnaire raisonné des sciences, des arts et des métiers* (Paris: Briasson, Le Breton, 1751–80), 6:472. Thomas Laqueur calls this the "two-sex model" in *Making Sex: Body and Gender from the Greeks to Freud* (Cambridge: Harvard University Press, 1990), viii, 149–92; see also Schiebinger, who uses the phrase "biological divergence" in *The Mind Has No Sex?,* 190.

7. Schiebinger, *The Mind Has No Sex?,* 195–200.

8. Pierre Roussel, *Système physique et moral de la femme* (1775; Paris: Caille and Ravier, 1809), 16.

9. Ibid., 18. For a fuller discussion of Roussel's *Système,* see Michèle Le-Doeuff, *The Philosophical Imaginary,* trans. Colin Gordon (London: Athlone, 1989), 144–70. See also Anne Vila, *Enlightenment and Pathology: Sensibil-*

ity in the Literature and Medicine of Eighteenth-Century France (Baltimore: Johns Hopkins University Press, 1998), 243–55.

10. Denis Diderot, "Sur les femmes," in *Qu'est-ce qu'une femme?*, ed. Elizabeth Badinter (Paris: P.O.L., 1989), 170.

11. Denis Diderot, *Éléments de physiologie,* in *Oeuvres complètes de Diderot,* ed. J. Assézat (Paris: Garnier Frères, 1875), 391–92.

12. See Schiebinger, *The Mind Has No Sex ?,* 216.

13. Linda Timmermans, *L'accès des femmes à la culture (1598–1715)* (Paris: Honoré Champion, 1993), 819.

14. Ibid., 52.

15. Anne-Thérèse de Lambert, "Réflexions nouvelles sur les femmes par une Dame de la Cour de France" (1727; in *Oeuvres,* ed. Robert Granderoute, Paris: Honoré Champion, 1990), 223, 218. For an overview on this topic, see Jean Bloch, "Discourses of Female Education in the Writings of Eighteenth-Century French Women," in *Women, Gender, and Enlightenment,* ed. Sarah Knott and Barbara Taylor (New York: Palgrave Macmillan, 2005), 243–58.

16. Anne-Marie Armelin, *Preuves de noblesse pour l'entrée à la maison royale de l'enfant-Jésus,* Les cahiers nobles 34 et 35 (Paris, 1968), n. p.

17. Jean-Jacques Rousseau, *Émile* (Paris: Garnier-Flammarion, 1966), 473; Rousseau, *Emile,* trans. Barbara Foxley (London: Dent, 1957), 327. On Rousseau's views about women's education, see Trouille, *Sexual Politics.*

18. Rousseau, *Émile,* 558–59, *Emile* 389, translation modified.

19. Quoted in Fraisse, *Reason's Muse,* 153.

20. Janet Whatley, "Sophie de Grouchy de Condorcet," in *The Feminist Encyclopedia of French Literature*, ed. Eva Martin Sartori (Westport, CT: Greenwood Press, 1999), 123.

21. Olwen Hufton, "Women, Work, and Family," in *A History of Women in the West,* ed. Natalie Zemon Davis and Arlette Farge (Cambridge: Belknap Press, 1993), 3:26.

22. Vivien Jones, ed. and intro., *Women in the Eighteenth Century: Constructions of Femininity* (London: Routledge, 1990), 14.

23. Adrienne Rogers, "Woman and the Law," in *French Women and the Age of Enlightenment,* ed. Samia I. Spencer (Bloomington: Indiana University Press, 1984), 35, 43.

24. DeJean, *Tender Geographies,* 149–50.

25. Rogers, "Woman and the Law," 37.

26. Carla Hesse, "Reading Signatures: Female Authorship and Revolutionary Law in France, 1750–1850," *Eighteenth-Century Studies* 22 (1989): 476.

27. Julie Hardwick, "Seeking Separations: Gender, Marriages, and Household Economies in Early Modern France," *French Historical Studies* 21.1 (1998): 160.

28. Lieselotte Steinbrügge, *The Moral Sex: Woman's Nature in the French Enlightenment,* trans. Pamela Selwyn (New York: Oxford University Press, 1995).

29. Rousseau, *Émile,* 471, *Emile,* 325; Rousseau, *Émile,* 475, *Emile,* 328, emphasis added.

30. Fraisse, *Reason's Muse,* 100.

31. These points are engaged by Fraisse and Steinbrügge as well as by Corinne Harol, "Faking It: Female Virginity and Pamela's Virtue," *Eighteenth-Century Fiction* 16.2 (2004): 197–216. In Rousseau's words, "Il n'y a pas de bruyantes que les folles; les femmes sages ne font point de sensation" (*Émile* 511); "Fools make a stir, good women pass unnoticed" (*Emile* 352).

32. *Encyclopédie* 13:776.

33. Christine de Pizan, *Le Livre de la Cité des Dames* (1405; trans. Earl Jeffrey Richards as *The Book of the City of Ladies,* New York: Persea, 1982), ¶ I.8.3, 18.

34. Joan Kelly, "Early Feminist Theory and the *Querelle des Femmes,* 1400–1789," in Kelly, *Women, History, and Theory* (Chicago: University of Chicago Press, 1984), 65, 83, 80.

35. David Hall and Roger Ames, *Anticipating China: Thinking Through the Narratives of Chinese and Western Culture* (Albany: State University of New York Press, 1995), 167.

36. Paul Hazard, *The European Mind, 1680–1715* (Cleveland: World Publication Company, 1968), v.

37. Immanuel Kant, "An Answer to the Question: 'What is Enlightenment?,'" trans. H. B. Nisbet, *Kant: Political Writings,* ed. Hans Reiss (Cambridge: Cambridge University Press, 1991), 54.

38. Kant, "What is Enlightenment?," 54.

39. Immanuel Kant, *Observations on the Feeling of the Beautiful and Sublime,* trans. John T. Goldthwaite (Berkeley: University of California Press, 1960), 78. Anne Dacier was a distinguished classicist, known for publishing prose translations of the *Iliad* and the *Odyssey.*

40. *Encyclopédie* 13:774.

41. Michel Malherbe, "Reason," in *The Cambridge History of Eighteenth-Century Philosophy,* ed. Knud Haakonssen (New York: Cambridge University Press, 2006), 319.

42. Gary Hatfield, "Reason," in *Encyclopedia of the Enlightenment,* ed. Alan Charles Kors (Oxford: Oxford University Press, 2003), 3:405.

43. D'Alembert, "Discours préliminaire," *Encyclopédie* 1:i–ii.

44. Janet Todd, *Sensibility: An Introduction* (New York: Methuen, 1986), 7, quoted in Vera Grayson, *The Genesis and Reception of Mme de Graffigny's Lettres d'une Péruvienne and* Cénie. *SVEC* 336 (Oxford: Voltaire Foundation, 1996), 90.

45. Helvétius, *Oeuvres complètes* (Paris: Didot, 1795), 3:264, 1:223, quoted in Guy Besse, Introduction to Helvétius, *De l'Esprit,* ed. Besse (Paris: Éditions sociales, 1959), 40.

46. Denis Diderot, *Pensées philosophiques* (1746; in *Oeuvres philosophiques,* ed. Paul Vernière, Paris: Garnier, 1961), 9–10.

47. Vila, *Enlightenment and Pathology,* 3.

48. Rousseau, *Émile,* 507; *Emile,* 349.

49. Rousseau, *Émile,* 507; *Emile,* 350.

50. Rousseau, *Émile,* 475; *Emile,* 328.

51. Hazard, *The European Mind,* vii.

52. James Schmidt, "Civility, Enlightenment, and Society: Conceptual Confusions and Kantian Remedies," *American Political Science Review* 92.1 (1998): 422.

53. Hatfield, "Reason," 408. In "Feminist Perspectives on the Self," Diana Meyers, too, dismisses what she calls Enlightenment's "instrumental rationality" for its "privileging of reason over other capacities." Actually, this claim rests upon some confusion, because privileging reason would not necessarily entail privileging instrumental rationality. Meyers, "Feminist Perspectives on the Self," in *The Stanford Encyclopedia of Philosophy,* ed. Edward N. Zalta, 1999. http://plato.stanford.edu/entries/feminism-self/. For a sustained response to Horkheimer and Adorno, see Stephen Eric Bronner, *Reclaiming the Enlightenment: Toward a Politics of Radical Engagement* (New York: Columbia University Press, 2004).

54. For a postmodernist account in which an astonishing variety of phenomena are ascribed to Enlightenment, see John Gray, *Enlightenment's Wake* (New York: Routledge, 1997). Susan Wilson offers a balanced assessment in "Postmodernism and the Enlightenment," in *The Enlightenment World,* ed. Martin Fitzpatrick et al. (London: Routledge, 2004), 648–59.

55. Daniel Gordon, "On the Supposed Obsolescence of the French Enlightenment," in *Postmodernism and the Enlightenment: New Perspectives in Eighteenth-Century French Intellectual History,* ed. Gordon (New York: Routledge, 2001), 212, 214.

56. Dena Goodman, "Difference: An Enlightenment Concept," in *What's Left of Enlightenment? A Postmodern Question,* ed. Keith Michael Baker and Peter Hanns Reill (Stanford: Stanford University Press, 2001), 129–47.

57. Julie Candler Hayes, *Reading the French Enlightenment: System and Subversion* (Cambridge: Cambridge University Press, 1999), 21.

58. Susan Hekman, "Reply to Hartsock, Collins, Harding, and Smith," in *The Feminist Standpoint Theory Reader: Intellectual and Political Controversies,* ed. Sandra Harding (New York: Routledge, 2004), 271.

59. Susan Hekman, *Gender and Knowledge: Elements of a Postmodern Feminism* (Boston: Northeastern University Press, 1990), 9.

60. Jane Flax, *Disputed Subjects: Essays on Psychoanalysis, Politics and Philosophy* (New York: Routledge, 1993), 30.

61. See, for example, Elizabeth Grosz, "Bodies and Knowledges: Feminism and the Crisis of Reason," in *Feminist Epistemologies,* ed. Linda Alcoff and Elizabeth Potter (New York: Routledge, 1993), 187–215.

62. Meyers, "Feminist Perspectives"; see also Diana Meyers, ed., *Feminists Rethink the Self* (Boulder, CO: Westview, 1997).

63. Schmidt, "Civility, Enlightenment," 426; see also James Schmidt, "What Enlightenment Project?," *Political Theory* 28.6 (2000): 734–57.

64. Marie Fleming, "Women's Place in Communicative Reason," in *Women and Reason,* ed. Elizabeth D. Harvey and Kathleen Okruhlik (Ann Arbor: University of Michigan Press, 1992), 258; see also the excellent and much-anthologized analysis of Habermas in Nancy Fraser, "What's Critical about

Critical Theory? The Case of Habermas and Gender," *New German Critique* 35 (1985): 97–131.

65. Seyla Benhabib, *Situating the Self: Gender, Community and Postmodernism in Contemporary Ethics* (New York: Routledge, 1992), 3, 8.

66. Pauline Johnson, "The Antinomies of the Age of Enlightenment," chap. 2 in Johnson, *Feminism as Radical Humanism* (Boulder, CO: Westview, 1994), 27.

67. Anne Mellor, "Feminist Theory," in *Encyclopedia of the Enlightenment*, ed. Alan Kors (New York: Oxford University Press, 2003), 2:39.

68. See, for example, Sara Maza, "The Diamond Necklace Affair Revisited (1785–1786): The Case of the Missing Queen," in *Eroticism and the Body Politic*, ed. Lynn Hunt (Baltimore: Johns Hopkins University Press, 1991), 63–89.

69. Dena Goodman, *The Republic of Letters: A Cultural History of the French Enlightenment* (Ithaca: Cornell University Press, 1994), 104, 53, emphasis added.

70. In his 600-page tome *Le Monde des salons: Sociabilité et mondanité à Paris au XVIIIe siècle* (Paris: Fayard, 2006), Antoine Lilti argues, in fact, that Goodman *overstates* the intellectual contributions of the *salonnières*.

71. See, for example, Judith P. Zinsser and Julie Candler Hayes, eds., *Émilie Du Châtelet: Rewriting Enlightenment Philosophy and Science* (Oxford: Voltaire Foundation, 2006); Bonnie Arden Robb, *Félicité de Genlis: Motherhood in the Margins* (Newark: University of Delaware Press, 2008).

72. See Jonathan Israel, *Radical Enlightenment: Philosophy and the Making of Modernity 1650–1750* (Oxford: Oxford University Press, 2001) and *Enlightenment Contested: Philosophy, Modernity, and the Emancipation of Man 1670–1752* (Oxford: Oxford University Press, 2006). See also Charles W. Mills, "Defending the Radical Enlightenment," in *Social Philosophy Today: Truth and Objectivity in Social Ethics,* ed. Cheryl Hughes (Charlottesville: Philosophy Documentation Center, 2003), 9–29. A notable exception is Karen Offen, "Reclaiming the European Enlightenment for Feminism," in *Perspectives on Feminist Political Thought in European History: From the Middle Ages to the Present,* ed. Tjitske Akkerman and Siep Stuurman (London: Routledge, 1998), 85–103.

73. In the French context, sometimes Du Châtelet is held up as "the" Enlightenment woman; witness the title of Élizabeth Badinter and Danielle Muzerelle's edited collection *Madame du Châtelet, la femme des Lumières* (Paris: Bibliothèque nationale de France, 2006).

74. Dorinda Outram, *The Enlightenment,* 2nd ed. (Cambridge: Cambridge University Press, 2005); Mellor, "Feminist Theory," 39–44; Claire Colebrook, *Gender* (New York: Palgrave Macmillan, 2004).

75. Karen Offen also affirms that some eighteenth-century thinkers made the distinction between sex and gender. See Offen, "Reclaiming the Enlightenment," 85.

76. Halperin writes: "[W]e are so far from remembering Foucault that there is little point in entertaining the possibility of forgetting him." "Forgetting Foucault: Acts, Identities, and the History of Sexuality," *Representations* 63 (1998): 94.

77. Michel Foucault, "What is Enlightenment?," trans. Catherine Porter et al., in *Ethics: Subjectivity and Truth*, ed. Paul Rabinow (New York: The New Press, 1997), 312, 319.

78. Hayes, *Reading the French Enlightenment*, 14.

79. DeJean, *Tender Geographies*, 91.

80. Jean-Jacques Rousseau, *Julie, ou la Nouvelle Héloïse* (Paris: Garnier-Flammarion, 1967), 4.

81. Lambert, "Réflexions," 214.

82. Rousseau, *Émile*, 537; *Emile*, 372.

83. Nicolas-Edme Restif de la Bretonne, *La Paysanne pervertie* (Paris: Garnier, 1972), 355, quoted in Colette Piau-Gillot, "Comment s'échapper du second rayon? ou le parcours littéraire de Marie-Jeanne Riccoboni," *Littératures Classiques* 31 (1997): 168.

84. Louis-Sébastien Mercier, *Le Tableau de Paris*, ed. and selected Jeffry Kaplow (Paris: Maspero, 1982), 166.

85. Mercier, *Tableau*, 166–67.

86. Ibid., 169.

87. Nicolas-Edme Restif de la Bretonne, *Les Parisiennes, ou XL caractères généraux pris dans les moeurs actuelles* (Neuchâtel and Paris: Guillot, 1787), 3:147.

88. Restif de la Bretonne, *Les Parisiennes*, 149.

89. "Coquetterie," in *Encyclopédie* 4:183.

90. Rousseau, *Émile*, 509; *Emile*, 351.

91. Rousseau, *Émile*, 503; *Emile*, 347.

92. Rousseau, *Émile*, 516–17; *Emile*, 356.

93. Rousseau, *Émile*, 627; *Emile*, 443.

94. Rousseau, *Émile*, 476; *Emile*, 329.

95. Mary Wollstonecraft, *A Vindication of the Rights of Woman*, 2nd ed. (1792; New York: Norton, 1987), 28.

96. *Encyclopédie*, 12:509b.

97. On Graffigny, see Charlotte Simonin, "Cléomène et Caton: deux figures de philosophe dans le théâtre de Madame de Graffigny," in *Le Philosophe sur les planches: l'image du philosophe dans le théâtre des Lumières 1680–1815*, ed. Pierre Hartmann (Strasbourg: Presses universitaires de Strasbourg, 2004), 64; on Riccoboni, see Emily Crosby, *Une romancière oubliée: Madame Riccoboni* (1924; Geneva: Slatkine Reprints, 1970), chapter 3; on Charrière, see Henri Coulet, "Isabelle de Charrière, femme des Lumières?," in *Une Européenne: Isabelle de Charrière en son siècle*, ed. Doris Jakubec and Jean-Daniel Candaux (Hauterive-Neuchâtel: Attinger, 1994), 10. As discussed in chapter 4, Charrière is the only one of these three writers sometimes defended against this assertion.

98. Gravelot [pseudonym of Hubert François Bourguignon d'Anville] and Cochin, *Iconologie par figures ou traité complet des allégories, emblèmes etc.* 4 vols. (Paris: Lattré, n.d. [1791]) 4:119, quoted in Sheriff, "Decorating Knowledge," 169.

99. Etienne Bonnot, abbé de Condillac, *Essai sur l'origine des connaissances humaines*, in *Oeuvres complètes* (Paris: 1821–22; rpt Geneva, 1970), 1:102, quoted in Sheriff, "Decorating Knowledge," 161.

100. Sheriff, "Decorating Knowledge," 154.

101. Georges May, "Observations on an Allegory: The Frontispiece of the *Encyclopédie,*" *Diderot Studies* 16 (1973): 160, 161.

102. Lionel Gossman, "What Was Enlightenment?," in *A New History of French Literature,* ed. Denis Hollier (Cambridge: Harvard University Press, 1989), 489.

103. See Hayes, *Reading the French Enlightenment;* Brewer, *The Discourse of Enlightenment.*

104. Daniel Gordon, Introduction, *Postmodernism and the Enlightenment: New Perspectives in Eighteenth-Century French Intellectual History,* ed. Gordon (New York: Routledge, 2001), 3.

105. See Ricoeur, *Time and Narrative;* Benhabib, *Situating the Self;* Alasdair MacIntyre, *After Virtue: A Study in Moral Theory* (Notre Dame: University of Notre Dame Press, 1984); Martha Nussbaum, *Love's Knowledge: Essays on Philosophy and Literature* (New York: Oxford University Press, 1990) and *Poetic Justice: The Literary Imagination and Public Life* (Boston: Beacon Press, 1995); Taylor, *Sources of the Self.*

106. For example, Taylor commits a slippage when he writes that "we must inescapably understand our lives in narrative form, as a 'quest,'" *Sources,* 52. Oversimplifying narrative identity, Taylor collapses "narrative" and "quest" as if the two terms were synonymous. Moreover, his focus on socially privileged authors and protagonists leads him to describe narrative as "stories of linear development, progress stories" and "construals of life as growth," *Sources,* 105. Narratives by women authors, for example, tend to present more complex scenarios.

107. Louise d'Épinay and Lambert both wrote educational works for women. On eighteenth-century conduct books, see the work of Nadine Bérenguier, for example "The Politics of Happy Matrimony: Cerfvol's *La Gamologie ou l'éducation des filles destinées au mariage,*" *Studies in Eighteenth-Century Culture* 29 (2000): 173–200, and her *Conduct Books in Eighteenth-Century France: Girls' Education and Enlightenment Discontents* (Ashgate, forthcoming).

108. Carla Hesse discusses the philosophical import of nineteenth-century literature; my analysis suggests that she places the emergence of this phenomenon a century too late. See Hesse, *The Other Enlightenment: How French Women Became Modern* (Princeton: Princeton University Press, 2001), 130–53.

109. Note, however, that a sentimental novel like Rousseau's *Julie* was widely interpreted as a guide to conduct in the real world. For a useful discussion of the relative values assigned to sentimental and to libertine novels, see Nancy K. Miller, "Cultural Memory and the Art of the Novel: Gender and Narrative in Eighteenth-Century France," chapter 4 in Miller, *French Dressing,* 69–79.

110. Mauzi, *L'idée,* 10.

111. Mauzi calls her text the only eighteenth-century discourse on happiness worth reading, *L'idée,* 9; see also Barbara Whitehead, "The Singularity of Mme Du Châtelet: An Analysis of the *Discours sur le bonheur,*" *SVEC* 1 (2006): 255–76.

112. Joanna Russ, *How to Suppress Women's Writing* (Austin: University of Texas Press, 1983), 65–66.

113. Madelyn Gutwirth, "ASECS Women's Caucus Response," in *A History of the ASECS Women's Caucus 1975–2005*, ed. Alison Conway (American Society for Eighteenth-Century Studies, 2005), 9–10.

2. REASON, GENDER, AND MASQUERADE

1. *Recueil des oeuvres de Madame Du Boccage* (Lyon, 1764), 243, quoted in Grayson, *The Genesis*, 110.

2. Colin Harrison, "Les portraits de Mme de Graffigny," *SVEC* 12 (2004): 195–211.

3. Editors' introduction to Françoise de Graffigny, *Correspondance de Mme de Graffigny* (hereafter abbreviated *CG*), ed. J. A. Dainard et al. (Oxford: Voltaire Foundation, 1985–2008), 9:xxi. This more authentic portrait, which may have been painted by Charles-François Chéron, was likely copied from a portrait of Graffigny by Maurice Quentin de La Tour. English Showalter graciously provided this clarification in a personal communication, October 29, 2008.

4. For a useful discussion of these plays, see Perry Gethner, "Les *pièces nouvelles* de Graffigny: de la comédie sentimentale au drame," *SVEC* 12 (2004): 41–49.

5. See Jonathan Mallison's 2002 edition of the novel (Oxford: Voltaire Foundation), which includes a lengthy introduction; see Grayson, *Genesis and Reception;* and see Simon Davies, *Lettres d'une Péruvienne, 1977–1997:* The Present State of Studies," *SVEC* 05 (2000): 295–324.

6. Graffigny describes this visit to the Châtelet estate at Cirey, in the Champagne region, in *CG* 1:287–88. See Marie-Thérèse Inguenaud, "La Grosse et le Monstre: Histoire d'une haine," *SVEC* 1 (2006): 65–90.

7. Jack Undank, "Grafigny's Room of Her Own," *French Forum* 13.3 (1988): 299.

8. Diane Fourny, "Language and Reality in Françoise de Graffigny's *Lettres d'une Péruvienne,*" *Eighteenth-Century Fiction* 4 (1992): 237, quoted in Grayson, *The Genesis*, 102.

9. December 13, 1744, *CG* 6:98, quoted in English Showalter, *Françoise de Graffigny: Her Life and Works, SVEC* 11 (Oxford: Voltaire Foundation, 2004), 323; also in *Françoise de Graffigny: Choix de lettres,* ed. English Showalter (Oxford: Voltaire Foundation, 2001), 106.

10. February 9, 1749, *CG* 9:416.

11. Showalter, *Graffigny,* 272–73.

12. Ibid., 128.

13. Graffigny Papers XLII 16 (hereafter abbreviated GP); quoted in *CG* 1:7.

14. Dorothy S. Packer explains: "The term 'vaudeville' was the name given a song whose melody was well-known and to which a new topical, satirical text had been added." " 'La Calotte' and the 18th-Century French Vaudeville," *Journal of the American Musicological Society* 23.1 (1970): 63.

15. August 15, 1745, *CG* 6:535.

16. De Jaucourt, "Momus," in *Encyclopédie* (1765), 10:635. Momus is a perennial figure in French literature—particularly theater—of the seventeenth and eighteenth centuries. See Dominique Quéro, *Momus philosophe: Recherches sur une figure littéraire du XVIIIe siècle* (Paris: Honoré Champion, 1995).

17. Françoise de Graffigny, "La Réunion du bon sens et de l'esprit," Gen. Mss. 353, GP, Box 67, vol. 83, Beinecke Library, Yale University, scene three. Hereafter abbreviated *RBSE;* references are to the scene.

18. This scene recalls the debate illustrated in Lafayette's *La Princesse de Clèves* (1678), where Mme de Chartres introduces her daughter to the court only to have her fall in love with the unattainable M. de Nemours, eventually occasioning the novel's tragic conclusion.

19. Pierre Bayle, *Dictionnaire historique et critique* (1697) s.v. "Pierre Bunel," 254.

20. [René] Descartes, *Méditations métaphysiques* (1641; Paris: Larousse, 1973), 19; René Descartes, *Discourse on Method and Meditations on First Philosophy,* trans. Donald A. Cress. 4th ed. (Indianapolis: Hackett, 1998), 49.

21. January 19, 1745, Graffigny, *Choix de lettres,* 108.

22. Showalter, *Graffigny,* 130.

23. July 1747, *CG,* 8:420.

24. Showalter, *Graffigny,* 313.

25. Ibid., 207.

26. September 12, 1749, quoted in Charlotte Simonin, "Cléomène et Caton," 59.

27. Cf. Zilia who writes of the authors of books: "Je comprends qu'ils sont à l'âme ce que le soleil est à la terre, et que je trouverais avec eux toutes les lumières . . . dont j'ai besoin." Graffigny, *Lettres d'une Péruvienne,* 160; "I realize that they are to the soul what the Sun is to the earth and that in their company I would find all the lights of learning . . . I need." Graffigny, *Letters from a Peruvian Woman,* trans. David Kornacker (New York: Modern Language Association, 1993), 88–89.

28. The term comes from Judith Butler, *Gender Trouble: Feminism and the Subversion of Identity* (New York: Routledge, 1990), xi.

29. August 20, 1747, *CG* 8:464.

30. August 29, 1747, *CG* 8:471.

31. May 30, 1748, *CG* 9:134.

32. September 13, 1747, *CG* 8:489.

33. See Graffigny's letter of April 3–4, 1749, *CG* 9:471, 473n.4.

34. March 14, 1749, *CG* 9:447. Louis de Bourbon-Condé, comte de Clermont, was a great-grandson of the Grand Condé; he was the patron of other writers as well, including La Chaussée. See Grayson, *The Genesis,* 48.

35. Charlotte Simonin, "Phaza, la 'fille-garçon' de Madame de Graffigny," in *Le Mâle en France, 1715–1830: Représentations de la masculinité,* ed. Katherine Astbury and Marie-Emmanuelle Plagnol-Diéval (New York: Peter Lang, 2004), 54.

36. August 29, 1747, *CG* 8:471.

37. Graffigny, *Phaza,* in *Oeuvres posthumes de Madame de Grafigny* (Paris: Segaud, 1775), 53. Subsequent textual references are to the page number.

38. Raymonde Robert, *Le conte de fées littéraire en France de la fin du XVIIe à la fin du XVIIIe siècle* (Nancy: Presses universitaires de Nancy, 1981), 327.

39. Robert, *Le conte de fées,* 328.

40. Lewis C. Seifert, "Fairy Tales," in *The Feminist Encyclopedia of French Literature,* ed. Eva Martin Sartori (Westport, CT: Greenwood Press, 1999), 199.

41. Daniel Gerould, ed. and intro, *Gallant and Libertine: Divertissements and Parades of Eighteenth-Century France* (New York: Performing Arts Journal Publications, 1983), 8.

42. Graffigny, *Oeuvres posthumes,* vii–viii.

43. Joan Riviere, "Womanliness as a Masquerade," (1929) in *Gender,* ed. Anna Tripp (New York: Palgrave, 2000), 130.

44. Note that Graffigny herself married at sixteen.

45. August 22, 1747, *CG* 8:466.

46. Graffigny's letters show that she liked to coin words, particularly nouns ending in the suffix *-erie* (which appears in French words such as *causerie,* "chat," or *féerie,* "fairy play"). Other Graffigny neologisms include *fillerie,* from the verb *filer,* "to spin textiles," *parlerie,* from *parler,* "to speak," and *lecticerie,* from *lectrice,* "a woman reader." *CG* 8:95, 9:122, 9:450.

47. July 17, 1739, quoted in Showalter, *Graffigny,* 54. On Quinault, see Judith Curtis, *"Divine Thalie": The Career of Jeanne Quinault, SVEC* 8 (Oxford: Voltaire Foundation, 2007).

48. Letter to Devaux, August 1, 1745, *CG* 6:509.

49. Sarah R. Cohen, "Masquerade as Mode in the French Fashion Print," in *The Clothes That Wear Us: Essays on Dressing and Transgressing in Eighteenth-Century Culture,* ed. Jessica Munns and Penny Richards (Newark: University of Delaware Press, 1999), 178–79.

50. June 25, 1750, *CG* 10:574.

51. English Showalter, "A Woman of Letters in the French Enlightenment: Madame de Graffigny," *British Journal for Eighteenth-Century Studies* 1 (1978): 98.

52. April 30, 1751, Graffigny, *Choix de lettres,* 198.

53. Margaret Wise, "Cross-Dressing," in *The Feminist Encyclopedia of French Literature,* ed. Sartori, 135.

54. *CG* 8:490.

55. April 30, 1748, *CG* 9:82–85.

56. Cohen, "Masquerade as Mode," 176.

57 Stephen Heath, "Joan Riviere and the Masquerade," in *Gender,* ed. Tripp, 143.

58. Graffigny, *Lettres d'une Péruvienne,* 204; *Letters from a Peruvian Woman,* 149.

59. Riviere, "Womanliness as a Masquerade," 131, 132, 133.

60. Heath, "Joan Riviere," 143.

61. Butler, *Gender Trouble,* xi.

62. Ibid., 25.

63. Judith Butler, *Bodies That Matter: On the Discursive Limits of "Sex"* (New York: Routledge, 1993), 94–95, 235–36.

64. Butler, *Gender Trouble,* 22.

65. Showalter, *Graffigny,* 206. Even more striking is Simonin's literalist interpretation of the conclusion in "La fille-garçon."

66. Grayson, *The Genesis,* 85.

67. Friedrich Nietzsche, "On the Uses and Disadvantages of History for Life," in *Untimely Meditations,* trans. R. J. Hollingdale (Cambridge: Cambridge University Press, 1983), 92.

68. October 1733, *CG* 1:5–6.

69. January 7, 1744, *CG* 5:12; see also *CG* 5:16 n.5, quoted in English Showalter, "The Beginnings of Madame de Graffigny's Literary Career: A Study in the Social History of Literature," in *Essays on the Age of Enlightenment in Honor of Ira O. Wade,* ed. Jean Macary (Geneva and Paris: Droz, 1977), 297.

70. Riviere, "Womanliness as a Masquerade," 130.

71. Russ, *How to Suppress,* 20, 22, 99.

72. Butler, *Gender Trouble,* 52.

73. August 22, 1745, *CG* 6:549.

74. Graffigny wrote about the public's perception of her: "j'ai deux réputations parfaitement opposées, grâce aux ingrats, et au Monstre" [I have two perfectly opposed reputations, thanks to the ingrates and the Monster], August 29, 1747, *CG* 8:471.

75. English Showalter, "'Madame a fait un livre: Madame de Graffigny, Palissot et *Les Philosophes,*" *British Journal for Eighteenth-Century Studies* 1 (1978): 89–104; also Showalter, *Graffigny,* 286.

76. Quoted in Showalter, "Madame a fait un livre," 115.

77. 1.5.157, quoted in Showalter, "Madame a fait un livre," 123.

78. 1.1.145, quoted in ibid., 121.

79. Quoted in Grayson, *The Genesis,* 108.

80. Quoted in ibid., 121. Graffigny was quite upset upon learning of Roy's epigram; see *CG* 11:31–34.

81. Guillaume-Thomas Raynal, *Nouvelles littéraires manuscrites (1747–1755),* bound with *Correspondance littéraire, philosophique et critique par Grimm, Diderot, Raynal, Meister, etc.,* 1 (Paris: Garnier Frères, 1877), 132 (letter 14), quoted in Janet Altman, "A Woman's Place in the Enlightenment Sun: The Case of F. de Graffigny," *Romance Quarterly* 38.3 (1991): 264.

82. Chant IX, vol. 3, 142, quoted in Showalter, "Madame a fait un livre," 122; see also Showalter, *Graffigny,* 231.

83. Marivaux, *Spectateur français,* quoted in Gossman, "Literature and Society," 312–13.

84. May 12, 1748, *CG* 9:105.

85. Quoted in Grayson, *The Genesis,* 88.

86. Grayson, *The Genesis,* 88.

87. Graffigny persuaded Clermont to participate in a scheme where she pretended not to know the play was being staged; thus she could "make money without ruining her reputation." Grayson, *The Genesis,* 67.

88. Graffigny, *Cénie,* in *Femmes dramaturges en France (1650–1750): Pièces choisies,* ed. and intro. Perry Gethner (1750; Paris: Papers on French Seventeenth Century Literature, 1993), 330, emphasis added.

89. July 11, 1747, *CG* 8:419.

90. Graffigny, *Lettres d'une Péruvienne,* 222; *Letters from a Peruvian Woman,* 173.

91. September 6, 1747, *CG* 8:478.

92. September 10, 1747, *CG,* 8:488.

93. December 9, 1749, quoted in Showalter, *Graffigny,* 176.

94. Quoted in Showalter, *Graffigny,* 267, 268.

95. Quoted in ibid., 251.

3. Reason as Remedy

1. May 15, 1765, *Mme Riccoboni's Letters to David Hume, David Garrick and Sir Robert Liston: 1764–1783,* ed. and intro. James Nicholls, *SVEC* 149 (Oxford: Voltaire Foundation, 1976), 44.

2. May, "Observations," 165.

3. The first French translation of *Pamela,* entitled *Pamela, ou la vertu recompensée,* was published in London in 1741. See Sarah W. R. Smith, *Samuel Richardson: A Reference Guide* (Boston: GK Hall and Co, 1984), 11. Rousseau's *Julie* contains a footnote lauding Riccoboni, in Letter II of Part Five. See Colette Piau-Gillot, "Comment s'échapper du second rayon? ou le parcours littéraire de Marie-Jeanne Riccoboni," *Littératures Classiques* 31 (1997), 166. The passionate language of Riccoboni's Fanni Butlerd may have influenced Rousseau's Julie. Moreover, Antoinette Sol has documented Riccoboni's substantial influence on another famous novelist, Laclos. See her *Textual Promiscuities.*

4. See Emily Crosby, *Une romancière oubliée: Madame Riccoboni* (1924; Geneva: Slatkine Reprints, 1970), 24. Cecilia Beach lists four *compliments* authored by Riccoboni, in 1735, two in 1739, and 1744. Cecilia Beach, *French Women Playwrights before the Twentieth Century: A Checklist* (Westport, CT: Greenwood, 1994), 47. Riccoboni coauthored the plays *Le siège de Grenade* (1745); *Les Caquets,* an imitation of Goldoni (1761); *Sophie ou le Mariage caché,* written with Thérèse Biancolelli (1770); *Il n'y a plus d'enfants* (1767); and *Le Double piège* (1768).

5. January 1772, *Mme Riccoboni's Letters,* 227–28.

6. Mercier, *Le Tableau de Paris,* 168.

7. June 1764, *Correspondance littéraire,* vol. 4, 131.

8. Letter to Diderot, August 5, 1762, in Diderot, *Correspondance de Diderot,* ed. Georges Roth (Paris: Minuit, 1956), 4:91, quoted in Susan Lanser, *Fictions of Authority: Women Writers and Narrative Voice* (Ithaca: Cornell University Press, 1992), 56; the English translation is Lanser's.

9. *Mme Riccoboni's Letters,* 15.

10. This idea is reflected not only in Alan Kors's 1976 book on the topic but also in a recent encyclopedia article. Alan Kors, *D'Holbach's Coterie: An*

Enlightenment in Paris (Princeton: Princeton University Press, 1976); Alan Kors, "Holbach, Paul-Henri Thiry D'," in *Encyclopedia of the Enlightenment,* vol. 2, ed. Kors (Oxford: Oxford University Press, 2003), 213–15.

11. Crosby, *Une romancière oubliée,* 105.

12. Ibid., 105.

13. Ibid., 106.

14. Quoted in ibid., 111.

15. Crosby, *Une romancière oubliée,* 109.

16. Ibid., 118.

17. Joan Hinde Stewart, *Gynographs: French Novels by Women of the Late Eighteenth Century* (Lincoln: University of Nebraska Press, 1993), 105.

18. Servais Etienne, *Le genre romanesque en France depuis l'apparition de la "Nouvelle Héloïse" jusqu'aux approches de la Révolution* (Brussels: Lamertin, 1922) and Paul Ginisty, "Les souvenirs sentimentaux de Mme Riccoboni," in *Mémoires et souvenirs de comédiennes (XVIIIe siècle)* (Paris: Louis Michaud, 1914), quoted in Stewart, *Gynographs,* 20.

19. Aurora Wolfgang, "Fallacies of Literary History: The Myth of Authenticity in the Reception of *Fanni Butlerd,*" *SVEC* 304 (1992): 735–39; and Wolfgang, *Gender and Voice in the French Novel, 1730–1782* (London: Ashgate, 2004). For an example of the "myth of authenticity," see Colette Cazenobe, *Au malheur des dames: Le roman féminin au XVIIIe siècle* (Paris: Champion, 2006).

20. Jean-François Bastide, ed., *Le Monde* (Amsterdam and Paris: Bauche, Duchesne, et al., 1761), 3:7.

21. Some scholars use the title "L'Abeille" to refer to an entire section of the *Recueil de pièces détachées,* including the two parts of the essay *L'Abeille* as well as the short stories "L'Aveugle" and "Lettres de la princesse Zelmaïde." I use *L'Abeille* in a more restricted sense to refer to the two parts of the text explicitly entitled "L'Abeille" in the collection, following Crosby, 112 and Piau-Gillot, 170. Aside from eighteenth-century editions to be found in research libraries, a copy of the 1781–83 Humblot edition is available on microfilm in the "History of Women" series (New Haven, CT: Research Publications, 1975), reels 72 and 72, no. 474.

22. *Correspondance littéraire* vol. 4, May 1765, 435–36.

23. Suzan van Dijk, "Madame Riccoboni: Romancière ou journaliste?," *SVEC* 304 (1993): 773.

24. Marie Jeanne Riccoboni, *L'Abeille,* in *Recueil de pièces détachées* (Paris: Humblot, 1765), 228. Subsequent textual references are to this edition.

25. Bastide, *Le Monde* 3:12, 3:13.

26. Ibid., 4:41, 40.

27. Graffigny made a similar comment following a dinner in the company of intellectuals whose conversation she had followed and well understood. She remarked jokingly in a letter to Devaux dated September 4, 1739, that because she had spoken little, these companions probably doubted her intelligence. See Graffigny, *Choix,* 41.

28. Kevin Bourque, "'Tout est en désordre dans la ruche': Republican Discourse, Patriarchal Strategy, Gendered Labour and the Bees of the *Encyclo-*

pédie," SVEC 12 (2006): 361–76. See also Jeffrey Merrick, "Royal Bees: The Gender Politics of the Beehive in Early Modern Europe," *Studies in Eighteenth-Century Culture* 18, ed. John W. Yolton and Leslie Ellen Brown (East Lansing, MI: Colleagues Press, 1988): 7–37.

29. David Hume, who would later become a friend of Riccoboni's, adopted Mandeville's ideas in his *Treatise of Human Nature*, published in 1740, the same year in which Mandeville's *Fable* became available in French translation. See E. J. Hundert, ed. and intro. *Bernard Mandeville: The Fable of the Bees and Other Writings* (Indianapolis: Hackett, 1997), xxx.

30. Francis Bacon, *Novum Organon* (1620), quoted in R. S. Woolhouse, "Empiricism," *Encyclopedia of the Enlightenment*, ed. Kors, 1.394. See also Gary Hatfield, "Rationalism," in *Encyclopedia of the Enlightenment*, ed. Kors, 3.393. Here, I leave to the side Bacon's notorious gendered metaphors of science as a masculine force that must subjugate feminized Nature. See Lloyd, *Man of Reason*, 10–17.

31. Bastide, *Le Monde*, 4:40.

32. On the *bel-esprit*, see Elena Russo, *Styles of Enlightenment: Taste, Politics, and Authorship in Eighteenth-Century France* (Baltimore: Johns Hopkins University Press, 2007).

33. Descartes, *Discours de la méthode* (1637; Paris: Larousse, 1972), 38, 39; Descartes, *Discourse on Method*, 5, 6.

34. Rousseau, *Émile*, 350; *Emile*, 508.

35. Lanser, *Fictions of Authority*, 53.

36. January 2, 1772, *Mme Riccoboni's Letters*, 227.

37. See Anne Coudreuse, "Pleurer en bref: le pathétique dans l'*Histoire du marquis de Cressy*, nouvelle de Mme Riccoboni," *Littératures classiques* 62 (2007): 149–56, especially 152–53, 155.

38. Quoted in Jean-Auguste Jullien, *Histoire anecdotique et raisonnée du théâtre italien, depuis son rétablissment en France jusqu'à l'année 1769* (Paris: Lacombe, 1769), 4:430.

39. Letter to Garrick, 1772, *Mme Riccoboni's Letters*, 227.

40. Olga B. Cragg, introduction to Marie Jeanne Riccoboni, *Histoire du marquis de Cressy* (1758), ed. Cragg, *SVEC* 266 (Oxford: Voltaire Foundation, 1989), 6.

41. Riccoboni, *Histoire de Cressy*, 95. Hereafter abbreviated *HC*.

42. For an analysis of the theatrical aspect of this death scene, see Ruth Thomas, "Marriage as Theatre in the Novels of Madame Riccoboni," *Dalhousie French Studies* 56 (2001): 129.

43. Letter to Liston, April 28, 1773, *Mme Riccoboni's Letters*, 304.

44. Stéphanie-Félicité de Genlis, *De l'influence des femmes sur la littérature française* (1811), quoted in Stewart, *Gynographs*, 84.

45. *Année littéraire* 4 (1758), 128, quoted in Cragg, introduction to Riccoboni, *Cressy*, 26.

46. Gossman, "What Was Enlightenment?," 491. See also Robert Favre, *La Mort dans la littérature et la pensée françaises au Siècle des Lumières* (Presses universitaires de Lyon, 1978), especially chapter 11: "Du Suicide au Sacrifice Héroïque." For primary texts from the English context, see *The History of*

234 NOTES TO CHAPTER 3

Suicide in England, 1650–1850, 2 vols., ed. Donna T. Andrew (London: Pickering & Chatto, 2009–10).

47. See Arlette Farge, *Subversive Words: Public Opinion in Eighteenth-Century France,* trans. Rosemary Morris (University Park: Pennsylvania State University Press, 1994), 96–97, 139, 140–42.

48. *Correspondence littéraire, philosophique et critique* par Grimm, Diderot, Raynal, Meister, etc, ed. Maurice Tourneaux (Paris 1877–1881), 1:365, quoted in Cragg, introduction to Riccoboni, *Cressy,* 28.

49. Letter to Liston, March 6, 1771, *Mme Riccoboni's Letters,* 190. For another example, see Riccoboni's letter to Liston dated May 21, 1777, *Mme Riccoboni's Letters,* 412–13.

50. Letter to Liston, December 5, 1773, *Mme Riccoboni's Letters,* 324.

51. Jeffrey Merrick, "Suicide and Politics in Pre-Revolutionary France," *Eighteenth-Century Life* 30.2 (2006): 34, 43.

52. Merrick, "Suicide," 42.

53. See English Showalter, "Writing Off the Stage: Women Authors and Eighteenth-Century Theater," *Yale French Studies* 75 (1988): 101–5.

54. Nancy K. Miller, "The Exquisite Cadavers: Women in Eighteenth-Century Fiction," *Diacritics* (1975): 37.

55. *Mme Riccoboni's Letters,* 328.

56. Raymond Trousson, *Socrate devant Voltaire, Diderot et Rousseau: La conscience en face du mythe* (Paris: Minard, 1967), 6–7. For a lively and more recent discussion, see Emily Wilson, *The Death of Socrates* (Cambridge: Harvard University Press, 2007). See also Dominique Lanni, "La mort de Socrate, de Voltaire à Bernardin de Saint-Pierre," in *Le philosophe sur les planches: l'image du philosophe dans le théâtre des Lumières,* ed. Pierre Hartmann (Strasbourg: Presses universitaires de Strasbourg, 2004), 287–94.

57. Grimm, *Correspondance litteraire,* August 1, 1762, 5:134, quoted in Trousson, *Socrate,* 19.

58. See Clifford Orwin, "Rousseau's Socratism," *The Journal of Politics* 60.1 (1998): 174–87.

59. Felicia Berger Sturzer, "Literary Portraits and Cultural Critique in the Novels of Marie Jeanne Riccoboni," *French Studies* 50 (1996): 404.

60. While the context for Spivak's remark is a discussion of East Indian *sati,* or widow sacrifice, her fine analysis is pertinent here. Gayatri Spivak, *A Critique of Postcolonial Reason: Toward a History of the Vanishing Present* (Cambridge: Harvard University Press, 1999), 299.

61. Plato, *Phaedo,* in *Plato: Complete Works,* ed. John M. Cooper (Indianapolis: Hackett, 1997), 58e.

62. Plato, *Phaedo* 64a.

63. Sol, *Textual Promiscuities,* 192.

64. Piau-Gillot, "Comment s'échapper du second rayon?," 166–67.

65. Nicolas-Edme Restif de la Bretonne, *Les Contemporaines,* vols. 39–40. (1785; Geneva: Slatkine Reprints, 1988), 24.

66. May 15, 1765, *Mme Riccoboni's Letters,* 44.

67. Letter to Liston, November 15, 1776, *Mme Riccoboni's Letters,* 389.

68. January 26, 1777, *Mme Riccoboni's Letters,* 395.

69. See Cragg's introduction to Marie Jeanne Riccoboni, *Lettres de Mylord Rivers à Sir Charles Cardigan* (1776; Geneva: Droz, 1992), 20. The first edition of the novel bears the date "1777," but it probably appeared in late 1776.

70. *Mme Riccoboni's Letters,* 149–50.

71. September 11, 1774, *Mme Riccoboni's Letters,* 341.

72. Friedrich Melchior Grimm, *Correspondance littéraire,* October 1776, quoted in Piau-Gillot, "Comment s'échapper," 171.

73. February 11, 1777, *Mme Riccoboni's Letters,* 398–99.

74. Lanser, *Fictions of Authority,* 58.

75. Riccoboni, *Lettres de Mylord Rivers,* 75. Hereafter abbreviated *MR.*

76. April 11, 1773, *Mme Riccoboni's Letters,* 302.

77. *Mme Riccoboni's Letters,* 398–99. See also Plato's *Phaedrus* for discussion of such texts.

78. See, for example, Michèle Bissière, "Graffigny, Riccoboni, et la tradition des *Lettres persanes,*" *Postscript* 12 (1995), 15.

79. August 10, 1766, *Mme Riccoboni's Letters,* 81.

80. August 26, 1772, *Mme Riccoboni's Letters,* 270.

81. *Mme Riccoboni's Letters,* 349.

82. Letter to Mr. Thickness, in response to his request for biographical information, quoted in Crosby, *Une romancière oubliée,* 14.

83. Louis Van Delft, *Les Spectateurs de la vie: Généalogie du regard moraliste* (Sainte-Foy, Québec: Presses de l'Université Laval, 2006).

84. *Tablettes de l'homme du monde* (1715), 39ff., quoted in Mauzi, *L'Idée du bonheur,* 135.

85. Quoted in D'Origny, *Annales* 1:208.

86. February 19, 1772, *Mme Riccoboni's Letters,* 234; March 23, 1777, *Mme Riccoboni's Letters,* 401.

87. Riccoboni, *Lettres de Mistriss Fanni Butlerd à Mylord Charles Alfred* (1757), ed. and intro. Joan Hinde Stewart (Geneva: Droz, 1979), 118.

88. Cragg, introduction to Riccoboni, *Cressy,* 33–34.

89. Susan Lanser has argued that mid-eighteenth-century women's texts evince a lack of "authoriality," that is, strong, authoritative narrative voices. See Lanser, *Fictions,* 48–49. Though Lanser acknowledges the third-person female narrator of *Cressy,* she argues that this narrative voice lacks "outspokenness" and that it is "restrict[ed] . . . almost entirely to representational acts," 50–51. The analysis offered here takes issue with that interpretation.

90. *Mme Riccoboni's Letters,* 26.

91. *Symposium* 189d. For other Platonic dialogues, I refer to the Hackett volume edited by Cooper; for the *Symposium,* however, see the excellent translation and edition by Robin Waterfield in *Plato: Symposium.* World's Classics (Oxford: Oxford University Press, 1994).

92. Plato, *Symposium* 204b.

93. March 6, 1771, *Mme Riccoboni's Letters,* 187.

94. Letter to Liston, May 1775, *Mme Riccoboni's Letters,* 353.

95. Ibid., January 20, 1779, *Mme Riccoboni's Letters,* 429.

96. *Mme Riccoboni's Letters,* 392.

97. May 14, 1771, *Mme Riccoboni's Letters,* 203.

98. *Mme Riccoboni's Letters,* 148, 149.

99. Letter to Garrick, July 1772, *Mme Riccoboni's Letters,* 267.

100. Riccoboni, *Mylord Rivers,* 66.

101. March 6, 1771, *Mme Riccoboni's Letters,* 191.

102. Letter to Liston, July 21, 1772, *Mme Riccoboni's Letters,* 263; *Mme Riccoboni's Letters,* 278.

103. July 17, 1772, *Mme Riccoboni's Letters,* 268.

104. Riccoboni, undated letter to Laclos, in Choderlos de Laclos, *Oeuvres complètes.* Pléiade (Paris: Gallimard, 1951), 686. On this epistolary exchange, see Janie Vanpée, "Dangerous Liaisons 2: The Riccoboni-Laclos Sequel," *Eighteenth-Century Fiction* 9.1 (1996): 51–70.

105. January 20, 1779, *Mme Riccoboni's Letters,* 429.

106. November 22, 1772, *Mme Riccoboni's Letters,* 280.

107. Elizabeth Heckendorn Cook, *Epistolary Bodies: Gender and Genre in the Eighteenth-Century Republic of Letters* (Stanford: Stanford University Press, 1996).

108. February 19, 1775, *Mme Riccoboni's Letters,* 350.

109. Roger Chartier, *The Cultural Origins of the French Revolution,* trans. Lydia Cochrane (Durham: Duke University Press, 1991), 30.

110. Quoted in Laclos, *Oeuvres complètes,* 689. See Vanpée, "Dangerous Liaisons," 69.

4. Reading Reason

1. *Encyclopédie* 9:605.

2. A foundational text is Brian Street, *Literacy in Theory and Practice* (New York: Cambridge University Press, 1984); see also Ellen Cushman et al., eds., *Literacy: A Critical Sourcebook* (Boston: Bedford–St. Martin's, 2001); and Bill Cope and Mary Kalantzis, eds., *Multiliteracies: Literacy Learning and the Design of Social Futures* (London: Routledge, 2000).

3. Roger Chartier, "Reading and Reading Practices," in *Encyclopedia of the Enlightenment,* ed. Kors (Oxford: Oxford University Press, 2003), 3:399–404. See also Chartier, *Cultural Origins,* 69.

4. This remark comes from a letter to David-Louis Constant d'Hermenches dated April 22–26, 1767, in which the author describes meeting David Hume. It appears in *Oeuvres complètes d'Isabelle de Charrière/Belle de Zuylen,* ed. Jean-Daniel Candaux et al. (Amsterdam: van Oorschot, Geneva: Slatkine, 1979), 2:39. Hereafter abbreviated *OC.*

5. The English translation comes from Isabelle de Charrière, *There Are No Letters Like Yours: The Correspondence of Isabelle de Charrière and Constant d'Hermenches,* trans. and with intro. and annotations by Janet Whatley and Malcolm Whatley (Lincoln: University of Nebraska Press, 2000), 8. Hereafter abbreviated *Correspondence.*

6. September 9, 1762, *OC* 1:129, *Correspondence,* 12.

7. Cecil Courtney, Roundtable presentation on "La place d'Isabelle de Charrière dans l'histoire littéraire," conference *Belle van Zuylen/ Isabelle de Charrière: Education & création,* Utrecht, April 7, 2005.

8. Beauvoir writes, melodramatically: "Mais ce n'est pas sa raison qui a éteint en elle cette flamme de vie . . . : c'est le mariage qui a lentement assassiné l'éclatante Belle de Zuylen" [But it is not her reason that extinguished in her this flame of life . . . ; it is marriage that slowly assassinated the brilliant Belle de Zuylen]. Simone de Beauvoir, *Le deuxième sexe* (Paris: Gallimard, 1949), 2:319.

9. Joke J. Hermsen, "Now Foolish Then Wise: Belle van Zuylen's Game with Sexual Identity," in *Hypatia's Daughters: Fifteen Hundred Years of Women Philosophers,* ed. Linda Lopez McAlister (Bloomington: Indiana University Press, 1996), 165–80.

10. Marie-Hélène Chabut, *"Les lettres trouvées dans des porte-feuilles d'émigrés* d'Isabelle de Charrière: Violence politique et violence domestique, ou pour une 'raison sensible,'" in *Violence et fiction jusqu'à la Révolution,* ed. Martine Debaisieux and Gabrielle Verdier (Tübingen: G. Narr, 1998), 403–10. See also Marie-Hélène Chabut, "Isabelle de Charrière écrivaine et lectrice des Lumières," in *Belle de Zuylen / Isabelle de Charrière: Education, creation, reception,* ed. Suzan van Dijk et al. (Amsterdam: Rodopi, 2006), 137, 142.

11. Emma Rooksby, "Moral Theory in the Fiction of Isabelle de Charrière: The Case of *Three Women," Hypatia* 20.1 (2005): 1–20. See also Rooksby's introduction to the Modern Language Association edition of *Three Women* (2007).

12. See, for example, Madeleine Dobie, "Romantic Psychology and Kantian Ethics in the Novels of Isabelle de Charrière," *Eighteeth-Century Fiction* 10.3 (1998): 303–24. See also Hesse, *The Other Enlightenment,* 104–29.

13. Stewart, *Gynographs,* 105.

14. Ibid., 109.

15. Susan K. Jackson, "Publishing Without Perishing: Isabelle de Charrière a.k.a. la mouche du coche," in *Going Public: Women and Publishing in Early Modern France,* ed. Dena Goodman and Elizabeth Goldsmith (Ithaca: Cornell University Press, 1995), 205. See Claire Jaquier, "Un roman à deux coups," chapter 5 in *L'Erreur des désirs: Romans sensibles au XVIIIe siècle* (Lausanne: Payot, 1998), 139–50, and Monique Moser-Verrey, "Leaving the Castle: The Avenues of Creation," 29.

16. Jean-Daniel Candaux et al., in *OC* 8:95.

17. See Jacqueline Letzter, "Isabelle de Charrière's *Sainte Anne,* or a Woman's Wayward Quest for Knowledge," *Studies in Eighteenth-Century Culture* 26 (1998): 209–30; Marie-Hélène Chabut, "Louvoyer pour innover: *Trois femmes* d'Isabelle de Charrière," in *Écriture de la ruse,* ed. Elzbieta Grodek (Amsterdam: Rodopi, 2000), 241–51; Susan Lanser, "Toward a Feminist Narratology," in *Feminisms: An Anthology of Literary Theory and Criticism,* rev. ed., ed. Robyn R. Warhol and Diane Price Herndl (New Brunswick, NJ: Rutgers University Press, 1997), 674–93; Lanser, *Fictions of Authority.*

18. *OC* 8:106, *Letters of Mistress Henley Published by Her Friend,* trans. Philip Stewart and Jean Vaché (New York: Modern Language Association, 1993), 15. Hereafter abbreviated *Letters.*

19. See Kees van Strien, "Genesis and Reception of *Portrait de Zélide,"* in *Belle de Zuylen / Isabelle de Charrière: Education, creation, reception,* ed. Suzan van Dijk et al. (Amsterdam: Rodopi, 2006), 151.

20. September 9, 1762, *OC* 1:129, *Correspondence*, 12 (translation modified).

21. The author of an anonymous *Analyse du Portrait de Zélide* writes: "Zélide est épicurienne ou pour le moins dans l'intention de le devenir" [Zélide is Epicurean or at least intends to become so], quoted in van Strien, "Genesis," 162.

22. September 9, 1762, *OC* 1:129, *Correspondence*, 12.

23. Kees van Strien, *Isabelle de Charrière (Belle de Zuylen) Early Writings: New Material From Dutch Archives* (Louvain and Paris: Editions Peeters, 2005), 31.

24. Cornelis van Engelen, *De Denker*, 3, 1766, no. 157, December 30, 1765, p.411. Translated by and quoted in van Strien, *Isabelle de Charrière*, 30.

25. See the complete text reproduced in Kees van Strien "Genesis and Reception," 155–63; also in Kees van Strien, *Isabelle de Charrière*.

26. Quoted in van Strien, "Genesis and Reception," 161.

27. Quoted in ibid., 158.

28. Quoted in ibid., 163.

29. Van Strien, "Genesis and Reception," 153. Perhaps one reason why van Strien sees echoes of Rousseau in the *Portrait* is that there are some other links between Rousseau and Charrière—for example, her *Plainte et défense de Thérèse Levasseur* (1789). See Raymond Trousson, "Madame de Charrière et Jean-Jacques Rousseau," *Lettre de Zuylen et du Pontet* 30 (2005): 12–15.

30. Van Strien, "Genesis and Reception," 154.

31. Rousseau, *Émile*, 32; *Emile*, 2, translation modified.

32. Guillemette Samson, *La présence masculine dans le théâtre d'Isabelle de Charrière* (Paris: Champion, 2005). See also Yvette Went-Daoust, "L'oeuvre dramatique d'Isabelle de Charrière: Classicisme et renouvellement," *Études sur le XVIIIe siècle* 28 (2000): 35–45.

33. Guillemette Samson, "Le thème de l'éducation dans les comédies d'Isabelle de Charrière," in *Belle de Zuylen / Isabelle de Charrière*, ed. van Dijk et al., 192, 194.

34. Samson, *La présence masculine*, 7.

35. Ibid., 15.

36. Letzter, "Isabelle de Charrière's *Sainte Anne*," 212.

37. Candaux et al., Introduction to *Élise ou l'université*, *OC* 7:409.

38. See editors' comments in *OC* 7:410.

39. May 30, 1794, *OC* 4:446.

40. Went-Daoust, "L'oeuvre dramatique," 40.

41. Van Strien, "Genesis and Reception," 152.

42. The potentially ennobling and progressive role of eighteenth-century motherhood is the central theme of Lesley Walker, *A Mother's Love: Crafting Feminine Virtue in Enlightenment France* (Lewisburg, PA: Bucknell University Press, 2008).

43. Quoted in van Strien, "Genesis and Reception," 160.

44. *Allgemeine Literatur-Zeitung*, quoted in *OC* 7:411.

45. October 22, 1792, *OC* 3:428.

46. Samson, *La présence masculine*, 131.

47. Plato, *Phaedo* 62d.

48. Quoted in *OC* 7:411.

49. Letter to Huber, August 17, 1794, *OC* 4:525.

50. Monique Moser-Verrey, "Leaving the Castle: The Avenues of Creation," in *Belle de Zuylen / Isabelle de Charrière,* ed. van Dijk et al., 17–45.

51. Suellen Diaconoff, *Through the Reading Glass: Women, Books, and Sex in the French Enlightenment* (Albany: State University of New York Press, 2005), 109.

52. Ibid., 26–27 ff.

53. Samson, "Le thème de l'éducation," 193.

54. Ibid., 196.

55. See Michèle Mat-Hasquin, "Dramaturgie et démystification dans les comédies d'Isabelle de Charrière," *Études sur le XVIIIe siècle* 8 (1981), especially 55–57, 60, 63, 65.

56. Samson, *La présence masculine,* 83.

57. February 13, 1799, *OC* 5:541.

58. It is held at the Bibliothèque Publique et Universitaire de Neuchâtel, "Fragments," MS 1387 / 13/ 2. I am deeply grateful to Valérie Cossy and Suzan van Dijk for sending me a copy of the typescript. The estimate of the text's date of composition comes from Jeroom Vercruysse, "The Publication of the *Oeuvres complètes:* Navigating the Risky Waters of the Unforeseeable," *Eighteenth-Century Life* 13.1 (1989), 75.

59. Vercruysse, "The Publication," 74.

60. Ibid., 75, 76.

61. Valérie Cossy, "Isabelle de Charrière, Frances Burney et le métier d'écrivain," in *Une Européenne: Isabelle de Charrière en son siècle,* ed. Doris Jakubec and Jean-Daniel Candaux (Hauterive-Neuchâtel: Attinger, 1994), 126. Charrière's *Trois femmes* opens by posing a similar question.

62. Cecil P. Courtney, *Belle van Zuylen and Philosophy* (Utrecht: Faculteit der Letteren Universiteit Utrecht, 1995), 9.

63. Henri Coulet, "Isabelle de Charrière, femme des Lumières?," 9, 12, 20.

64 *OC* 1:216, *Correspondence,* 88.

65. *OC* 1:217, *Correspondence,* 89.

66. *OC* 1:218, *Correspondence,* 90.

67. *OC* 1:163, *Correspondence,* 48.

68. July 3, 1797, *OC* 5:331.

69. Courtney, *Belle van Zuylen,* 28.

70. Kant, "What is Enlightenment?," 54.

71. *OC* 1:163–64, *Correspondence,* 49.

72. June 19, 1764, *OC* 1:195.

CONCLUSION

1. That association was again highlighted when the French newsmagazine *Le Nouvel observateur* published an issue (dated January 3, 2008) on Simone de Beauvoir, choosing as the cover image a nude photograph of the dis-

tinguished feminist philosopher. Feminists in France picketed the magazine's headquarters and an international community of scholars expressed outrage. http://hebdo.nouvelobs.com/hebdo/parution/p20080103/.

2. Michèle Le Doeuff, *The Sex of Knowing,* trans. Kathryn Hamer and Lorraine Code (New York: Routledge, 2003), 171.

3. See http://www.guerrillagirls.com.

4. Descartes, *Discours,* 60, *Discourse,* 16–17, emphasis added.

5. April 15, 1766, *Mme Riccoboni's Letters,* 67.

6. October 23–November 6, 1762, *OC* 1:142–43, *Correspondence,* 29.

7. See Peter Gay, "The Living Enlightenment," The Tanner Lectures on Human Values, delivered at University of Toronto, October 7, 1996.

8. Le Doeuff, *The Sex of Knowing,* 192.

9. Hilda Smith, "Intellectual Bases," 32; Timothy J. Reiss, *The Meaning of Literature* (Ithaca: Cornell University Press, 1992), 267.

10. See Hesse, *The Other Enlightenment,* 31–55; Wolfgang, *Gender and Voice,* 7–11.

11. [Marie Jean Antoine Caritat, marquis de] Condorcet, "Sur l'admission des femmes au droit de cité," in *Oeuvres de Condorcet,* vol. 10 (Paris: Firmin Didot, 1847), 124–25.

12. Le Doeuff, *The Sex of Knowing,* 213.

13. Joan Landes, *Visualizing the Nation: Gender, Representation, and Revolution in Eighteenth-Century France* (Ithaca: Cornell University Press, 2001), 30.

14. Joan Landes, *Women and the Public Sphere in the Age of the French Revolution* (Ithaca: Cornell University Press, 1988), 145, 170.

15. Johnson, "The Antinomies," 41.

16. Alison Jaggar, "Love and Knowledge: Emotion and Feminist Epistemology," in *Women, Knowledge, and Reality: Explorations in Feminist Philosophy,* ed. Ann Garry and Marilyn Pearsall (New York: Routledge, 1989), 150.

17. Diaconoff, *Through the Reading Glass,* 207; Lesley Walker expresses this same concern in *A Mother's Love,* 195.

18. Offen, "Reclaiming the Enlightenment," 99.

19. Alison M. Jaggar, "Freethinking?," in *Singing in the Fire: Stories of Women in Philosophy,* ed. Linda Martín Alcoff (New York: Rowman and Littlefield, 2003), 69.

20. See "Entre érotisme et perversité, 'Thérèse philosophe' fascine," *Le Monde,* April 13, 2007.

21. As Robin Morgan writes in an essay about the Clinton campaign, "Goodbye to All That (#2)": "*We have tried* reason, persuasion, reassurances, and being extra-qualified, only to learn it never was about qualifications after all." http://www.womensmediacenter.com/ex/contents/020108_main.html.

22. Judith Ezekiel, "*Le Women's Lib:* Made in France," *European Journal of Women's Studies* 9.3 (2002): 354. Ezekiel offers an illuminating discussion of the *parité* debates, and suggests that in France *parité* is "a euphemism for 'equality' and even 'feminism,'" 355. On this topic, see also Geneviève Fraisse, "La controverse des sexes, le cas de la parité," in *La controverse des sexes* (Paris: Presses universitaires de France, 2001), 311–24.

23. For a full account of the remarks and their aftermath, see "Chronicle of a Controversy" at the Anita Borg Institute for Women and Technology website, http://www.anitaborg.org.

24. On the brain research, see Simon Baron-Cohen, *The Essential Difference: The Truth about the Male and Female Brain* (New York: Basic Books, 2003). See also Steven Pinker, *The Blank Slate: The Modern Denial of Human Nature* (New York: Viking, 2002). For a feminist critique, see Victoria L. Bergvall, "Ideologies of Nature and Nurture in Language and Gender Research," paper presented at IGALA3, the International Gender and Language Association Conference, Cornell University, Ithaca, NY, June 7, 2004. Harvey C. Mansfield, *Manliness* (New Haven: Yale University Press, 2006).

25. Virginia Valian, *Why So Slow? The Advancement of Women* (Cambridge: MIT Press, 1998), 11.

26. "A Study on the Status of Women Faculty in Science at MIT," in *The MIT Faculty Newsletter* 11.4 (1999) http://web.mit.edu/fnl/women. On the persistence of gender inequities at MIT, see Nancy Hopkins, "Diversification of a University Faculty: Observations on Hiring Women Faculty in the Schools of Science and Engineering at MIT," 2006. http://web.mit.edu/fnl/volume/184/hopkins.html.

27. Karen Jones, "Gender and Rationality," in *The Oxford Handbook of Rationality,* ed. Alfred R. Mele and Piers Rawling (Oxford: Oxford University Press, 2004), 301.

28. Jones, "Gender and Rationality"; Herta Nagl-Docekal, *Feminist Philosophy,* trans. Katharina Vester (Boulder, CO: Westview, 2004), 88, 121; Hilda L. Smith, "Intellectual Bases for Feminist Analyses: The Seventeenth and Eighteenth Centuries," in *Women and Reason,* ed. Elizabeth D. Harvey and Kathleen Okruhlik (Ann Arbor: University of Michigan Press, 1992), 22–23. On a similar paradox in postmodern thought, see Susan Wilson, "Postmodernism and the Enlightenment," 655–56.

29. Jones, "Gender and Rationality," 302; Nagl-Docekal, *Feminist Philosophy,* 97.

30. Nagl-Docekal, *Feminist Philosophy,* 119–20.

31. Ibid., 128.

32. Ibid., 132.

33. Fraisse, *Reason's Muse,* 191.

34. Jones, "Gender and Rationality," 315.

35. Helen Longino, "Circles of Reason: Some Feminist Reflections on Reason and Rationality," *Episteme* 2.1 (2005): 79.

36. Longino, "Circles of Reason," 82.

37. Miranda Fricker, "Feminism in Epistemology: Pluralism without Postmodernism," in *The Cambridge Companion to Feminism in Philosophy,* ed. Fricker and Jennifer Hornsby (Cambridge: Cambridge University Press, 2000), 157.

38. Ibid., 159, 160.

39. See, for example, Lorraine Code, "Taking Subjectivity into Account," in *Feminist Epistemologies,* ed. Linda Alcoff and Elizabeth Potter (New York: Routledge, 1993). See also Lorraine Code, *What Can She Know? Feminist*

Theory and the Construction of Knowledge (Ithaca: Cornell University Press, 1991).

40. See Jean Grimshaw, "Philosophy, Feminism and Universalism," *Radical Philosophy* 76 (1996): 19; and Alcoff and Potter, "Introduction: When Feminisms Intersect Epistemology," in *Feminist Epistemologies,* 1–14.

41. Iris Young, "Impartiality and the Civic Public: Some Implications of Feminist Critiques of Moral and Political Theory," in *Throwing Like a Girl and Other Essays in Feminist Philosophy and Social Theory* (Bloomington: Indiana University Press, 1990), 96, quoted in Robin Schott, introduction to *Feminist Interpretations of Immanuel Kant,* ed. Schott (University Park: Pennsylvania State University Press, 1997), 8.

42. Benhabib, *Situating the Self,* 6, 5.

43. Sandra Harding, *Whose Science? Whose Knowledge? Thinking from Women's Lives* (Ithaca: Cornell University Press, 1991), 124. See also Sandra Harding, "Rethinking Standpoint Epistemology: 'What Is Strong Objectivity'?," in *Feminist Epistemologies,* ed. Alcoff and Potter, 49–82.

44. These texts, originally published in the journal *Signs* in 1997, were reprinted in *The Feminist Standpoint Theory Reader: Intellectual and Political Controversies,* ed. Sandra Harding (New York: Routledge, 2004), 225–71. Harding provides a useful overview in "Introduction: Standpoint Theory as a Site of Political, Philosophic, and Scientific Debate," 1–15.

45. Hekman, "Reply," 271.

46. This is the main argument in Ezekiel, *"Le Women's Lib."*

47. Alcoff and Potter, eds., *Feminist Epistemologies.* See particularly Lynn Hankinson Nelson, "Epistemological Communities," 121–59; Nancy Tuana and Sandra Morgen, eds. *Engendering Rationalities* (Albany: State University of New York Press, 2001).

48. Nagl-Docekal, *Feminist Philosophy,* 92.

49. Judith Richards, "The Struggle to Naturalize Literary Studies," in *Engendering Rationalities,* ed. Tuana and Morgen, 316–17.

50. Johnson, "The Antinomies," 44.

51. Ibid., 45.

52. Ibid., 26.

53. Dena Goodman, "Difference: An Enlightenment Concept," in *What's Left of Enlightenment? A Postmodern Question,* ed. Keith Michael Baker and Peter Hanns Reill (Stanford: Stanford University Press, 2001), 132–36.

54. Baker and Reill, introduction to *What's Left of Enlightenment?,* 2.

55. Lawrence E. Klein, "Enlightenment as Conversation," in *What's Left of Enlightenment?,* ed. Baker and Reill, 150.

56. September 6, 1764, *OC* 1:295, *Correspondence,* 170.

57. Klein, "Enlightenment as Conversation," 164.

58. Gordon, "On the Supposed Obsolescence," 220. For remarks in a similar spirit, see Susan Wilson, "Postmodernism and the Enlightenment," 658.

59. Iris Marion Young, "Structural Injustice and Political Responsibility," keynote address, annual meeting of the Society for Phenomenology and Existential Philosophy, Chicago, October 2002. See also Paul Ricoeur's insights

about narrative and the work of the "productive imagination" in *Time and Narrative* vol. 2, especially 68–70.

60. Ludwig Wittgenstein, *On Certainty* (New York: Harper Torchbooks, 1972), ¶ 378, quoted in Lorraine Code, "The Unicorn in the Garden," in *Women and Reason*, ed. Harvey and Okruhlik, 276.

61. *Mme Riccoboni's Letters,* 406.

62. Claire de Duras, *Ourika: The Original French Text* (New York: Modern Language Association, 1994), 27; Duras, *Ourika: An English Translation*, trans. John Fowles (New York: Modern Language Association, 1994), 27, translation modified.

Bibliography

Adorno, Theodor, and Max Horkheimer. *Dialectic of Enlightenment: Philosophical Fragments.* 1969. Edited by Gunzelin Schmid Noerr. Translated by Edmund Jephcott. Stanford: Stanford University Press, 2002.

Alcoff, Linda, and Elizabeth Potter, eds. *Feminist Epistemologies.* New York: Routledge, 1993.

Altman, Janet. "A Woman's Place in the Enlightenment Sun: The Case of F. de Graffigny." *Romance Quarterly* 38.3 (1991): 261–72.

Armelin, Anne-Marie. *Preuves de noblesse pour l'entrée à la maison royale de l'enfant-Jésus,* Les cahiers nobles 34 et 35. Paris, 1968.

Bacon, Francis. *Novum Organon.* 1620. Translated and edited by Peter Urbach and John Gilson. Chicago: Open Court, 1994.

Badinter, Élizabeth, and Danielle Muzerelle, eds. *Madame du Châtelet, la femme des Lumières.* Paris: Bibliothèque nationale de France, 2006.

Baker, Keith Michael, and Peter Hans Reill, ed. and intro. *What's Left of Enlightenment? A Postmodern Question.* Stanford: Stanford University Press, 2001.

Baron-Cohen, Simon. *The Essential Difference: The Truth about the Male and Female Brain.* New York: Basic Books, 2003.

Bastide, Jean-François. *Le Monde.* Vols. 3 and 4. Amsterdam and Paris: Bauche, Duchesne et al., 1761.

Bayle, Pierre. *Dictionnaire historique et critique.* Rotterdam: Reinier Leers, 1697.

Beach, Cecilia, comp. *French Women Playwrights before the Twentieth Century: A Checklist.* Westport, CT: Greenwood, 1994.

Beauvoir, Simone de. *Le deuxième sexe.* 2 vols. Paris: Gallimard, 1949.

Benhabib, Seyla. *Situating the Self: Gender, Community and Postmodernism in Contemporary Ethics.* New York: Routledge, 1992.

Bissière, Michèle "Graffigny, Riccoboni, et la tradition des *Lettres persanes,*" *Postscript* 12 (1995): 9–21.

Bloch, Jean. "Discourses of Female Education in the Writings of Eighteenth-Century French Women." In *Women, Gender, and Enlightenment.* Edited by Sarah Knott and Barbara Taylor. New York: Palgrave Macmillan, 2005. 243–58.

Bourque, Kevin. "'Tout est en désordre dans la ruche': Republican Discourse, Patriarchal Strategy, Gendered Labour and the Bees of the *Encyclopédie,*" *SVEC* 12 (2000). 301–70.

Brewer, Daniel. *The Discourse of Enlightenment in Eighteenth-Century France: Diderot and the Art of Philosophizing.* Cambridge: Cambridge University Press, 1993.

Bronner, Stephen Eric. *Reclaiming the Enlightenment: Toward a Politics of Radical Engagement.* New York: Columbia University Press, 2004.

Butler, Judith. *Bodies that Matter: On the Discursive Limits of "Sex."* New York: Routledge, 1993.

———. *Gender Trouble: Feminism and the Subversion of Identity.* New York: Routledge, 1990.

Cazenobe, Colette. *Au malheur des dames: Le roman féminin au XVIIIe siècle.* Paris: Champion, 2006.

Chabut, Marie-Hélène. "Isabelle de Charrière écrivaine et lectrice des Lumières." In *Belle de Zuylen / Isabelle de Charrière: Education, creation, reception.* Ed. Suzan van Dijk, Valérie Cossy, Monique Moser-Verrey, and Madeleine van Strien-Chardonneau. Amsterdam: Rodopi, 2006. 127–47.

———. "*Les lettres trouvées dans des porte-feuilles d'émigrés* d'Isabelle de Charrière: Violence politique et violence domestique, ou pour une 'raison sensible.'" In *Violence et fiction jusqu'à la Révolution.* Edited by Martine Debaisieux and Gabrielle Verdier. Tübingen: G. Narr, 1998. 403–10.

———. "Louvoyer pour innover: *Trois femmes* d'Isabelle de Charrière." In *Ecriture de la ruse.* Edited by Elzbieta Grodek. Amsterdam: Rodopi, 2000. 241–51.

Charrière, Isabelle de. "Des Auteurs et des livres." Unpublished manuscript. Bibliothèque Publique et Universitaire de Neuchâtel, "Fragments," MS 1387 / 13/ 2.

———. *Letters of Mistress Henley Published by Her Friend.* Translated by Philip Stewart and Jean Vaché. New York: Modern Language Association, 1993.

———. *Oeuvres complètes d'Isabelle de Charrière / Belle de Zuylen.* 10 vols. Edited by Jean-Daniel Candaux et al. Amsterdam: van Oorschot, Geneva: Slatkine, 1979.

———. *There Are No Letters Like Yours: The Correspondence of Isabelle de Charrière and Constant d'Hermenches.* Translated and with introduction and annotations by Janet Whatley and Malcolm Whatley. Lincoln: University of Nebraska Press, 2000.

Chartier, Roger. *The Cultural Origins of the French Revolution.* Translated Lydia Cochrane. Durham, NC: Duke University Press, 1991.

———. "Reading and Reading Practices" in Kors, *Encyclopedia of the Enlightenment.* Vol. 3. Oxford: Oxford University Press, 2003. 399–404.

Code, Lorraine. "Taking Subjectivity into Account." In *Feminist Epistemologies.* Edited by Linda Alcoff and Elizabeth Potter. New York: Routledge, 1993. 15–48.

Cohen, Sarah R. "Masquerade as Mode in the French Fashion Print." In *The Clothes That Wear Us: Essays on Dressing and Transgressing in Eighteenth-Century Culture.* Edited by Jessica Munns and Penny Richards. Newark: University of Delaware Press, 1999. 174–207.

Colebrook, Claire. *Gender.* New York: Palgrave Macmillan, 2004.

Condillac, Etienne Bonnot, abbé de. *Essai sur l'origine des connaissances humaines,* in *Oeuvres complètes.* Paris: 1821–22; rpt Geneva, 1970.

Condorcet [Marie Jean Antoine Caritat, marquis de]. "Sur l'admission des femmes au droit de cite." In *Oeuvres de Condorcet.* Vol. 10. Paris: Firmin Didot, 1847.

Cook, Elizabeth Heckendorn. *Epistolary Bodies: Gender and Genre in the Eighteenth-Century Republic of Letters.* Stanford: Stanford University Press, 1996.

Cope, Bill, and Mary Kalantzis, eds., *Multiliteracies: Literacy Learning and the Design of Social Futures.* London: Routledge, 2000.

Cossy, Valérie. "Isabelle de Charrière, Frances Burney et le métier d'écrivain." In *Une Européenne: Isabelle de Charrière en son siècle.* Edited by Doris Jakubec and Jean-Daniel Candaux. Hauterive-Neuchâtel: Attinger, 1994. 125–40.

Coudreuse, Anne. "Pleurer en bref: le pathétique dans l'*Histoire du marquis de Cressy,* nouvelle de Mme Riccoboni." *Littératures classiques* 62 (2007): 149–56.

Coulet, Henri. "Isabelle de Charrière, femme des Lumières?" In *Une Européenne: Isabelle de Charrière en son siècle.* Edited by Doris Jakubec and Jean-Daniel Candaux. Hauterive-Neuchâtel: Attinger, 1994. 9–23.

Courtney, Cecil P. *Belle van Zuylen and Philosophy.* Utrecht: Faculteit der Letteren Universiteit Utrecht, 1995.

———. Roundtable presentation on "La place d'Isabelle de Charrière dans l'histoire littéraire," presented at the conference *Belle van Zuylen / Isabelle de Charrière: Education & création,* Utrecht, April 7, 2005.

Cragg, Olga B. Introduction to Riccoboni, *Histoire du marquis de Cressy.* 1758. Edited by Cragg. *SVEC* 266. Oxford: Voltaire Foundation, 1989: 1–123.

Crosby, Emily A. *Une romancière oubliée: Madame Riccoboni.* 1924. Geneva: Slatkine Reprints, 1970.

Curtis, Judith. *"Divine Thalie": The Career of Jeanne Quinault, SVEC* 8. Oxford: Voltaire Foundation, 2007.

Cushman, Ellen, et al., eds., *Literacy: A Critical Sourcebook.* Boston: Bedford–St. Martin's, 2001.

Davies, Simon. *"Lettres d'une Péruvienne,* 1977–1997: The Present State of Studies," *SVEC* 05 (2000): 295–324.

DeJean, Joan. *Tender Geographies: Women and the Origins of the Novel in France.* New York: Columbia University Press, 1991.

Descartes, René. *Discourse on Method and Meditations on First Philosophy.* Translated by Donald A. Cress. 4th ed. Indianapolis: Hackett, 1998.

———. *Discours de la méthode.* 1637. Paris: Larousse, 1972.

———. *Méditations métaphysiques.* 1641. Paris: Larousse, 1973.

Diaconoff, Suellen. *Through the Reading Glass: Women, Books, and Sex in the French Enlightenment.* Albany: State University of New York Press, 2005.

Dictionnaire de L'Académie française, 4th edition, 1762. http://www.lib.uchi-gaco/edu/efts/ARTFL/projects/dicos/ACADEMIE/QUATRIEME/

Diderot, Denis. *Correspondance de Diderot.* 16 vols. Edited by Georges Roth. Paris: Minuit, 1956.

———. *Éléments de physiologie* in *Oeuvres complètes de Diderot.* Edited by J. Assézat. Paris: Garnier Frères, 1875.

———. *Pensées philosophiques.* 1746. In *Oeuvres philosophiques.* Edited by Paul Vernière. Paris: Garnier, 1961.

———. "Sur les femmes." *Qu'est-ce qu'une femme?* Edited by Elizabeth Badinter. Paris: P.O.L., 1989. 163–85.

Dijk, Suzan van. "Madame Riccoboni: Romancière ou journaliste?" *SVEC* 304 (1993): 772–75.

Dijk, Suzan van, et al., eds. *Belle de Zuylen / Isabelle de Charrière: Education, creation, reception.* Amsterdam: Rodopi, 2006.

Dobie, Madeleine. "Romantic Psychology and Kantian Ethics in the Novels of Isabelle de Charrière." *Eighteeth-Century Fiction* 10.3 (1998): 303–24.

Du Boccage, Anne-Marie Fiquet. *Recueil des oeuvres de Madame Du Boccage.* Lyon, 1764.

Duras, Claire de. *Ourika: The Original French Text.* New York: MLA, 1994. Translated by John Fowles as *Ourika: An English Translation.* New York: MLA, 1994.

Encyclopédie, ou dictionnaire raisonné des sciences, des arts et des métiers. 17 vols. Paris: Briasson, Le Breton, 1751–65. Facsimile Stuttgart-Bad Cannstatt: Frommann, 1966.

Étienne, Servais. *Le genre romanesque en France depuis l'apparition de la "Nouvelle Héloïse" jusqu'aux approches de la Révolution.* Brussels: Lamertin, 1922.

Ezekiel, Judith. "*Le Women's Lib:* Made in France." *European Journal of Women's Studies* 9.3 (2002): 345–61.

Farge, Arlette. *Subversive Words: Public Opinion in Eighteenth-Century France.* Translated by Rosemary Morris. University Park: Pennsylvania State University Press, 1994.

Favre, Robert. *La Mort dans la littérature et la pensée françaises au Siècle des Lumières.* Lyon: Presses universitaires de Lyon, 1978.

Flax, Jane. *Disputed Subjects: Essays on Psychoanalysis, Politics and Philosophy.* New York: Routledge, 1993.

Fleming, Marie. "Women's Place in Communicative Reason." In *Women and Reason.* Edited by Elizabeth D. Harvey and Kathleen Okruhlik. Ann Arbor: University of Michigan Press, 1992. 245–62.

Foucault, Michel. "What is Enlightenment?" Translated by Catherine Porter et al. In *Ethics: Subjectivity and Truth.* Edited by Paul Rabinow. New York: The New Press, 1997. 303–19.

Fourny, Diane. "Language and Reality in Françoise de Graffigny's *Lettres d'une Péruvienne.*" *Eighteenth-Century Fiction* 4 (1992): 221–38.

Fraisse, Geneviève. *Reason's Muse: Sexual Difference and the Birth of Democracy*. Translated by Jane Marie Todd. Chicago: University of Chicago Press, 1994.

Fraser, Nancy. "What's Critical about Critical Theory? The Case of Habermas and Gender." *New German Critique* 35 (1985): 97–131.

Fricker, Miranda. "Feminism in Epistemology: Pluralism without Postmodernism." In *The Cambridge Companion to Feminism in Philosophy*. Edited by Miranda Fricker and Jennifer Hornsby. Cambridge: Cambridge University Press, 2000. 146–65.

Furetière, Antoine. *Le Dictionnaire universel d'Antoine Furetière*. 1690. 3 vols. Paris: Le Robert, 1978.

Gay, Peter. "The Living Enlightenment," The Tanner Lectures on Human Values, delivered at University of Toronto, October 7, 1996.

Gerould, Daniel, ed. and intro. *Gallant and Libertine: Divertissements and Parades of Eighteenth-Century France*. New York: Performing Arts Journal Publications, 1983.

Gethner, Perry. "Notice" on Françoise de Graffigny's *Cénie*. In *Femmes dramaturges en France (1650–1750) Pièces choisies*. Edited by Gethner. Paris: Papers on French Seventeenth Century Literature, 1993. 317–27.

———. "Les *pièces nouvelles* de Graffigny: de la comédie sentimentale au drame." *SVEC* 12 (2004): 41–49.

Ginisty, Paul. "Les souvenirs sentimentaux de Mme Riccoboni." In *Mémoires et souvenirs de comédiennes (XVIIIe siècle)*. Paris: Louis Michaud, 1914.

Goodman, Dena. "Difference: An Enlightenment Concept." In *What's Left of Enlightenment? A Postmodern Question*. Edited by Keith Michael Baker and Peter Hanns Reill. Stanford: Stanford University Press, 2001. 129–47.

———. *The Republic of Letters: A Cultural History of the French Enlightenment*. Ithaca: Cornell University Press, 1994.

Gordon, Daniel. "On the Supposed Obsolescence of the French Enlightenment." In *Postmodernism and the Enlightenment: New Perspectives in Eighteenth-Century French Intellectual History*. Edited by Daniel Gordon. New York: Routledge, 2001. 201–21.

Gordon, Daniel, ed. and intro. *Postmodernism and the Enlightenment: New Perspectives in Eighteenth-Century French Intellectual History*. New York: Routledge, 2001.

Gossman, Lionel. "Literature and Society in the Early Enlightenment: The Case of Marivaux." *MLN* 82.3 (1967): 306–33.

———. "What Was Enlightenment?" In Hollier, ed. *A New History of French Literature*. Cambridge: Harvard University Press, 1989. 487–95.

Graffigny, Françoise de. *Cénie*. 1750. In *Femmes dramaturges en France (1650–1750): Pièces choisies*. Edited and introduction by Perry Gethner. Paris: Papers on French Seventeenth Century Literature, 1993. 315–87.

———. *Correspondance de Mme de Graffigny*. Edited by J. A. Dainard et al. 12 vols. to date. Oxford: Voltaire Foundation, 1985–2008.

———. *Françoise de Graffigny: Choix de lettres.* Edited by English Showalter. Oxford: Voltaire Foundation, 2001.

———. *Letters from a Peruvian Woman.* Translated by David Kornacker. New York: Modern Language Association, 1993.

———. *Lettres d'une Péruvienne.* 1747 or 1748. Edited and introduction by Jonathan Mallinson. Oxford: Voltaire Foundation, 2002.

———. *Oeuvres posthumes de Madame de Grafigny.* Paris: Segaud, 1770. Includes *Phaza.*

———. "La Réunion du bon sens et de l'esprit." Unpublished manuscript. Gen. Mss. 353, Graffigny Papers, Box 67, vol.83, Beinecke Library, Yale University.

Gravelot [pseudonym of Hubert François Bourguignon d'Anville] and Cochin. *Iconologie par figures ou traité complet des allégories, emblèmes etc.* 4 vols. Paris: Lattré, n.d. [1791].

Gray, John. *Enlightenment's Wake.* New York: Routledge, 1997.

Grayson, Vera. *The Genesis and Reception of Mme de Graffigny's* Lettres d'une Péruvienne *and* Cénie. *SVEC* 336. Oxford: Voltaire Foundation (1996): 1–152.

Grimm, Baron de. *Correspondance littéraire.* Paris: Longchamps: F. Buisson, 1813.

Grimshaw, Jean. "Philosophy, Feminism and Universalism." *Radical Philosophy* 76 (1996): 19–28.

Grosz, Elizabeth. "Bodies and Knowledges: Feminism and the Crisis of Reason." In *Feminist Epistemologies.* Edited by Linda Alcoff and Elizabeth Potter. New York: Routledge, 1993. 187–215.

Gutwirth, Madelyn. "ASECS Women's Caucus Response." In *A History of the ASECS Women's Caucus 1975–2005.* Edited by Alison Conway. American Society for Eighteenth-Century Studies, 2005. 7–10.

Habermas, Jürgen. *The Structural Transformation of the Public Sphere: An Inquiry into a Category of Bourgeois Society.* 1962. Translated by Thomas Burger with Frederick Lawrence. Cambridge: MIT Press, 1989.

Hall, David L., and Roger T. Ames. *Anticipating China: Thinking Through the Narratives of Chinese and Western Culture.* Albany: State University of New York Press, 1995.

Halperin, David. "Forgetting Foucault: Acts, Identities, and the History of Sexuality." *Representations* 63 (1998): 93–120.

Harding, Sandra, ed. *The Feminist Standpoint Theory Reader: Intellectual and Political Controversies.* New York: Routledge, 2004.

Harding, Sandra. *Whose Science? Whose Knowledge? Thinking from Women's Lives.* Ithaca: Cornell University Press, 1991.

Hardwick, Julie. "Seeking Separations: Gender, Marriages, and Household Economies in Early Modern France." *French Historical Studies* 21.1 (1998): 157–80.

Harol, Corrine. "Faking It: Female Virginity and Pamela's Virtue." *Eighteenth-Century Fiction* 16.2 (2004): 197–216.

Harrison, Colin. "Les portraits de Mme de Graffigny." In *Françoise de Graffigny, femme de lettres. Écriture et réception.* Edited by Jonathan Mallinson. *SVEC* 12 (2004): 195–211.

Harth, Erica. *Cartesian Women: Versions and Subversions of Rational Discourse in the Old Regime.* Ithaca: Cornell University Press, 1992.

Hatfield, Gary. "Rationalism." In *Encyclopedia of the Enlightenment.* Vol. 3. Edited by Alan Charles Kors. Oxford: Oxford University Press, 2003. 392–98.

Hatfield, Gary. "Reason." In *Encyclopedia of the Enlightenment.* Vol. 3. Edited by Alan Charles Kors. Oxford: Oxford University Press, 2003. 404–9.

Hayes, Julie Candler. *Reading the French Enlightenment: System and Subversion.* Cambridge: Cambridge University Press, 1999.

Hazard, Paul. *La crise de la conscience européenne, 1680–1715.* Paris: Fayard, 1961. Translated as *The European Mind, 1680–1715.* Cleveland: World Publication Company, 1968.

Heath, Stephen. "Joan Riviere and the Masquerade." In *Gender.* Edited by Anna Tripp. New York: Palgrave, 2000. 139–53.

Hekman, Susan J. *Gender and Knowledge: Elements of a Postmodern Feminism.* Boston: Northeastern University Press, 1990.

———. "Reply to Hartsock, Collins, Harding, and Smith." In *The Feminist Standpoint Theory Reader: Intellectual and Political Controversies.* Edited by Sandra Harding. New York: Routledge, 2004. 269–71.

Helvétius. *De l'Esprit.* Edited and introduction by Guy Besse. Paris: Éditions sociales, 1959.

Hermsen, Joke J. "Now Foolish Then Wise: Belle van Zuylen's Game with Sexual Identity." In Linda Lopez McAlister, ed., *Hypatia's Daughters: Fifteen Hundred Years of Women Philosophers.* Bloomington: Indiana University Press, 1996. 165–80.

Hesse, Carla. *The Other Enlightenment: How French Women Became Modern.* Princeton: Princeton University Press, 2001.

———. "Reading Signatures: Female Authorship and Revolutionary Law in France, 1750–1850." *Eighteenth-Century Studies* 22 (1989): 469–87.

Hollier, Denis, ed. *A New History of French Literature.* Cambridge: Harvard University Press, 1989.

Hufton, Olwen. "Women, Work, and Family." *A History of Women in the West.* Vol. 3. Edited by Natalie Zemon Davis and Arlette Farge. Cambridge: Belknap Press, 1993. 15–45.

Hunt, Lynn. *The Family Romance of the French Revolution.* Berkeley: University of California Press, 1993.

Inguenaud, Marie-Thérèse. "La Grosse et le Monstre: Histoire d'une haine." *SVEC* 1 (2006): 65–90.

Israel, Jonathan. *Enlightenment Contested: Philosophy, Modernity, and the Emancipation of Man 1670–1752.* Oxford: Oxford University Press, 2006.

———. *Radical Enlightenment: Philosophy and the Making of Modernity 1650–1750.* Oxford: Oxford University Press, 2001.

Jackson, Susan K. "Publishing Without Perishing: Isabelle de Charrière a.k.a. la mouche du coche." In Dena Goodman and Elizabeth Goldsmith, eds., *Going Public: Women and Publishing in Early Modern France*. Ithaca: Cornell University Press, 1995.

Jaggar, Alison M. "Freethinking?" In *Singing in the Fire: Stories of Women in Philosophy*. Edited by Linda Martín Alcoff. New York: Rowman and Littlefield, 2003. 57–70.

———. "Love and Knowledge: Emotion and Feminist Epistemology." In *Women, Knowledge, and Reality: Explorations in Feminist Philosophy*. Edited by Ann Garry and Marilyn Pearsall. New York: Routledge, 1989.

Jaquier, Claire. "Un roman à deux coups." Chap. 5 in Jaquier, *L'Erreur des désirs: Romans sensibles au XVIIIe siècle*. Lausanne: Payot, 1998. 139–50.

Jensen, Katharine Ann. *Writing Love: Letters, Women, and the Novel in France, 1605–1776*. Carbondale: Southern Illinois University Press, 1995.

Johnson, Pauline. "The Antinomies of the Age of Enlightenment." Chap. 2 in Johnson, *Feminism as Radical Humanism*. Boulder, CO: Westview, 1994.

Jones, Karen. "Gender and Rationality." In *The Oxford Handbook of Rationality*. Edited by Alfred R. Mele and Piers Rawling. Oxford: Oxford University Press, 2004. 301–19.

Jones, Vivien, ed. and intro. *Women in the Eighteenth Century: Constructions of Femininity*. London: Routledge, 1990.

Jullien, Jean-Auguste. *Histoire anecdotique et raisonnée du théâtre italien, depuis son rétablissment en France jusqu'à l'année 1769*. 7 vols. Paris: Lacombe, 1769.

Kant, Immanuel. "An Answer to the Question: 'What is Enlightenment?'" Translated by H. B. Nisbet. In *Kant: Political Writings*. Edited by Hans Reiss. Cambridge: Cambridge University Press, 1991. 54–60.

———. *Observations on the Feeling of the Beautiful and Sublime*. Translated by John T. Goldthwaite. Berkeley: University of California Press, 1960.

Karp, Sergueï, ed. *Être dix-huitiémiste*. Ferney-Voltaire: Centre international d'étude du XVIIIe siècle, 2003.

Kelly, Joan. "Early Feminist Theory and the *Querelle des Femmes*, 1400–1789." Chap. 4 in Kelly, *Women, History, and Theory*. Chicago: University of Chicago Press, 1984.

Klein, Lawrence E. "Enlightenment as Conversation." In *What's Left of Enlightenment? A Postmodern Question*. Edited by Keith Michael Baker and Peter Hanns Reill. Stanford: Stanford University Press, 2001. 148–66.

Kors, Alan Charles. *D'Holbach's Coterie: An Enlightenment in Paris*. Princeton: Princeton University Press, 1976.

———. "Holbach, Paul-Henri Thiry D'." In *Encyclopedia of the Enlightenment*. Vol. 2. Edited by Kors. Oxford: Oxford University Press, 2003. 213–15.

Kors, Alan Charles, ed. *Encyclopedia of the Enlightenment*. 4 vols. New York: Oxford University Press, 2003.

Laclos, Choderlos de. *Oeuvres complètes*. Pléiade. Edited by Laurent Versini. Paris: Gallimard, 1951.

Lambert, Anne-Thérèse de. "Réflexions nouvelles sur les femmes par une Dame de la Cour de France." 1727. In *Oeuvres*. Edited by Robert Granderoute. Paris: Honoré Champion, 1990.

Landes, Joan. *Visualizing the Nation: Gender, Representation, and Revolution in Eighteenth-Century France*. Ithaca: Cornell University Press, 2001.

———. *Women and the Public Sphere in the Age of the French Revolution*. Ithaca: Cornell University Press, 1988.

Lanni, Dominique. "La mort de Socrate, de Voltaire à Bernardin de Saint-Pierre." In *Le philosophe sur les planches: l'image du philosophe dans le théâtre des Lumières*. Edited by Pierre Hartmann. Strasbourg: Presses universitaires de Strasbourg, 2004. 287–94.

Lanser, Susan Sniader. *Fictions of Authority: Women Writers and Narrative Voice*. Ithaca: Cornell University Press, 1992.

———. "Toward a Feminist Narratology." In *Feminisms: An Anthology of Literary Theory and Criticism*, rev. ed. Edited by Robyn R. Warhol and Diane Price Herndl. New Brunswick: Rutgers University Press, 1997. 674–93.

Laqueur, Thomas. *Making Sex: Body and Gender from the Greeks to Freud*. Cambridge: Harvard University Press, 1990.

LeDoeuff, Michèle. *The Philosophical Imaginary*. Translated by Colin Gordon. London: Athlone, 1989.

———. *The Sex of Knowing*. Translated by Kathryn Hamer and Lorraine Code. New York: Routledge, 2003.

Letzter, Jacqueline. "Isabelle de Charrière's *Sainte Anne*, or a Woman's Wayward Quest for Knowledge." *Studies in Eighteenth-Century Culture* 26 (1998): 209–30.

Lilti, Antoine. *Le Monde des salons: Sociabilité et mondanité à Paris au XVIIIe siècle*. Paris: Fayard, 2006.

Lloyd, Genevieve. *The Man of Reason: "Male" and "Female" in Western Philosophy*. 2nd ed. Minneapolis: University of Minnesota Press, 1993.

Longino, Helen. "Circles of Reason: Some Feminist Reflections on Reason and Rationality." *Episteme* 2.1 (2005): 79–88.

MacIntyre, Alasdair. *After Virtue: A Study in Moral Theory*. Notre Dame: University of Notre Dame Press, 1984.

Malherbe, Michel. "Reason." In *The Cambridge History of Eighteenth-Century Philosophy*. Edited by Knud Haakonssen. New York: Cambridge University Press, 2006. 319–42.

Mallinson, Jonathan. Introduction to Françoise de Graffigny, *Lettres d'une Péruvienne*. Edited by Jonathan Mallinson. Oxford: Voltaire Foundation, 2002. 1–92.

Mandeville, Bernard. *Bernard Mandeville: The Fable of the Bees and Other Writings*. Edited and introduction by E. J. Hundert. Indianapolis: Hackett, 1997.

Mansfield, Harvey C. *Manliness*. New Haven: Yale University Press, 2006.

Mat-Hasquin, Michèle. "Dramaturgie et démystification dans les comédies d'Isabelle de Charrière." *Études sur le XVIIIe siècle* 8 (1981): 53–66.

Mauzi, Robert. *L'Idée du bonheur dans la littérature et la pensée françaises au XVIIIe siècle.* 4th ed. Paris: Armand Colin, 1969.

May, Georges. "Observations on an Allegory: The Frontispiece of the *Encyclopédie.*" *Diderot Studies* 16 (1973): 159–74.

Maza, Sara. "The Diamond Necklace Affair Revisited (1785–1786): The Case of the Missing Queen." In *Eroticism and the Body Politic.* Edited by Lynn Hunt. Baltimore: Johns Hopkins University Press, 1991. 63–89.

Mellor, Anne K. "Feminist Theory." In *Encyclopedia of the Enlightenment.* Vol. 2. Edited by Kors. New York: Oxford University Press, 2003. 39–44.

Mercier, Louis-Sébastien. *Le Tableau de Paris.* Introduction and selections by Jeffry Kaplow. Paris: François Maspero, 1982.

Merrick, Jeffrey. "Royal Bees: The Gender Politics of the Beehive in Early Modern Europe." In *Studies in Eighteenth-Century Culture* 18. Edited by John W. Yolton and Leslie Ellen Brown. East Lansing, MI: Colleagues Press, 1988. 7–37.

———. "Suicide and Politics in Pre-Revolutionary France." *Eighteenth-Century Life* 30.2 (2006): 32–47.

Meyers, Diana. "Feminist Perspectives on the Self." In *The Stanford Encyclopedia of Philosophy.* Edited by Edward N. Zalta. 1999. http://plato.stanford.edu/entries/feminism-self/.

Meyers, Diana, ed. *Feminists Rethink the Self.* Boulder, CO: Westview, 1997.

Miller, Nancy K. "The Exquisite Cadavers: Women in Eighteenth-Century Fiction." *Diacritics* (1975): 37–43.

———. *French Dressing: Women, Men and Ancien Régime Fiction.* New York: Routledge, 1995.

Mills, Charles W. "Defending the Radical Enlightenment." In *Social Philosophy Today: Truth and Objectivity in Social Ethics.* Edited by Cheryl Hughes. Charlottesville: Philosophy Documentation Center, 2003. 9–29.

Morgan, Robin. "Goodbye to All That (#2)." http://www.womensmediacenter.com/ex/contents/020108_main.html.

Moser-Verrey, Monique. "Leaving the Castle: The Avenues of Creation." In *Belle de Zuylen / Isabelle de Charrière: Education, creation, reception.* Edited by Suzan van Dijk, Valérie Cossy, Monique Moser-Verrey, and Madeleine van Strien-Chardonneau. Amsterdam: Rodopi, 2006. 17–45.

Moya, Paula. *Learning From Experience: Minority Identities, Multicultural Struggles.* Berkeley: University of California Press, 2002.

Nagl-Docekal, Herta. *Feminist Philosophy.* Translated by Katharina Vester. Boulder, CO: Westview, 2004.

Nicholls, James. Introduction to *Mme Riccoboni's Letters to David Hume, David Garrick and Sir Robert Liston: 1764–1783.* Edited by James Nicholls. *SVEC* 149. Oxford: Voltaire Foundation, 1976. 11–30.

Nietzsche, Friedrich. "On the Uses and Disadvantages of History for Life." In *Untimely Meditations.* Translated by R. J. Hollingdale. Cambridge: Cambridge University Press, 1983. 57–123.

Nussbaum, Martha. *Love's Knowledge: Essays on Philosophy and Literature.* New York: Oxford University Press, 1990.

———. *Poetic Justice: The Literary Imagination and Public Life.* Boston: Beacon Press, 1995.

Offen, Karen. "Reclaiming the European Enlightenment for Feminism." In *Perspectives on Feminist Political Thought in European History: From the Middle Ages to the Present.* Edited by Tjitske Akkerman and Siep Stuurman (London: Routledge, 1998), 85–103.

O'Neal, John C. *The Authority of Experience: Sensationist Theory in the French Enlightenment.* University Park: Pennsylvania State University Press, 1996.

Orwin, Clifford. "Rousseau's Socratism." *The Journal of Politics* 60.1 (1998): 174–87.

Outram, Dorinda. *The Enlightenment.* 2nd ed. Cambridge: Cambridge University Press, 2005.

Packer, Dorothy S. "'La Calotte' and the 18th-Century French Vaudeville." *Journal of the American Musicological Society* 23.1 (1970): 61–83.

Piau-Gillot, Colette. "Comment s'échapper du second rayon? ou le parcours littéraire de Marie-Jeanne Riccoboni." *Littératures Classiques* 31 (1997): 165–76.

Pinker, Steven. *The Blank Slate: The Modern Denial of Human Nature.* New York: Viking, 2002.

Pizan, Christine de. *Le Livre de la Cité des Dames.* 1405. Translated by Earl Jeffrey Richards as *The Book of the City of Ladies.* New York: Persea, 1982.

Plato: Complete Works. Edited by John M. Cooper. Indianapolis: Hackett, 1997.

Plato. *Symposium.* Translated and edited by Robin Waterfield. New York: Oxford University Press, 1994.

Poullain de la Barre, François. *De l'égalité des deux sexes.* Paris: Jean Du Puis, 1673.

Quéro, Dominique. *Momus philosophe: Recherches sur une figure littéraire du XVIIIe siècle.* Paris: Honoré Champion, 1995.

Ravel, Jeffrey. "France." In *Encyclopedia of the Enlightenment.* Edited by Alan Kors. Vol. 2. New York: Oxford University Press, 2003. 60–65.

Raynal, Guillaume-Thomas. *Nouvelles littéraires manuscrites (1747–1755),* bound with *Correspondance littéraire, philosophique et critique par Grimm, Diderot, Raynal, Meister, etc.,* 1. Paris: Garnier Frères, 1877.

Reiss, Timothy J. *The Meaning of Literature.* Ithaca: Cornell University Press, 1992.

Restif de la Bretonne, Nicolas-Edme. *Les Contemporaines.* Vols. 39–40. Geneva: Slatkine Reprints, 1988.

———. *Les Parisiennes, ou XL caractères généraux pris dans les moeurs actuelles.* 4 vols. Neuchâtel and Paris: Guillot, 1787.

———. *La Paysanne pervertie.* Paris: Garnier, 1972.

Riccoboni, Marie Jeanne. *L'Abeille*. In *Recueil de pièces détachées*. Paris: Humblot, 1765.

———. *Histoire du marquis de Cressy*. 1758. Edited by Olga B. Cragg. *SVEC* 266 (Oxford: Voltaire Foundation, 1989): 1–123.

———. *Lettres de Mistriss Fanni Butlerd à Mylord Charles Alfred*. 1757. Edited and introduction by Joan Hinde Stewart. Geneva: Droz, 1979.

———. *Lettres de Mylord Rivers à Sir Charles Cardigan*. 1776. Introduction and notes Olga B. Cragg. Geneva: Droz, 1992.

———. *Mme Riccoboni's Letters to David Hume, David Garrick and sir Robert Liston: 1764–1783*. Edited by James Nicholls. *SVEC* 149 (Oxford: Voltaire Foundation, 1976): 11–471.

Richards, Judith. "The Struggle to Naturalize Literary Studies." In *Engendering Rationalities*. Edited by Nancy Tuana and Sandra Morgen. Albany: State University of New York Press, 2001. 315–33.

Ricoeur, Paul. *Time and Narrative*. 3 vols. Translated by Kathleen McLaughlin and David Pellauer. Chicago: University of Chicago Press, 1984.

Riviere, Joan. "Womanliness as a Masquerade." 1929. In *Gender*. Edited by Anna Tripp. New York: Palgrave, 2000. 130–38.

Robb, Bonnie Arden. *Félicité de Genlis: Motherhood in the Margins*. Newark: University of Delaware Press, 2008.

Robert, Raymonde. *Le conte de fées littéraire en France de la fin du XVIIe à la fin du XVIIIe siècle*. Nancy: Presses universitaires de Nancy, 1981.

Rogers, Adrienne. "Woman and the Law." In *French Women and the Age of Enlightenment*. Edited by Samia I. Spencer. Bloomington: Indiana University Press, 1984. 33–48.

Rooksby, Emma. "Moral Theory in the Fiction of Isabelle de Charrière: The Case of *Three Women*." *Hypatia* 20.1 (2005): 1–20.

Rorty, Richard. "The Humanistic Intellectual: Eleven Theses." Chap. 8 in *Philosophy and Social Hope*. New York: Penguin, 1999.

Rousseau, Jean-Jacques. *Émile, ou de l'éducation*. 1762. Paris: Garnier-Flammarion, 1966. Translated by Barbara Foxley as *Emile*. London: Dent, 1957.

———. *Julie, ou la nouvelle Héloïse*. Paris: Garnier-Flammarion, 1967.

Roussel, Pierre. *Système physique et moral de la femme*. 1775. Paris: Caille and Ravier, 1809.

Russ, Joanna. *How to Suppress Women's Writing*. Austin: University of Texas Press, 1983.

Russo, Elena. *Styles of Enlightenment: Taste, Politics, and Authorship in Eighteenth-Century France*. Baltimore: Johns Hopkins University Press, 2007.

Samson, Guillemette. *La présence masculine dans le théâtre d'Isabelle de Charrière*. Paris: Honoré Champion, 2005.

———. "Le Thème de l'éducation dans les comédies d'Isabelle de Charrière." In *Belle de Zuylen / Isabelle de Charrière: Education, creation, reception*. Edited by Suzan van Dijk, Valérie Cossy, Monique Moser-Verrey and Madeleine van Strien-Chardonneau. Amsterdam: Rodopi, 2006. 187–98.

Schiebinger, Londa. "Feminine Icons: The Face of Early Modern Science." *Critical Inquiry* 14 (Summer 1988): 661–91.

———. *The Mind Has No Sex? Women in the Origins of Modern Science*. Cambridge: Harvard University Press, 1989.

Schmidt, James. "Civility, Enlightenment, and Society: Conceptual Confusions and Kantian Remedies." *American Political Science Review* 92.1 (1998): 419–27.

Schott, Robin May. Introduction to *Feminist Interpretations of Immanuel Kant*. Edited by Schott. University Park: Pennsylvania State University Press, 1997. 1–20.

Scott, Joan W. "Experience." In *Feminists Theorize the Political*. Edited by Judith Butler and Joan W. Scott. New York and London: Routledge, 1992. 22–40.

Seifert, Lewis C. "Fairy Tales." In *The Feminist Encyclopedia of French Literature*. Edited by Eva Martin Sartori. Westport, CT: Greenwood Press, 1999. 198–200.

Sheriff, Mary. "Decorating Knowledge: The Ornamental Book, the Philosophic Image and the Naked Truth." *Art History* 28.2 (April 2005): 151–73.

Showalter, Elaine. "Feminist Criticism in the Wilderness." In *The New Feminist Criticism: Essays on Women, Literature, and Theory*. Edited by Elaine Showalter. New York: Pantheon Books, 1985. 243–70.

Showalter, English. "The Beginnings of Madame de Graffigny's Literary Career: A Study in the Social History of Literature." *Essays on the Age of Enlightenment in Honor of Ira O. Wade*. Edited by Jean Macary. Geneva and Paris: Droz, 1977. 293–304.

———. *Françoise de Graffigny: Her Life and Works*. SVEC 11. Oxford: Voltaire Foundation, 2004.

———. "'Madame a fait un livre': Madame de Graffigny, Palissot et *Les Philosophes*." *Recherches sur Diderot et sur l'*Encyclopédie 23 (October 1997): 109–25.

———. "A Woman of Letters in the French Enlightenment: Madame de Graffigny." *British Journal for Eighteenth-Century Studies* 1 (1978): 89–104.

———. "Writing Off the Stage: Women Authors and Eighteenth-Century Theater." *Yale French Studies* 75 (1988): 95–111.

Simonin, Charlotte. "Cléomène et Caton: deux figures de philosophe dans le théâtre de Madame de Graffigny." In *Le Philosophe sur les planches: l'image du philosophe dans le théâtre des Lumières 1680–1815*. Edited by Pierre Hartmann. Strasbourg: Presses universitaires de Strasbourg, 2004. 55–67.

———. "Phaza, la 'fille-garçon' de Madame de Graffigny." In *Le Mâle en France, 1715–1830: Représentations de la masculinité*. Edited by Katherine Astbury and Marie-Emmanuelle Plagnol-Diéval. New York: Peter Lang, 2004. 51–62.

Smith, Dorothy. "Comment on Hekman's 'Truth and Method: Feminist Standpoint Theory Revisited.'" In *The Feminist Standpoint Theory Reader: Intellectual and Political Controversies*. Edited by Sandra Harding. New York: Routledge, 2004. 263–68.

258 BIBLIOGRAPHY

Smith, Hilda L. "Intellectual Bases for Feminist Analyses: The Seventeenth and Eighteenth Centuries." In *Women and Reason*. Edited by Elizabeth D. Harvey and Kathleen Okruhlik. Ann Arbor: University of Michigan Press, 1992. 19–38.

Smith, Sarah W. R. *Samuel Richardson: A Reference Guide*. Boston: GK Hall and Co, 1984.

Sol, Antoinette. *Textual Promiscuities: Eighteenth-Century Critical Rewriting*. Lewisburg, PA: Bucknell University Press, 2002.

Spivak, Gayatri. *A Critique of Postcolonial Reason: Toward a History of the Vanishing Present*. Cambridge: Harvard University Press, 1999.

Steinbrügge, Lieselotte. *The Moral Sex: Woman's Nature in the French Enlightenment*. Translated by Pamela Selwyn. New York: Oxford University Press, 1995.

Stewart, Joan Hinde. *Gynographs: French Novels by Women of the Late Eighteenth Century*. Lincoln: University of Nebraska Press, 1993.

Strien, Kees van. "Genesis and Reception of *Portrait de Zélide*." In *Belle de Zuylen/Isabelle de Charrière: Education, creation, reception*. Edited by Suzan van Dijk, Valérie Cossy, Monique Moser-Verrey and Madeleine van Strien-Chardonneau. Amsterdam: Rodopi, 2006. 149–66.

———. *Isabelle de Charrière (Belle van Zuylen) Early Writings: New Material From Dutch Archives*. Louvain and Paris: Editions Peeters, 2005.

Sturzer, Felicia Berger. "Literary Portraits and Cultural Critique in the Novels of Marie Jeanne Riccoboni." *French Studies* 50 (1996): 400–12.

Taylor, Charles. *Sources of the Self: The Making of the Modern Identity*. Cambridge: Harvard University Press, 1989.

Thomas, Ruth. "Marriage as Theatre in the Novels of Madame Riccoboni." *Dalhousie French Studies* 56 (2001): 125–32.

Timmermans, Linda. *L'accès des femmes à la culture (1598–1715)*. Paris: Honoré Champion, 1993.

Todd, Janet. *Sensibility: An Introduction*. New York: Methuen, 1986.

Trouille, Mary Seidman. *Sexual Politics in the Enlightenment: Women Writers Read Rousseau*. Albany: State University of New York Press, 1997.

Trousson, Raymond, ed. and intro. *Romans de femmes du XVIIIe siècle*. Paris: Laffont, 1996.

———. *Romans libertins du XVIIIe siècle*. Paris: Laffont, 1993.

Trousson, Raymond. *Socrate devant Voltaire, Diderot et Rousseau: La conscience en face du mythe*. Paris: Minard, 1967.

Tuana, Nancy, and Sandra Morgen, eds. *Engendering Rationalities*. Albany: State University of New York Press, 2001.

Undank, Jack. "Grafigny's Room of Her Own." *French Forum* 13.3 (1988): 297–318.

Valian, Virginia. *Why So Slow? The Advancement of Women*. Cambridge: MIT Press, 1998.

Van Delft, Louis. *Les Spectateurs de la vie: Généalogie du regard moraliste*. Sainte-Foy, Québec: Presses de l'Université Laval, 2006.

Vanpée, Janie. "Dangerous Liaisons 2: The Riccoboni-Laclos Sequel." *Eighteenth-Century Fiction* 9.1 (1996): 51–70.

Vanpée, Janie. "'Tout à la vérité parle en elles, mais un langage équivoque': The *Encyclopédie*'s Ambiguous Definition of Woman." *SVEC* 304 (1992): 749–52.

Vercruysse, Jeroom. "The Publication of the *Oeuvres complètes:* Navigating the Risky Waters of the Unforeseeable." *Eighteenth-Century Life* 13.1 (1989): 69–78.

Vila, Anne. *Enlightenment and Pathology: Sensibility in the Literature and Medicine of Eighteenth-Century France.* Baltimore: Johns Hopkins University Press, 1998.

Walker, Lesley. *A Mother's Love: Crafting Feminine Virtue in Enlightenment France.* Lewisburg, PA: Bucknell University Press, 2008.

Warner, Marina. *Monuments and Maidens: The Allegory of the Female Form.* Berkeley: University of California Press, 2001.

Went-Daoust, Yvette. "L'Oeuvre dramatique d'Isabelle de Charrière: Classicisme et renouvellement." *Études sur le XVIIIe siècle* 28 (2000): 35–45.

Whatley, Janet. "Sophie de Grouchy de Condorcet." In *The Feminist Encyclopedia of French Literature.* Edited by Eva Martin Sartori. Westport, CT: Greenwood Press, 1999. 123–24.

Whitehead, Barbara. "The Singularity of Mme Du Châtelet: An Analysis of the *Discours sur le bonheur.*" *SVEC* 1 (2006): 255–76.

Wilson, Emily. *The Death of Socrates.* Cambridge: Harvard University Press, 2007.

Wilson, Susan. "Postmodernism and the Enlightenment." In *The Enlightenment World.* Edited by Martin Fitzpatrick et al. London: Routledge, 2004. 648–59.

Wise, Margaret. "Cross-dressing." In *The Feminist Encyclopedia of French Literature.* Edited by Eva Martin Sartori. Westport, CT: Greenwood Press, 1999. 135–36.

Wolfgang, Aurora. "Fallacies of Literary History: The Myth of Authenticity in the Reception of *Fanni Butlerd.*" *SVEC* 304 (1992): 735–39.

———. *Gender and Voice in the French Novel, 1730–1782.* London: Ashgate, 2004.

Wollstonecraft, Mary. *A Vindication of the Rights of Woman.* 1792. Edited by Carol Poston. 2nd ed. New York: Norton, 1987.

Woolhouse, R. S. "Empiricism." In *Encyclopedia of the Enlightenment.* Vol. 1. Edited by Alan Charles Kors. Oxford: Oxford University Press, 2003. 394–98.

Young, Iris Marion. "Structural Injustice and Political Responsibility." Keynote address presented at the annual meeting of the Society for Phenomenology and Existential Philosophy, Chicago, IL, October 2002.

Zinsser, Judith P., and Julie Candler Hayes, eds. *Émilie Du Châtelet: Rewriting Enlightenment Philosophy and Science.* Oxford: Voltaire Foundation, 2006.

Index

Cahiers Isabelle de Charrière / Belle de Zuylen Papers, 216
Cartesianism. *See* Descartes
Cartésiennes, 25, 27, 35, 45
Caylus, comte de, 83
Cazenobe, Colette 232n. 19
Chabut, Marie-Hélène, 156, 237n. 17
Chambrier d'Oleyres, Jean-Pierre de, 169
Charrière, Charles-Emmanuel de, 154, 157
Charrière, Isabelle de, 17, 21, 22, 26–28, 35, 38, 40, 41, 44, 45, 50, 51, 53, 55, 58, 62, 63, 97, 151–94, 201, 214; reception of her work, 107, 154–56, 158, 165–69, 175, 191, 198, 216
—Works of: "Des Auteurs et des livres," 151, 153, 155, 187–90, 192, 193; *Brusquet,* 169; *Élise ou l'université,* 151, 155, 169, 170–87, 189, 190, 192, 193, 199; *L'Émigré,* 169; *L'Extravagant,* 185; *Les Femmes,* 173–74; *L'Inconsolable,* 169; *Lettres de mistriss Henley publiées par son amie,* 126, 157–60, 184; *Lettres trouvées dans des porte-feuilles d'émigrés,* 156; *Le Noble,* 154, 161, 185, 187; *Oeuvres complètes d'Isabelle de Charrière,* 156, 158, 170, 188; *Portrait de Zélide,* 151, 160–68, 173, 175, 179, 183, 187, 189, 190, 192, 193, 199, 200; *Sainte-Anne,* 170; *Trois femmes,* 156, 157, 199
Chartier, Roger, 149, 153
Chevert, François de, 216
Chevrier, François-Antoine, 99
Clermont, Louis de Bourbon-Condé, comte de, 83, 100; private theatre at Berny, 85
Clinton, Hillary, 205, 206
Cochin *fils,* Charles-Nicholas, 31, 59
Code, Lorraine, 241–42n. 39
Cohen, Sarah R., 90, 229n. 49
Colebrook, Claire, 51

Comédie Française, 65, 82, 85, 121, 131
Comédie italienne, 71, 72, 83, 89, 108, 121, 140
commedia dell'arte, 67, 72, 73
compliments, 108, 121
Condillac, Étienne Bonnot, marquis de, 43, 59
Condorcet, Marie Jean Antoine Caritat, marquis de, 36, 202–03
Constant, Benjamin, 155, 156, 157, 169
Constant, Samuel de, 157
Constant d'Hermenches, David-Louis, 155, 157, 161, 162, 191, 193, 199, 214
convents and convent schools, 35, 37, 116, 118, 14
Cook, Elizabeth Heckendorn, 147
Cope, Bill, 236n. 2
coquetry, and coquettes, 56–57, 59, 65, 67, 74, 79, 80, 82, 87, 93, 104, 170–87, 200, 206
cornflowers (*bleuets*), 174, 181, 183, 186
Correspondance littéraire, 112, 125
Cossy, Valérie, 190
Coudreuse, Ann, 233n. 37
Coulet, Henri, 191, 225n. 97
Counter-Reformation, 35
Courtney, Cecil, 155, 191, 192
Coyer, l'abbé Gabriel-François, 90
Cragg, Olga, 111, 122, 141, 142
Crosby, Emily, 110–11, 225n. 97, 232n. 21
cross-dressing, 86, 88–90, 93, 94
cup, 28, 106, 108, 121–23, 128, 148, 151, 198
Curtis, Judith, 229n. 47
Cushman, Ellen, 153

Dacier, Anne, 442
Darnton, Robert, 19
Davies, Simon, 227n. 5
Declaration of the Rights of Man and of the Citizen, 203
DeJean, Joan, 54, 60, 69